SIDE AFFECTS

SIDE AFFECTS

ON

BEING TRANS

AND

FEELING BAD

HIL MALATINO

UNIVERSITY OF MINNESOTA PRESS
MINNEAPOLIS LONDON

The University of Minnesota Press gratefully acknowledges the financial assistance provided for the publication of this book by the Rock Ethics Institute at Penn State University.

Chapter 1 was originally published as "Future Fatigue: Trans Intimacies and Trans Presents (or How to Survive the Interregnum)," *TSQ* 6, no. 4 (2019). Chapter 4 was originally published as "Tough Breaks: Trans Rage and the Cultivation of Resilience," *Hypatia: A Journal of Feminist Philosophy* 34, no. 1 (2019). Chapter 5 was originally published as "Beyond Burnout," in *Trans Care* (Minneapolis: University of Minnesota Press, 2020).

Published by the University of Minnesota Press
111 Third Avenue South, Suite 290
Minneapolis, MN 55401-2520
http://www.upress.umn.edu

ISBN 978-1-5179-1208-6 (hc)
ISBN 978-1-5179-1209-3 (pb)
Library of Congress record available at https://lccn.loc.gov/2021053052.

Printed in the United States of America on acid-free paper

The University of Minnesota is an equal-opportunity educator and employer.

31 30 29 28 27 26 25 24 23   10 9 8 7 6 5 4 3 2

CONTENTS

INTRODUCTION

BEING TRANS, FEELING BAD

Some days (weeks, months, years), being trans feels bad. To say so isn't particularly insightful—it's merely factic. Yet there's not much available cultural space for actually existing trans people to think through, let alone speak of, such bad feeling with any degree of nuance or complexity. Instead, we're more or less trapped within a contemporary discursive field that toggles between the celebratory tokenization and hypervisibility that's part and parcel of the *longue durée* of the supposed "transgender tipping point," on the one hand, and the virulently phobic conservative framings of trans subjectivity as irreal, inauthentic, and threatening that are deployed in order to further foreclose our life chances, on the other. Spectacularized accounts of trans death and suffering—especially the death and suffering of Black and brown trans women—are rife and circulate both as a form of white leftist virtue signaling and as a well-meaning liberal sob story that presents trans lives as single-note portraits of oppression and traumatization. The genres of trans living are whittled down to just a few: hero worship, demonology, victimology.

As for the tropes available to dramatize the felt experience of transition, there are similarly limited options: dysphoria and euphoria, feeling terrible or feeling great, and feeling so in a deeply individuated way, about one's personal and specific gender, with the experience of transition (whether surgical, hormonal, both, or neither) imagined as the way one shifts from one affective pole to the other. On the face of it, feeling bad might be thought synonymously with dysphoria, as if dysphoria was the proper name for the ensemble of bad feelings that inform and transform trans arts of living. Some of us might be thankful that at least being trans isn't framed as disorder any longer; at least we've moved from psychopathology to a more gently medicalized discourse of distress about the mismatch of assigned sex and gender identity. Nevertheless, it's still a diagnostic for a discrete, atomized individual, and the realm of negative affect that accompanies the diagnostic refers only to those bad feelings that attach more or less directly to one's experience of this mismatch. This produces the narrative of transition as entrée into a kind of gender euphoria, one where each gender-affirming step carries one further away from negativity, one where a kind of giddiness and pleasure sweeps one up in moments of gendered recognition that feel right, even if the recognition is only taking place between yourself and a mirror.

I don't dispute the realness of either dysphoria or euphoria. I've experienced both, even cried the first time I buttoned up a shirt after the drains were removed from my chest following top surgery. But even in that moment—the one from my own biography closest to some form of gender euphoria—I remember thinking, "Oh, this is very trans-positive after-school special of me." By which I mean this: even these moments of affirmation are mediated by the deeply bifurcated affective discourse that governs tropes of trans representation. I experienced my happiness about my flat chest in that snap-button plaid as a particularly overdetermined kind of Trans Happiness™, one that I've seen packaged and sold many times over. This isn't to say it wasn't genuine; rather, it's to point out that when we see, over and again, such single-note representations, something deeply significant falls out of the picture: the durability of negativity, the bad feelings that persist before, during, and after such moments of euphoria, the bad feelings that aren't ameliorated by such euphoria, the bad feelings that transition doesn't, can't possibly, eliminate.

I remember feeling palpably relieved the fall morning in 2018 that I read Andrea Long Chu's *New York Times* opinion piece "My New Vagina Won't Make Me Happy" (subtitle: "And It Shouldn't Have To") because, finally, someone had said it in a paper of record: transition won't deliver you into some promised land of gendered bliss, but this in no way means that you shouldn't pursue it, and it definitely doesn't mean you should be systematically prevented from doing so. Describing dysphoria in a stunning series of similes, she writes that it "feels like being unable to get warm, no matter how many layers you put on. It feels like hunger without appetite. It feels like getting on an airplane to fly home, only to realize mid-flight that this is it: You're going to spend the rest of your life on an airplane. It feels like grieving. It feels like having nothing to grieve."[1] This was testimony to the durability of negative affect in trans lives, before and beyond transition, and I was grateful for it. Transitioning doesn't have to be wholly curative, or even minimally happy-making, in order for it to be imperative. It doesn't have to guarantee survival in order to be necessary. At the conclusion of the piece, Chu insists on the right to feel bad, asserting that "the negative passions—grief, self-loathing, shame, regret—are as much a human right as universal health care, or food."[2] Trans people should not feel compelled to sweep self-narrative clean of such negative affect, or be corralled into associating bad feeling exclusively to the "pre-" of transition. Cis folks get to be understood as affectively complex and ambivalent in relation to all sorts of phenomena that are supposed to make one happy: gender, sex, marriage, body modification, children, food. Why not trans people?

Taking this further: Is there a trans specificity to certain ways of feeling bad? Are there certain kinds of negative affect that tend to attend trans experience? *Side Affects* argues that there is, and that there are. Saying so doesn't render trans lives tragic or univocally traumatized, nor does it mean that all trans folks experience such negative affect with the same intensity, with the same duration, or in the same kinds of combinations. Indeed, some folks may not resonate at all with the suite of bad feelings described herein. That said, each of the not-so-great feelings discussed in this book—fatigue, numbness, envy, rage, burnout—appear consistently enough across a wide range of trans cultural production and experience that they felt weighty enough to tarry with, significant enough to deserve substantive analysis.

The book was composed through what I think of as a method of affective attunement: a heightened, though not always necessarily conscious, awareness to the affective dimensions of trans living that resonated with, intensified, or otherwise modulated my own felt experience and, further, manifested regularly enough to become part of a trans affective commons. The phrase "affective attunement" comes to us through the work of developmental psychologist Daniel Stern, who used the phrase to describe a dimension of maternal relation to an infant characterized by the mother's practice of intuiting the child's affective state, internalizing it, and relaying it back to the infant in a way that grounds a caring interrelation.[3] Here, I'm not concerned with infant/ caker relations, but I am rather deeply preoccupied with the practices of caring interrelationality, and failures thereof, that shape trans modes of being-in-the-world. Examining the forms that negative affect takes necessarily means grappling with such failures of care, but doing so through attending to affective attunement means that the resonance of negative affect across trans experiences is itself a kind of caring interrelationality: it's about bearing witness to and feeling with each other. My hope is that, though the chapters are grounded in difficult-to-endure affects that track across more or less intense experiences, the experience of reading and thinking with them is a partial balm, at least to trans readers. I hope some readers experience the kind of relief I felt in the aftermath of encountering Chu's piece and that the method of staying attuned to trans negativity distills it, clarifies it, and thus makes it a little easier to bear.

One thing became obvious to me over the course of drafting this book, though it was already the implicit hunch that animated the work: negative affect is ordinary for trans folk. It is part of our mundane, woven into the everyday rhythms of our living. We live with it, alongside it, in it. Ordinary affects, as Kathleen Stewart writes, are "public feelings that begin and end in broad circulation, but they're also the stuff that seemingly intimate lives are made of. They give circuits and flows the forms of a life."[4] Ordinary affects give form to a life, which is not to say they bestow subjectivity or grant identity. Rather, they work to shape forms of experiential resonance that cut across discrete differences in subject position and identity. When I write about trans negativity in this book, I'm marking the ways in which negative affect gives form to trans lives, with *trans* used as inclusive of anyone who understands themselves as hailed by that word, anyone who claims that word as a partial descriptor of selfhood or lived experience. There are other aspects of identity and experience that modulate negative affect, that dampen or intensify it, that make it more or less difficult to endure, and these primarily have to do with questions of privilege and oppression, of structural position within a broader milieu irrevocably shaped by the violence and expropriation endemic to white supremacist settler cisheteropatriarchy. It is also true that the names given to certain ensembles of negative affect in this book, the concatenated bad feelings discussed, are not at all exclusive to trans experience; the question, for me, is how this thing we might call "transness" is itself an intensifier of negative affect, ramping up experiences of fatigue, numbness, envy, rage, and burnout to such a point that they become integral parts of a trans affective commons. Unpacking the way to approach thinking through ordinary affects, Stewart writes that "the question they beg is not what they might mean in an order of representations, or whether they are good or bad in an overarching scheme of things, but where they might go and what potential modes of knowing, relating, and attending to things are already somehow present in them in a state of potentiality and resonance."[5] *Side Affects* is an attempt to do this, to think through what so-called bad feelings make possible, open up, shut down, disclose, and foreclose in relation to trans arts of living.

Ordinary affects, as Stewart points out, are also public feelings, feelings that "begin and end in broad circulation." Ann

Cvetkovich, in her essential account of public feelings, positions them directly in relation to negative affect. She writes that thinking with public feelings provides "an approach to trauma that focuses on the everyday and the insidious rather than the catastrophic, and that depathologizes trauma and situates it in a social and cultural frame rather than a medical one."[6] The traumas of the trans mundane are precisely what seem to never make it onto the mainstream politico-cultural scene. The focus remains tuned to the catastrophic, whether that catastrophe is the routine and recurrent homicide of trans women of color or the catastrophe of trans people merely existing in public space, heralding the end of the order of things (marriage, romance, reproduction, sex, safety, stability, truth). Cvetkovich goes on to parse the distinctions between different registers of trauma:

> The distinction between everyday and catastrophic trauma is also tied to the distinction between public and private, since often what counts as national or public trauma is that which is more visible and catastrophic, that which is newsworthy and sensational, as opposed to the small dramas that interest me because they draw attention to how structural forms of violence are so frequently lived, how their invisibility or normalization is another part of their oppressiveness. Situating trauma within the larger context of public feelings offers a more flexible approach to the unpredictable linkages among violence, affective experience, and social and political change.[7]

Side Affects is a sustained attempt to think through trans trauma-ordinariness, to think with mostly small-scale, everyday scenes shaped by forms of negativity that are too often occluded by a focus on the spectacular and the catastrophic. In doing so, I hope to trouble the structuring logic of the public/private divide that minimizes and delimits the broadcasting and legibility of the critical, unruly, and negative feelings of minoritized subjects and communities. Rendering such feelings public (shared, common, broadly circulating) intervenes in the liberal and neoliberal regulation of affect in the public sphere by confronting and countering the structures of feeling supported by "vocabularies of tolerance, diversity, and multiculturalism" that, as Cvetkovich points out, "are inadequate to, or that too conveniently package and manage, the messy legacies of history."[8] There are no warm fuzzies to be found here, no sentimental accounts of trans redemption-through-inclusion, no happily-ever-afters. In place of this, you'll find a commitment to staying with a troubling (in the sense of both troublemaking and troublesome) coterie of bad feelings, animated by the hope that such sustained tarrying with trans negativity tells us more about the existential impacts of transantagonism—how it's managed, how it's resisted, the forms that resilience and resistance take in the face of it—than any simple celebratory or victimological narrative can.

SIDE AFFECTS

The title of this book is an obvious malapropism of the phrase *side effects*, which indexes all that might happen alongside, in addition to, or on top of the intended effect of a given treatment. When I set out to begin work on this project, I thought that I would write a slantwise analysis of experiences of medical transition that would move beyond both affirmative discourses of medical transition as exclusively curative and against the transphobic demonization of transition as unnatural, irreal, and inauthentic. I wanted a more nuanced account of medical transition than those that then—and still—commonly circulated. I thought I would explore questions of ambivalence and unsurety in relation to hormonal and surgical transition in a way that didn't relegate indecision or affective gray area exclusively to the moments before transition is embarked upon. I also wanted to pay greater attention to the ways in which transition transforms embodied experience in ways that are certainly more affirming, but also strange, unsettling, surprising, and not always altogether desired. (Did I want to be more masculine? Yes. Did I want back hair? Not so much.)

To that end, I began articulating the project as guided by an attention to *side affects*—that is, experiences of transition that exceed what I, building on the work of Raymond Williams,[9] call "transnormative structures of feeling."[10] By this, I refer to transition narratives that rely on and thus reproduce hegemonic, intensively stereotypical accounts of what it is to "feel like" a man or a woman, importing these accounts (rooted, most often, in white bourgeois gendered norms and mores) into trans lifeworlds wherein they seem to fit strangely, if at all. Nevertheless, each repetition of such a narrative seems to further entrench and intensify a set of racialized, gender-normed limitations that work to determine how transition becomes legible and coherent— indeed, that come to shape and delimit what it means to transition at all.

So I started actively seeking out accounts of transition that sat in certain kind of tension with transnormative structures of feeling, that were messier, more ambivalent, more complex. I was in no small part motivated by a desire to find material that resonated with my own relationship to transition, which was circuitous, stop-start, and decades long, mediated by poverty, insurance exclusions, rurality, and a complicated, ongoing grappling with the cultural politics of white masculinity. While there was a growing literature within trans studies that was critical of medical gatekeeping and the racial, geographic, and economic stratification of access to transition, there wasn't much to be found—at least, in academic literature—on how such gatekeeping and stratification *feels*. There wasn't much written about the circulation of affect in trans lives, full stop.

Simultaneously, it was quite clear that myself and the trans folks in my life, intimately and tangentially, were all dealing with (or attempting to not deal with) recurrent, consistent, ongoing, and often overwhelming manifestations of negative affect, regardless of where we were at or what we desired in terms of hormonal and surgical transition. We were talking about this, too, though not in a public-facing way, and oftentimes obliquely or in a mode of communication that was comprised more of gesture and touch than word. The compounding effects of such negative affect impact our physical and emotional well-being and, interestingly, their intensity seems to be down-regulated through the practice of sharing them with one another. This squares with one of the key insights of Adam Frank and Elizabeth Wilson, who, in their writing on foundational affect theorist Silvan Tomkins, assert that "sociality—the bonds that hold us together—is always brokered through shared and inevitable bad feeling" and that such bonding through negativity can, at least sometimes, work to modulate negative affects so that they "come to be more or less tolerable."[11]

This form of sociality, wherein the circulation, resonance, and amplification of negative affect between trans subjects makes living with such difficult-to-endure feelings more bearable, forms a trans affective commons. Abolitionist queer and trans theorist Eric Stanley, in a crucial essay on the worldmaking practices of subjects "held against the wall of white cisnormativity," articulates both what an affective commons is and why it matters for survival, resilience, and resistance.[12] The term *affective commons*, which Stanley borrows from Lauren Berlant,[13] indexes "how affect, in particular disgust and hate, structures relation, even as nonrelation, in and through space" and specifically "how negative affect, or bad feelings, produce psychic bonds and collective energies" in practices of trans and queer worlding.[14] A commons is not a public but a counter to the structural violence engendered by the public/private divide so central to capitalist development. It is, as Stanley puts it, a "place, a structure of feeling, an idea" that "provides refuge in the ruins of capital's totality."[15] This is not to say that the commons is an innocent concept. Stanley is careful to point out how the radical left's articulation of it, and its enclosure and privatization, consistently elides the ongoing realities of settler coloniality and, in its big-tent articulation of a "we"—think of the "We are the 99%" slogan so central to the Occupy movement—"collapses difference through the quake of equivalence."[16] That said, it need not flatten or be inattentive to the differences engendered by uneven distributions of precarity, violence, and vulnerability. It can be thought, instead, as a means of gathering a motley and loose collectivity of "those disposed of and made disposable by latest capitalism" in solidarity by virtue of being dissatisfied with this world and working against its casually brutal reproduction.[17]

Trans folks, across axes of significant difference, are certainly among those disposed of and made disposable, and much of what binds a trans affective commons is precisely the negativity that arises in the face of quotidian and relentless encounters with disposability. Natal alienation, heightened surveillance and state regulation, high rates of unemployment or low-wage employment, houselessness, substance abuse, suicidality, mental health struggles, medical maltreatment: the terrible litany is so familiar. This familiarity makes it even more striking that the ensemble of bad feelings that attend such a litany—and that, I argue, actually render such a litany more survivable—have received short shrift. The negative affects so central to trans modes of living that they form an affective commons and link very different kinds of trans folks to one another through resonant and overlapping experiences of and with such negativity are consistently sidelined in hegemonic narratives of and discussions about trans experience. This is, of course, because it isn't trans people that set the coordinates of such discursive terrain, though we are nevertheless constrained by them. That's why I think of this book as grounded in the infrapolitical practices, intimacies, and empathies that circulate between and among trans folks. It doesn't write back to dominant discourses of trans exceptionalism or the spectacularized representations of the necropolitical dimensions of trans lives: the forms of social and political marginalization that produce poverty, precarity, homicide, and suicidality. Rather, it is written to the side of such discourses.

The "side" in *Side Affects* is multiple. The book thinks with feelings that comprise a trans affective commons, and this commons that coheres through negative affect exists to the side of prevailing public discourse, to the side of trans-inclusion debates, to the side of a focus on medical transition, and to the side of conversations about trans visibility. Like side effects, the affects discussed herein have been relatively neglected—underresearched, elided, understood as epiphenomenal, figured as aleatory and idiosyncratic rather than constitutive of trans being-in-the-world. Moving bad feelings to the center of a discussion of what, if anything, might link or be shared by disparate trans subjects is a way of reorienting the way trans experience is thought; it becomes less about a diagnosis, less about dysphoria, less about our personal relation to embodiment and transition, and instead about more or less shared affective orientations and habituations to relentlessly quotidian, hydra-headed forms of transantagonism. *Side Affects* is, thus, about trans practices of disidentification, detachment, and refusal, about the ways in which we're worn down and worn out, and about the feelings that motivate justice-oriented work, as well as the experience of demotivation when this work becomes too much to bear. It is about how trans bodies infold the affective force of the milieus they inhabit, about how this infolding of context transforms us and recalibrates our possibilities for survival and resistance.

In a way, all affects are side affects. If *affect* refers to a swirl of prepersonal intensities, and if those intensities become named and stabilized by becoming attached to an emotion, then affect is always, in some ways, happening alongside or to the side of conscious awareness, always in a before or beyond of cognition. As Brian Massumi writes, "Emotion is qualified intensity, the conventional, consensual point of insertion of intensity into semantically and semiotically formed progressions, into narrativizable action-reaction circuits, into function and meaning. It is intensity owned and recognized."[18] Part of what this book does is bring negative affective intensity from the periphery of awareness to the center in order to think about what it does, how it works. This has meant narrativizing it, putting it into language, telling a certain set of stories about how negative affect informs and transforms trans lives. *Side Affects* does a kind of translational work, recoding the intensity of sometimes overwhelming negative affect into a delimited set of bad feelings. There is always a certain reduction involved in this process; the accounts of bad feeling herein are inevitably going to fail to do justice to the affective complexity they attempt to name. But that's what happens when you work in words. No account of affective intensity is totalizing or totalizable; some complexity always escapes when a feeling is named.

But, as any therapist will tell you, it's imperative that one name bad feelings in order to begin the long process of working with and through them. The naming is both a resolution and an incipience. No affective commons is possible in the absence of such naming, such recognition. Collective naming is the way that feelings become public, which is to say that it is the way that feelings come to have transformative force. And while there's nothing immediately revolutionary about the suite of bad feelings addressed here, taken together they index something critical about the constraints under which trans subjects currently exist.

A crucial insight about negative affect is that it works to minimize the power of bodies—both particular bodies and collective bodies. Political philosopher John Protevi writes, glossing Deleuze and Spinoza, that affect is "the felt change in the power of the body," experienced "as sadness or joy," and this change in power is inherently political, because it affects one's ability to "form new and mutually empowering encounters."[19] Put differently: negative affect makes collective organizing in the service of trans justice difficult, insofar as it chips away at the physiological and psychological power of the body. This is why Deleuze wrote that it is in the interest of power to produce sad passions—it's a strategic way to demobilize a collective, to quite literally disempower bodies in order to prevent challenges to the status quo.[20]

But you can't just flip the joy switch. The influx and efflux of sad passions take their toll. They demand reckoning; there's no easy movement beyond them. This book is one way, perhaps, by which to reckon.

AN ENSEMBLE OF BAD FEELINGS
(AND A STUDY IN THE LIMITS OF HEALING)

Each chapter in *Side Affects* is organized around a particular bad feeling. Let me introduce them in their order of appearance: fatigue, numbness, envy, rage, burnout, and a concluding chapter on practices of trans healing. I struggled with how to order these chapters, in large part because establishing any sequence seemed to risk narrativizing a sequential order of negative affect, with one producing or preceding the next. But there isn't a reliable sequence to these bad feels: they often appear in combination, one doesn't necessarily follow from another, there's no beginning or end point, no definitive resolution. Sometimes, they stick around for only a little while; sometimes, they last a lifetime. Again, the imposed structure belies the affective complexity. I'm tempted to say, taking a cue from Deleuze and Guattari's *A Thousand Plateaus*, that you can jump in or out at any point, read the chapters in any order. This book seems particularly well-suited to such a reading practice.

Side Affects opens with fatigue, and specifically an examination of the experience of fatigue in relation to waiting to transition, waiting to inhabit the body you want in order to be the gender you are. Titled "Future Fatigue: Trans Intimacies and Trans Presents (or How to Survive the Interregnum)," the first chapter examines the ways in which we come to learn a teleology of transition, one that coheres through and is justified by its assumed endpoint, which then produces a temporal logic of transition as a process with a very clearly defined beginning, middle, and end. This teleology is reified and reinforced by vlogs and transition testimonials focused on surgical outcomes, by the practice of broadcasting the date one begins taking exogenous hormones on social media and deliberately framing that date as a kind of rebirth, by all of the ways in which folks signal transition as beginning with an injection or ingestion and ending after one is healed from major gender-affirming surgeries. I argue that there is an affective dimension to these narratives, one that frames the time spent ostensibly "pre" transition as bleak, characterized by depression and despondency, while the "post" of transition is understood to be affirmative, happy, safe, secure. Troubling such affective accounts of transition, I focus on how the figuration of the affirmative and affirming future actually produces intense anticipatory anxiety in a present moment wherein one's future desires are deferred, which can of course happen for many reasons—lack of parental support, limited or no access to trans-affirming medical care, lack of insurance or the funds to pay out of pocket for the desired treatments. This prompts a sense of dwelling in lag time, feeling left behind, out of temporal sync, forced to inhabit a present shaped by foreclosed futurity. This living in lag is exhausting. I call this "future fatigue," and it is closely allied to Berlant's articulation of cruel optimism.[21] It names what happens when you're worn out by your attachment to a future vision that is structurally foreclosed. I propose, over and against such exhausting futural attachments, a commitment to a t4t (trans-4trans) praxis of love in the interregnum—those long moments spent in-between, in waiting—suggesting that dwelling in the timespace of interregnum may be all we have, as dystopic and dysphoric as it may be.

The second chapter, "Fuck Feelings: On Numbness, Withdrawal, and Disorientation," explores the ways in which trans subjects learn to inure ourselves to hostile surroundings through the selective cultivation of numbness, a method of freezing out transantagonism and gendered misrecognition by affective withdrawal, social recessivity, and dissociation. Focusing on scenes of intercorporeal (mis)recognition, sexual and otherwise, I chart the recurrence of these modes of sensorial dampening in the service of postponing, delaying, or altogether refusing to feel what may be unbearably self-shattering. Thinking with Berlant's work on flat affect,[22] Gayle Salamon's writing on trans phenomenology and intercorporeality,[23] the depictions of rural white Southern transmasculinity in the documentaries *Deep Run* and *Southern Comfort*, and Casey Plett's imperative novel *Little Fish*, I theorize recession and withdrawal as a cultivated means of avoiding triggers, and thus minimizing the impact of difficult memories called up by moments of gendered misrecognition, and numbness as a means through which we survive such moments by dulling ourselves to their force. It's easy to stigmatize the means through which some of us prompt such numbness—I'm thinking explicitly of substance (ab)use—but to do so risks overlooking the survival functions the selective cultivation of numbness serves, even as it can simultaneously threaten that very survival.

"Found Wanting: On Envy," the third chapter, tracks a different relation to trans desires for embodied transformation, positioning the much maligned affect of envy (famously, one of the cardinal sins in Christian theology) as central to trans modes of becoming, though it is frequently disavowed. I follow Sianne Ngai's account of envy as an "affective *response* to a perceived inequality" rather than a moral failing rooted in a kind of pernicious and lusty greed that gives rise to a false sense of subjective lack.[24] Moving with this insight, I read transmasculine manifestations of envy, from Lou Sullivan's diaries to Paul Preciado's autotheoretical writing, as indexing a troubling and, in many ways, structurally foreclosed relation to white cis masculinity.[25] This means that the chapter grapples with the concept of penis envy, though it does so entirely to the side of traditional Freudian understandings of the irresolution of such envy as a manifestation of developmental psychopathology. Instead, I position it as an indicator of injustice and inequality, a fraught and ambivalent relation to the stratified powers and precarities erected upon the scaffolding of white cisheteropatriarchy, and ultimately argue that envy is a powerful indicator of the unjust allocation of bodily comfort and ease in transantagonistic worlds.

The book then turns to rage, examining the power of this overwhelming form of anger in relationship to questions of trans survival and resistance. The fourth chapter, "Tough Breaks: Trans Rage and the Cultivation of Resilience," counters hegemonic understandings of rage as a deleterious emotion, examining rage across two specific sites of trans cultural production—the prison letters of CeCe McDonald and the durational performance art of Cassils—in order to argue that it is integral to trans survival and flourishing. Theorizing rage as a justified response to unlivable circumstances that plays a key role in enabling trans subjects to detach from toxic relational dynamics in order to transition toward other forms of gendered subjectivity and intimate communality, I develop an account of what I call an "infrapolitical ethics of care" that indexes a web of communal practices that empathically witness and amplify rage, as well as support subjects during and after moments of grappling with overwhelming negative affect. I draw on the work of trans, queer, and feminist theoreticians who have theorized the productivities of so-called negative affects, particularly Sara Ahmed's work on willfulness and killing joy, María Lugones's writing on anger, Judith Butler's Spinozan reassessment of the vexed relations between self-preservation and self-destruction, and the rich account of trans rage provided by Susan Stryker.[26]

Expanding on my theorization of burnout in the small book that preceded this, *Trans Care,* chapter 5, "Beyond Burnout: On the Limits of Care and Cure," provides a genealogy of burnout, from its initial articulation in the context of the emergence of the free clinic movement in the United States on toward trans-specific articulations of burnout spanning the 1980s and 1990s.[27] The reasons for this historical focus are twofold: these are the decades that witnessed the emergence and consolidation of the World Professional Association for Transgender Health (WPATH), heralding a new era of gatekeeping authority in trans medicine, but they also—not coincidentally—witnessed significant, concerted trans activist efforts to transform such medical gatekeeping procedures in the name of increased trans livability and survival. Moving beyond the concept of burnout as a symptom of chronic overwork, I illustrate that burnout, in its original iteration, was a concept coined to name a specific conjuncture of care work (either unremunerated or poorly remunerated), overwork, and structural precarity on account of institutional, economic, social, and political marginalization. Reclaiming this more robust and holistic articulation of burnout enables me to position it as endemic and widespread among trans communities precisely because so many trans folks live and work within precisely this conjuncture.

Finally, I turn away from bad feelings and toward trans spirituality and healing practices, particularly those taken up by white trans subjects. The book's last chapter, "After Negativity? On Whiteness and Healing," is the verso-face of my sustained argument that negative affects do much more than chip away at one's ability to get by (though they certainly *do* do that!). I turned to trans healing practices, both practically and intellectually, after years of tarrying with and thinking through the productivity of negative affect in trans lives. But the more I thought about these healing practices, and the more I practiced (some of) them, the more I found that they do much more than merely heal: they also appropriate, exclude, and entrench individualized neoliberal models of self-transformation and self-care. This chapter analyzes several specific trans engagements with psychedelic and New Age culture from the 1960s (when an LSD researcher named Robert Masters wrote to Harry Benjamin, mid-twentieth-century sexological architect of trans treatment protocols, to see if he'd be interested in recruiting trans subjects for psychedelic research) through the gatherings of self-proclaimed trans shamans undertaken in the mountains of western North Carolina in the 1990s and early 2000s, documented within a series of newsletters published under the title *Gender Quest: The Quarterly Publication of Kindred Spirits*. Building on the scholarship of Arun Saldanha and Amanda J. Lucia, I examine how such practices reproduce white viscosity: they foment forms of social cohesion that make white bodies stick together, intensifying racial exclusions while presenting themselves as colorblind or, more perniciously, both racially conscious and in direct betrayal of white bourgeois spiritual and cultural norms.[28] I end with a meditation on such practices because we desperately need to bring collective, continued focus to bear on the practices of care, mutual aid, support, and healing that support living with and through, though perhaps never fully beyond, the bad feelings addressed here, while remaining cognizant of the ongoing legacy of trans-centered and trans-inclusive forms of spiritual and healing practice that have nevertheless worked to reproduce both white hegemony and stratified access to the tools and networks—spiritual, physical, practical—that might, and have historically sought, to support trans flourishing.

1

FUTURE FATIGUE

Trans Intimacies and Trans Presents (or How to Survive
the Interregnum)

> *Being a person next to someone feels precious, especially while*
> *so many forces in the world work with such violence to make*
> *sure I am not next to so many people, and although it is vio-*
> *lence, also, that brought me here in the first place, that is why I*
> *am next to who I am next to.*
>
> —T Fleischmann, *Time Is the Thing a Body Moves Through*

LAG: RETHINKING THE AFFECTIVE TEMPORALITIES OF TRANSITION

What makes a future bleak? Is it a question of one's orientation
to futurity? Is a future bleak because of the anticipation, anxiety,
and fear that imbues one's relationship to it? Is it a failure of ability to envision oneself happy in one's projections of the future?
Or a failure to envision oneself in any kind of future at all?

Sometimes, perhaps, what makes a future bleak is also that
which makes it promising. This is the key insight of Lauren Berlant's theorization of cruel optimism, their name for the affective complex that occurs when that which you profoundly desire

is also that which inhibits your flourishing, when that which you imagine to one day deliver happiness, security, comfort, or joy actually wears you down and out through your attachment to it.[1]

This chapter interprets certain visions of the future that circulate in hegemonic narratives of medicalized transition as generative of a form of cruel optimism that stems from the affective promises they offer. It explores the ways that teleological narratives of transition come coupled with corresponding affective narratives that frame life "pre" transition as characterized by a reductively bleak emotional surround and cathect life "post" transition to a bright-sided promise of social ease, domestic comfort, and existential peace. Building on Berlant's theorization of cruel optimism and the work of Tobias Raun and Laura Horak on video narratives of hormonal and surgical transition, I position the figuration of futurity in these narratives as generative of a form of intense anticipatory anxiety in the present, one that may actually impede the flourishing of trans subjects, particularly those who encounter difficulty accessing technologies of transition.[2] These teleological affective narratives generate an inhabitation of the present as a dwelling in lag—a form of being out of temporal sync, left behind, with the life one desires deferred (perhaps perennially). As an ameliorative to the effects of such cruelly optimistic futural narratives, I theorize a trans for trans (t4t) praxis of love, drawing on the fantastic and dystopic imaginaries at work in the fiction of Kai Cheng Thom and Torrey Peters in order to account for the creative and caring acts of trans intimacy that render life in the interregnum—in the moments during transition, which may very well not have a definite end—not only livable but also, sometimes, joyous.

Hegemonic transition narratives emanate from diverse sites. Sometimes, they are framed and marketed by medical specialists addressing trans folk as a surgical niche market. Other times, they are produced within DIY spaces of trans cultural production that document medical transition. In this chapter, I focus specifically on the futural narratives at work in the genre of trans vlogs concerned with documenting the impacts of transition produced by folks residing in the United States. These vlogs fulfill a crucial function for trans folks and communities, making specialized medical information accessible across disparate healthscapes, offering interactive forums for communication about experiences with hormones and surgery, and documenting the corporeal and affective changes that accompany medicalized forms of transition. They are a critical stopgap in the notoriously uneven terrain of trans health-care access in the United States, one shaped by a long legacy of rigorous and problematic gatekeeping, a historic and ongoing dearth of insurance coverage, high out-of-pocket fees, and a metrocentricity that makes it quite difficult for trans subjects in rural areas and small towns and cities to access transition-related care (as well as trans-competent medical care, broadly construed). The folks composing, editing, and posting these vlogs are engaged in forms of care labor for, and on behalf of, trans communities, documenting their own experiences in order to educate and potentially mitigate feelings of isolation and anomie. They perform, with a much wider reach, the work of trans community newsletters and magazines like *Chrysalis, AEGIS News,* the *Erickson Educational Foundation Newsletter,* and *Transgender Tapestry* that circulated throughout the 1970s, '80s, and '90s, informing scattered and disparate trans subjects and communities of developments in transition-related health care and advice on how to navigate a too-often byzantine and difficult process.

However, the imperative care labor of these vloggers is frequently shaped by an affective orientation to futurity that I interpret as a trans-specific, biomedicalized variant of the much-criticized "It Gets Better" genre of inspirational, affirmative messaging. The It Gets Better Project was initiated by gay journalist Dan Savage and his partner Terry Miller in 2010 as a social media campaign to address high instances of depression and suicidality among LGBTQ youth, a public response to the highly publicized suicides of teenagers like Billy Lucas and Tyler Clementi, who were bullied for being—or suspected of being— gay. The project seeks to offer hope to LGBTQ adolescents and teens with the repeated assurance that "it"—one's life and life chances, the degree of discrimination one encounters—improves significantly as one ages. This project was roundly critiqued by many prominent North American queer academics and activists almost immediately for failing to grapple with questions of intersectionality. Jasbir Puar penned a paradigmatic editorial in the *Guardian* that succinctly outlines the prevailing grounds for such critique, highlighting how "many . . . have been struck with how these deaths have been made to serve the purpose of highlighting an exceptional class of aspirational gay citizens at the expense of others. Part of the outrage and upset generated by these deaths is precisely afforded through a fundamental belief that things *are* indeed, better, especially for a particular class of white gay men."[3]

Unlike the initial, official iterations of the It Gets Better campaign, these vlogs are geared specifically toward trans folks that are contemplating or in the midst of transition, offering palliative reassurances that once one moves through the process of medical gatekeeping and accesses the forms of medical transition that comprise the normative ensemble of interventions, life improves on most all registers: economically, romantically, in terms of body image and self-esteem, social belonging, mental health, etc. Like the It Gets Better Project, however, they seek to offer reassurances and support in the face of high rates of depression and suicidality. The promise implicit in these narratives is that, as one takes steps to bring their embodiment in line with their gender identity, a radical metamorphosis takes place that makes the rhythms and patterns of everyday life easier, more bearable, less traumatic. Insofar as vloggers proffer this affective narrative, they echo and enhance the promissory narrative of transition articulated by trans-specialized medical professionals, whose practices and reputations rely upon such repetitions and amplifications, especially in the form of patient testimonials. Trans vloggers working in this genre are positioned proximally to the medical industry, radically lacking institutional power and authority but able to harness their communal social credit to attest to the promise of (and, sometimes, to critique) trans medical practice.

Tobias Raun, in an examination of trans male vloggers on the "digital *Wunderkammer*" of YouTube, understands this genre as offering a "database for the display of everyday trans life."[4] What strikes him, however, is how redundant this database is, establishing and reifying specific generic conventions in performances of transmasculine self-making. Raun provides an account of the specific tropes that shape the genre, including titling and cataloging vlogs by the number of months one has been on testosterone and assiduously detailing the transformations wrought by testosterone injections, a process through which testosterone becomes the "structuring principle" of the genre.[5] Raun highlights the ways in which "the drug and the camera are mutually constitutive, instantiating and confirming maleness, thereby allowing the vlogger and the viewer to witness the process (documenting effects) while also being a site for staging what and how to witness (performative effects)."[6] More than a visual record of transition, these videos also have a pedagogical or coaching function, directing the viewer's attention, establishing zones of corporeal significance (facial hair, the postsurgical chest) and showing us how to gaze, what to notice. This visual coaching does, indeed, do more than document the effects of transition—it also teaches us what constitutes the transition process. Raun concludes that "while trans male vlogs manifest potentials—and possible futures—they also create norms for how trans men look, feel, and talk about their transition, and how they vlog about it," operating as both "commencement and commandment."[7] These vlogs are part of a cultural ensemble that installs narratives of transnormativity, teaching viewers what transition is supposed to look like, what they might one day look like, operating as a visual litmus test against which one might measure their "progress" and gauge what the process and the "post" of transition might be. Inevitably, this entails self-objectification and anxiety, as it invites a practice of corporeal comparison (Will my chest hair grow in like his? Will my top surgery scars heal that well?) that, while undergirded by the hope of inhabiting something closer to one's corporeal ideal, hinges on an uncertain and projected future that may very well not turn out to be what one wishes. The affective surround produced by this kind of media is one of anticipation, in all its tense complexity, with all the desire, hope, fear, and dread that anticipation entails.

J. F. Miller comments on the transnormative assumptions that circulate in the trans vlogosphere, writing that many vlogs reflect the "mainstream media portrayal of trans people" insofar as they focus on "documenting the changing body during the early stages of hormone replacement therapy (HRT) or after various gender-affirming surgeries" and frame medical intervention "as a life-or-death step to achieving happiness."[8] In doing so, they fail to reflect the diversity of trans subjects and communities. Miller writes that "the privileging of such a limiting narrative has, among other negative outcomes, created damaging expectations for trans people who identify outside of a male/female binary or do not desire medical intervention," as well as those subjects who encounter substantial difficulty accessing the forms of medical transition they do desire, given that such access is intensively stratified.[9] This surfeit of transnormative narratives makes it difficult, Miller argues, to locate trans vlogs that offer alternative and critical accounts of trans experience, particularly those that foreground questions of race and racism in relation to trans identity and the politics of transition, refuse to overemphasize physical transformation, or depict nonbinary or nonmedically transitioning trans experiences. Though the trans vlog archive is vast, the most popular and readily accessible vlogs tend to reiterate, rather than destabilize, transnormative tropologies, producing a misleading sense of coherence that can result in viewers assuming, as Miller did early in his research, that trans YouTube is almost exclusively informed by the perspectives of class-privileged, white, straight, and binary trans subjects.[10]

By highlighting this, I don't mean to dismiss the crucial worldbuilding work done by even the most ostensibly transnormative vlogs. In a fundamentally transphobic institutional, political, and cultural environment, providing digital community and transition-related support is both radical and necessary. I call attention to the limits of these narratives only because I believe that other, additional forms of support, solidarity, and intimacy are needed in order to grapple with the all-too-common experience of lag and the negative affects associated with it. This is especially so because the shape of most trans lives doesn't mimic the progressive teleological contours of such narratives, and the ascendancy of these narratives has been far from frictionless, with a well-articulated trans critique of transnormative teleologies of medical transition dating back at least to the work of Sandy Stone in her foundational essay "The *Empire* Strikes Back" and continuing through the present, with important contributions from Dean Spade, Julian Carter, Jules Gill-Peterson, C. Riley Snorton, and others.[11] Rather, transnormativity and trans exceptionalism are aspirational fantasies that very, very few trans subjects are able to live out phenomenologically. Because the embodied reality of living in and through forms of transphobic violence is so often articulated with the indignities, harms, and aggressions that characterize poverty, disability, and debility, the inhabitation of perceptually queer forms of embodiment, and the differential and compounded violence that attends processes of racialization as nonwhite, the number of trans subjects who live in any kind of comfortable proximity to transnormativity is slim indeed. If there is a phenomenon that crosscuts much of trans experience—in this moment, in those zones of dispossession, extraction, expropriation, and brutal reterritorialization that some of us call North America—it is the experience of "near life," what Eric Stanley refers to as "that which emerges in the place of the question of humanity," a term that indexes the experience of living with one's humanity withheld, insistently interrogated, rarely ever assumed.[12]

Laura Horak builds on Raun's scholarship, unpacking the temporality of these narratives structured around hormonal transition, which she refers to as "hormone time."

> Hormone time is linear and teleological, directed toward the end of living full time in the desired gender. It borrows

a Christian temporal structure—time begins with moment of rupture and points in a particular direction. . . . While hormone time is not as grandiose, it also points toward a utopian future, in which the subject experiences harmony between the felt and perceived body.[13]

Hormone time is both teleological and utopian. The future is always better than the present, a site of promise, deliverance; transition is framed as a period of trial and potential distress that is rewarded with the experience of harmony, good feeling, corporeal comfort, and ease when navigating everyday social interactions. For this reason, Horak links hormone time to "straight time," writing that "it appropriates the 'straight' temporality of progress for radical ends—proving that trans self-determination is not only possible but viable and even joyful. Unlike 'straight' time, the goal is not children or the future of the nation but expansive trans subjects and communities."[14] Hormone time is quite distinct from reproductive futurism—a politics molded by a heterocisnormative investment in providing a better future for the Child—but nevertheless appropriates a teleological utopian temporality in order to provide hope to trans subjects and communities.[15] The futural horizon, the promised telos, is, as Horak writes, the moment of "harmony between the felt and perceived body."[16]

The trouble is that this horizon sometimes seems to be infinitely receding. When is one "post" transition? Who experiences such unity between feeling and perception, given how radically thrown—nonsovereign, out of one's control—modes of intersubjective corporeal perception are? Is there ever an experience of subjectivity-in-sociality that isn't, to some (significant) extent, shaped by dissonance and misrecognition, particularly if, as Berlant reminds us, "recognition is the misrecognition you can bear"?[17] Is there ever a moment where we are—transparently, in all our complexity, intuitively and deeply—known by those others we share space with? Where those others understand our bodyminds in precisely the ways in which we desire them to? Even if such moments are possible, or at least feel possible, that doesn't erase the prior years of consistent dissonance, misgendering, and misrecognition, nor does it easily transform the anxiety and fear that one cultivates as a product of living through such (routine, quotidian, incessant) moments.

What hormone time does—and what related futural narratives of medicalized transition do, such as those that prioritize top or bottom surgery (or both) as the sine qua non of a "completed" transition—is position biomedical intervention as necessary and fundamental to securing the future one desires, to achieving the promised moment of harmony between the felt and the perceived body. I want to push against this promissory narrative for a few different reasons. First, it encourages trans subjects to cathect hope for a more livable life to a for-profit medical industry that, too often, lacks empathy and sensitivity and treats trans subjects as a niche market rife for economic exploitation. This means that doctors become saviors, capable of enabling or disabling the possibility of a better future for trans subjects. It also means that the politics of access to forms of medical transition—which are simultaneously geographical, economic, racialized, and gendered, not to mention contingent on questions of employment, insurance, citizenship, and carceral status—aren't significantly engaged, and those that experience compromised access are encouraged to understand this as tantamount to a foreclosed future. If one is unable to access, or has compromised access to, the large ensemble of transition-related technologies, they are placed in a position of lag, their desired future deferred, perhaps perennially. Lag shapes the experience of saving up for transition, putting away a little bit of money each paycheck for specialist appointments not covered, or only partially covered, by insurance (if one has it). Economic considerations aside, the experience of lag structures transition at least as much as transition-related technologies themselves, manifesting in the days, months, and years before one takes steps toward transition and shaping the experience of waiting for each new appointment, each treatment, each follow-up visit. The tropic conventions of hormone time that shape the narratives of transition critiqued by Horak and Raun tend to downplay the affects that correspond to the temporal experience of lag. Lag often comes coupled with an experience of repeated, persistent, and dogged misrecognition, and allied forms of transphobic hostility operative at both macro and micro levels. This misrecognition wears away at the resilience of trans subjects and makes the daily arts of living more difficult—in other words, it produces fatigue. I think, largely, we invest in the promises of hormone time because we hope sincerely that one day this fatigue will lessen, subside, surcease.

Hormone time and related futural narratives are undergirded by the promise of a moment (not yet, but someday) when the relation between one's gendered sense of self and the way that self is perceived socially are aligned. Within this alluring future vision, recognition is conferred explicitly through social interaction, which is understood in a bifurcated manner—either folks get it right or get it wrong, and what they get right or wrong is explicitly linked back to questions of medical access, binary understandings of gender, and the gender-ideal aesthetic "success" of trans subjects. My concern with this understanding of the conferral of gendered recognition is that the granting of legibility lies solely with the perceiver rather than with the subject being perceived. If we take seriously the fact that access to technologies of transition is shaped by multiple, intersecting vectors of privilege (not to mention differing degrees of interest in and desire for medical transition) and that, both because of and despite this, many trans subjects experience "passing" only in discontinuous, situationally dependent ways, a teleological account of transition that ends with an experience of "harmony between the felt and perceived body" is radically inadequate; it doesn't begin to dignify the complexities of trans experiences of gendered (mis)recognition and the complicated interplay, linkages, and feedback loops that inform the relationship between the "felt" and "perceived" body.

The desire for this experience of harmony between the felt and perceived body is common to trans and cis folks alike—it undergirds all efforts to acquire and inhabit a body unlike the one inhabited at any present moment. I don't mean to suggest that an investment in the promise of experiencing such harmony is the province of trans folks exclusively, though the stakes of such hopes are often much higher for us. The experience, however durable or fleeting, of being recognized in gendered ways that resonate with how we understand ourselves is a form of legibility that isn't only pleasurable but quite crucial to survival, and this is true for both our own perception of our bodies and the ways in which others perceive them. What I am trying to think, however, is how trans subjects might (and do) cultivate forms of self-regard and intracommunal recognition that bolster our ability to see ourselves—and love ourselves, and each other—even as crucial forms of intersubjective gendered recognition are withheld, even as we don't pass as cis, even as we're deprived of the forms of social mooring that gendered legibility and recognition provides: even as we inhabit lag time.

I am accompanied by the work of Gayle Salamon as I think through the interrelation of trans recognition and livability. She draws on Merleau-Ponty's phenomenological account of perception and embodiment to develop the idea that perception is fundamentally relational and that, on account of this, the reality of the perceived body is always situationally coproduced. Therefore, the "reality" of the body always lies "'further on' than any objective perception," which means that the conferral of gendered recognition never lies solely with an external perceiver.[18] She goes on to clarify what this means for trans and gender-variant bodies:

> What one might read from the contours of the body is something less than the truth of that body's sex, which cannot be located in an external observation of the body, but exists instead in the relation between the material and the ideal, between the perceiver and the perceived, between the material particularity of any body and the network of forces and contexts that shape the material and the meaning of that body.[19]

The task, for Salamon and for myself, is how to develop relational ways of witnessing and perceiving trans and gender-variant bodies regardless of their relation to, positioning within, or investment in medicalized teleologies of transition.

Further, I want to suggest that, despite the proliferation of temporally linear, progressive, transnormative narratives, it would be deeply misled to understand them as offering nuanced experiential accounts of transition or trans experience. They move quickly to affirm an affective experience of embodiment characterized by comfort, joy, recognition, and pleasure and tarry with negative affect only insofar as they work to reassure subjects who might be dwelling in an existential space saturated with such affect that it will one day improve, especially if they heed the hegemonic pedagogy of transition offered. I think these narratives, while seeking to provide hope—to trans folk beginning to consider medical transition but also, perhaps, to cis audiences grappling with the affective politics of the transition of a loved one—also (albeit unintentionally) shut down possibilities for empathic identification across and exploration of the more difficult affective experiences of trans becoming—becomings that are often shaped by a dwelling in lag time and are no stranger to ensembles of negative affect that manifest in both routine and unpredictable ways.

I prefer to use the language of becoming rather than being because it offers a way of understanding trans experience that exists to the side of (though not incompatible with) hegemonic understandings of transition. Borrowing the term from Deleuze and Guattari's account in *A Thousand Plateaus* and drawing on its history of deployment within trans studies scholarship, I understand becoming as the unfolding of difference in time, as an experience of ontological shifts that don't necessarily cohere as shifts in identity at the level of representation.[20] Rather, becoming undermines the fixed, stable terms that give shape and sense to the taxonomies of identity offered up within a given milieu; as philosopher and Deleuze scholar Todd May glosses, "to become is to be part of a process by which the stable identities—the majorities—are dissolved in creative acts in which more fluid 'identities' are created, but only as the by-products of the process itself."[21] Placing emphasis on becoming enables me to think through some of the aspects of transition that fall to the wayside when the focus is solely on questions of representation, identity, and social legibility. This is not to suggest that political and scholarly emphasis on representation and recognition isn't important, only to call attention to the fact that these terms don't do justice to the affective textures of trans experience. Identity is a (very important) part-object in a broader ensemble of relations and shouldn't be taken as coidentical or coterminous with transness—or, rather, trans-ing.

Susan Stryker, Paisley Currah, and Lisa Jean Moore propose the concept of "trans-ing" in the introduction to a 2008 special issue of *Women's Studies Quarterly* entitled "Trans-" and concerned with the concept of transition, broadly conceived. They write:

> Rather than seeing genders as classes or categories that by definition contain only one kind of thing (which raises unavoidable questions about the masked rules and normativities that constitute qualifications for categorical membership), we understand genders as potentially porous and permeable spatial territories (arguably numbering more than two), each capable of supporting rich and rapidly proliferating ecologies of embodied difference.[22]

The understanding of gender fleshed out here shifts our attention away from questions of identity constitution ("classes or categories that by definition contain only one kind of thing") and toward questions of becoming. If gender isn't an identity but rather a territory that supports "rapidly proliferating ecologies of embodied difference," then "trans" names not a specific entity but a process; it is not a noun but an adjective. Trans-ing, then, "is a practice that takes place within, as well as across or between, gendered spaces. . . . A practice that assembles gender into contingent structures of association with other attributes of bodily being, and that allows for their reassembly."[23] Thinking of transition as a practice of "trans-ing" allows one to focus on how gender is a practice of assembly and reassembly, a process without a delimited outcome. I find this shift in perspective helpful when trying to think slantwise in relation to the emphasis on surgical and hormonal outcomes and normative gendered legibility that forcefully structures transnormative teleologies of transition. In order to think transition otherwise, especially to think through the aporias produced by such hegemonic accounts of transition, an emphasis on assemblage, process, and practice is key.

Another way to put this: I want to focus on transition as a journey rather than a destination, and a particularly unpredictable journey at that: one with shifting itineraries, detours, roadblocks, and breakdowns, comprised of various speeds and slownesses, with no given return "home" and no guarantee that home might not be profoundly changed if and when one does return. I want to focus on trans lives in interregnum, in the crucial and transformative moments between past and future, between the regime of what was and the promise of what might be. I don't understand the interregnum as the midpoint of a linear temporal narrative, however. It is a kind of nowness that shuttles transversally between different imaginaries of pasts and futures and remains malleable and differentially molded by these imaginaries. Typically understood as a moment between state regimes, or the moments between state failure and the installation of a new system of power, the meaning of the interregnum shifts if we refuse to place emphasis on what was and what might be and instead focus on the pause, the interim, as a moment of foment, generation, complexity, and fervor, rife with unexpected partnerships, chance events, and connections fortuitous and less so; a space of looseness and possibility, not yet overcoded and fixed in meaning, signification, or representative economy. What possibilities open up when we cease to run toward promissory futures from pasts that we're (sometimes, literally) dying to leave behind?

What I'm proposing is a trans-specific reconsideration of

queer theorizations of temporal drag: the refusal to embrace narratives of queer modernity and the attendant march toward ever-increasing progress on account of a stubborn attachment to an often-traumatic past, what Heather Love calls a "history of queer damage [that] retains its capacity to do harm in the present."[24] Like Love, I'm calling for a necessary grappling with the negativity that doesn't ever seem to stay planted firmly in the past, and the affects allied to the forms of social marginality and abjection that suffuse trans experience regardless of how passable-as-cis one may be in the wake of transition.

This isn't the same as an embrace of a queer temporality of developmental lag that solidifies through being positioned askew in relation to heteronormative reproductive time. This queer embrace of arrested development, articulated by Jack Halberstam in *In a Queer Time and Place* and trenchantly critiqued by Julian Carter, is the kind that refuses to grow up in order to embrace, instead, a form of not-quite-adulthood that "opens the space for same-sex bonding and polymorphous perversity" but also shuts down "the space for becoming-trans."[25] The inhabitation of the interregnum entails not the refusal to grow up but instead an approach to temporality that understands it as multiply enfolded rather than merely delayed or deferred. This is how Carter envisions what he calls "transitional time," writing that the folding of such time may produce a sense of lag, but it also might "heighten a body's sensitivity, invaginating it so that it touches itself in several different moments at once," and that these temporal "pleats may propel the body forward . . . toward an embodied future, even as that future is summoned into being in and through a body that does not yet exist, and while the body that does exist in the present is the medium for the future body's becoming-form."[26] Such an enfolded temporality is inevitably affectively complex, with traumas residual and fresh existing alongside—rather, knotted together with—moments of joy, hope, and recognition. As Gwen Benaway writes, in a beautiful essay on surgical transition and the long process of coming home to one's body, "the events that surround our becoming leave an imprint on us."[27] The memories of these events are carried with us and come to help constitute our divergent and overlapping experiences of embodiment. Meditating on the complexities of the relations between trans embodiment, selfhood, and temporality, and figuring her self and her body as a "we" in negotiation, Benaway offers the following account:

> Together, we imagined a possibility instead of an ending. This is the real story of bodies. Movement, joy, and release into new configurations. Our bodies do not need to be perfect or exactly as they were when we were born. We are not ruled by the shape we arrive in. We adapt, heal, and expand. Our bodies are not an ending, but a beginning. This is a truth I am willing to die for.[28]

While transnormative futural narratives envision the time of posttransition as characterized by the structure of feeling associated with domesticity—comfort, ease, happiness, safety—and are underwritten by the promise of finally feeling at home in one's skin, this affective narrative of what the body as home feels like belies the complex temporalities of transition. Benaway points out the ways that such a coming-home involves moving through trauma, grappling with the enormous existential difficulties and forms of violence, both structural and interpersonal, that attend processes of trans becoming. She argues that these experiences leave an imprint, that the traces of these events are, following Carter, always temporally enfolded within, part and parcel of, the experience of embodiment.

Some of the difficulties that attend affective experiences of transition have do with the forms of disconnection, withdrawal, and dissociation that often accompany it. As trans scholar Atalia Israeli-Nevo writes, in a meditation on her own (slow, circuitous) transition process:

> As trans subjects in this transphobic world, we are encouraged and forced into a position of not being present. We are dissociated from our bodies, our loved ones, and our

general environment. This dissociation throws us into a far future in which we are safe after we have passed and found a bodily and social home. However, this future is imagined and unreachable, resulting in us being out of time.[29]

When Israeli-Nevo articulates being "forced into a position of not being present," she's referring to the ensemble of strategies that trans subjects cultivate in response to consistent misrecognition, phobic response, and shunning. One of these responses is social withdrawal. If one's appearance in a situation or social world is contingent on misrecognition and encounters with macro- and microaggressions, they may do their best to limit or altogether avoid, to the best of their ability, such situations. Another related response is that of skepticism and mistrust. This entails a carefully considered curation of where and how one appears, among whom, in what kinds of built spaces. This means that any form of public or semipublic encounter is subject to premeditation and scrutiny with reference to the maintenance of one's physical and emotional well-being (though often one has very limited agency over whether or not to inhabit certain spaces and must appear and engage ones they'd rather avoid). If "being present" means occupying space with a degree of unself-consciousness, lack of anxiety, and without projections about what forms of violence might occur, then "being present" is a form of privilege that the majority of trans subjects lack. The word Israeli-Nevo gives to this complex experience is *dissociation*—detaching physically, psychologically, and emotionally from spaces, institutions, situations, relationships, and our own bodies, even as we must continue to inhabit them. In the midst of this dissociation, we are offered narratives about finding home and safety, but this is contingent on a process of medical transition that may be out of reach, differentially deferred, or not even desired; it is upon this narrative that we are encouraged to pin our hopes and dreams. Even for those of us who are able to access medical technologies of transition, the experience of dissociation, once endured, remains pleated into the present moment, a memory imprinted, informing our relationship to our own bodies and the multiple milieu they move with and within.

T4T: TRANS INTIMACIES AND TRANS PRESENTS (OR HOW TO SURVIVE THE INTERREGNUM)

Linear temporalities of transition have trouble holding the complexities that attend the enfolded time of transition. It isn't adequate to the task of dignifying the ways in which past trauma emerges suddenly in a present moment, the ways that negative affect that we might be tempted to associate with a closeted past or the turbulence of transition persists and endures, resonating across lifespans and irrefutably transforming the subjects so affected. I have found, in the speculative dystopic trans fictions of Kai Cheng Thom and Torrey Peters, disruptive reworkings of temporalities of transition that offer a more capacious frame through which to incorporate the ongoing lived effects of negative affect.[30] The dystopic visions they offer resist the tendency to link joyful affect to futural hope, even as they vividly depict the scrappy inventiveness, creativity, and intimacy cultivated by trans folks in order to survive in radically imperfect, irreparably broken worlds.

Kai Cheng Thom's *Fierce Femmes and Notorious Liars* takes place in a fantastic fictional near future that very much mirrors the North American present. The narrator—who is never named—leaves home in her late teens, running from a city called Gloom where she has lived with her parents, both Chinese migrants, and a beloved younger sister named Charity, toward the City of Smoke and Lights, a place where "the streets are crooked, and the light is heavy, and the air is stained ash grey from the glamorous cigarette lips of hungry ghosts swimming through the fog"; a place where "anything can happen if you dream it," where "you can be anything you want."[31] She has moved to the City of Smoke and Lights to transition, to "become nobody" in order to "become someone else."[32] She finds the Street of Miracles, a vice district populated by trans femmes and queers and cops and johns, and is quickly taken in by a circle of trans women and placed under the protective wing of Kimaya, a trans elder whose smile is "ancient and battered and mysterious, punctuated by several cracked teeth . . . from getting hit in the face by her boyfriend ten years ago, . . . from a police baton during a protest."[33] Kimaya's smile, which the narrator calls "bright and beautiful," is a living testimonial to the forms of trans resilience in the face of trauma that the narrator is about to be initiated into.[34] Over the course of the "confabulous memoir," she will fight (and kill) cops and johns in order to defend herself and her trans sisterhood, fall in love, navigate exploitative specialists in trans medicine, negotiate the difficulties of political solidarity through debates about the most effective modes of trans insurgency, struggle to find and afford a place to live, and cultivate strategies for ensuring her physical and emotional safety in situations of explicit transmisogynistic targeting.

Torrey Peters's novella *Infect Your Friends and Loved Ones* takes place in a dystopic near future where another unnamed narrator negotiates the fallout wrought by a global "contagion" that comes about when her on-again, off-again girlfriend, Lexi, invents a new form of bacteria that prevents human bodies from responding to endogenous hormonal production, ushering in an era wherein everyone—cis and trans folks alike—must rely on exogenous hormones in order to manifest gendered embodiment in the ways they desire. Over the course of the novel, we shuttle back and forth in time, with the orienting event that structures before and after being "contagion." This contagion is personal—the narrator is one of the first people infected, in a deliberate move by Lexi that would cease the narrator's biological responsiveness to androgens—but she is also a patient zero figure, initiating global contagion. It tweaks the temporal function of hormone injection and ingestion in mainstream trans narratives that, as Horak and Raun note, so often functions as a temporally structuring principle. In the novella, this moment is not individuated, not a tale of personal gender transformation, but an event of world-shifting magnitude; Peters even refers to trans folks in the novel as "antediluvian trans," situating contagion on par with the cataclysmic great biblical Flood. Because of the polysemy of the word *antediluvian*—which can also mean old-fashioned, behind-the-times—Peters also implicitly raises questions about how we might understand trans subjectivities in a near future where everyone partakes of exogenous hormonal body modification. It's worth noting that this near future is very much like the present, insofar as cis and trans folks alike routinely utilize exogenous hormones for all sorts of reasons.

Both books are animated by the questions that Alexis Lothian poses about the work of speculative dystopia, which she articulates as such: "A dystopian impulse leads us to ask: what do speculative narrative futures look and feel like without either a redemptive kernel of hope or an implicit acceptance of the way things are? And what pleasures . . . and politics grow from this kind of speculation?"[35] In other words, how can we think futurity without acquiescing to the narrative lures of optimism, salvation, rebirth, redemption? The genre of trans speculative dystopia, of which Peters and Thom are but two examples, offers us rich resources for envisioning such futures. They are part of a broader set of literatures theorized by Adrienne Maree Brown, Walidah Imarisha, and Sheree Renée Thomas as "visionary fiction," a term they use to distinguish speculative fiction that "has relevance towards building new, freer worlds from mainstream science fiction, which most often reinforces dominant narratives of power."[36]

The fact that Thom calls *Fierce Femmes* a "confabulous memoir" highlights the limitations of traditional (linear, redemptive) narrative strategies of trans memoir. Unpacking the portmanteau *confabulous* means, first, grasping that it is shaped by confabulation, a form of unintentional memory error that takes the form of fabricated or distorted retellings of experience; second, that it takes part in a process of fabulation, a postmodern narrative form emerging out of resistance to the conventions of both realism and romanticism, one that we most readily associate with magical realism in its combination of the mundane and the fantastic; and third, that such forms of revised and invented narratives are fabulous. A "confabulous memoir" offers us a way of getting at both the mundane and extraordinary valences of trans experiences and can only be enacted by leaving behind the dominant temporal and affective tropes of trans memoir. As Thom comments in an interview with *Teen Vogue*:

> [The book is] a struggle to break out of the memoir genre that trans women have been relegated to for a really long time, this idea that we are only important or readable as objects to study, as objects to be used as titillation for a cisgender audience. [This narrative of] us explaining our life story of being born in the wrong body and being oppressed and overcoming it and then assimilating into a happy cis-passing straight life. That is not the reality of the vast majority of trans women I know.[37]

The book begins with a critique of this narrative, opening with the narrator watching a wealthy white trans woman—a thinly veiled proxy for Caitlyn Jenner—who has just gotten "The Surgery" receive an "Upstanding Good Samaritan Pillar of the Community Award for, like, being brave or whatever."

> What really works me up is the *way* that this whole story is being told: Everyone look at this poor little trans girl desperate for a ~~fairy godmother~~doctor to give her boobs and a vagina and a pretty face and wear nice dresses! Save the trans girls! Save the whales! Put them in a zoo!
>
> It's actually a very old archetype that trans girl stories get put into: this sort of tragic, plucky-little-orphan character who is just supposed to suffer through everything and wait, and if you're good and brave and patient (and white and rich) enough, then you get the big reward. . . . which is that you get to be just like everybody else who is white and rich and boring. And then you marry the prince or the football player and live boringly ever after. We're like

Cinderella, waiting to go to the ball. Like the Little Mermaid, getting her tail surgically altered and her voice removed, so that she can walk around on land. Those are the stories we get, these days.

Or, you know, the ones where we're dead.[38]

The character slippage Thom's narrator highlights—between fairy godmother and doctor—highlights the messianic temporal structure that tends to characterize transition, shifting the register to a princess narrative, which (like narratives of being saved by religion) charts a move from wretchedness and despair to effulgence and fulfillment. Thom's narrator also raises the question of deservedness: Who is a good trans person? Who is an ideal candidate for transition? The long history of medical gatekeeping around transition is the obvious target of commentary here; the "~~fairy godmother~~doctor" the arbiter of whether one might become what they so desire. The proper affective disposition in relation to this phenomenon is one of deference and hope—one is exhorted to fulfill the role of the "tragic, plucky-little-orphan character" or the rare and endangered species in need of rescue ("Save the trans girls! Save the whales! Put them in a zoo!"). The orphan, the endangered species: both are figures of severely curtailed agency, victims of their environment almost entirely dependent on the good will, grace, and assistance of others. Importantly, in the case of the endangered species, these others are often precisely those who did the harm in the first place! These metaphors suggest trans girls are radically unable to save themselves, though desperately in need of saving. What Thom's narrator suggests here is that trans girls are consistently framed as both radically vulnerable and incapable of saving themselves—a disempowering, deleterious, and limiting trope if ever there was one. Further, she suggests that the possibility of rescue is not just predicated on the successful performance of deference, desire, and gratitude but also explicitly tied to racial and economic privilege—being "good and brave and patient (and white and rich) enough." One is worth saving only if they already bear certain markers of existential value, only if they already, in Foucauldian terms, count as part of the population conceptualized as worthy of life, rather than cathected to the slow process of neglect that characterizes the phenomenon of neglect that so profoundly shapes his articulation of biopolitics as the "the power to 'make' live and 'let' die."[39] Thom's narrator highlights the radically bifurcated mainstream narratives of trans femme existence; they vacillate between princess narratives and accounts of brutal homicide, and the difference between the two hinges on questions of racial and economic status. Temporally speaking, this is a vacillation between the brightest of futures and no future, between hope and the radical negation of hope. Both of these temporalities yoke (and reduce) the complexities of trans experience to a future, either promised or foreclosed. Both temporalities place trans presents, and trans presences (the forms in which we manifest here, now, whatever those may be), under erasure.

What Thom's novel does, instead, is radically refuse a futural narrative of redemption by grounding the story in the complicated intimacies of a group of trans femmes living and loving alongside one another, supporting each other, arguing with each other, forming an "all-trans girl vigilante gang" with each other, making love, breaking up, reconciling.[40] We shuttle to the past from time to time, through memory narratives offered by several different characters, but the bulk of the book takes place in a now wherein the narrator is learning, gradually, hard lessons about self-care and the importance of trans communality in a broader necropolitical context wherein violence is routinized, normalized, and rarely contested unless by trans subjects themselves. At the conclusion of the book, the narrator even explicitly refuses attachment to a fairy-tale ending: the arrival of her prince. She meets and falls for a trans guy named Josh, a graduate student from a wealthy family who is kind, generous, and committed to building a future with the narrator; he invites her to move into his (extraordinarily fancy) condo, bankrolled by his family, and encourages her to go to college in order to take writing classes.

While discussing this turn of events with her elder protectress Kimaya, she pauses to envision their future together:

> And now I'm going to move in with him, and he keeps on saying I should think about auditing classes at the University and probably I could get a scholarship and what a great writer I could be with my "gift for storytelling." And then I'll get published and become a super-famous Transgender Writer and we'll get married and be a Transgender Power Couple and have Transgender Children and raise them on a cloud of Transgender Happiness™.
>
> And the thing is, I *want* that. I want it so, so bad.[41]

But she also senses that Josh is pushing her toward this fairy-tale ending, toward the fulfillment of their promise as a Trans Power Couple; she resents this projection, while also being lured by it. She then turns to Kimaya and asks, "What do you think the difference is between hunger and love?" Kimaya responds, after some deliberation: "Hunger is a story you get stuck in. Love's the story that takes you somewhere new."[42] Thom gives vivid shape here to both the absolutely understandable lure of transnormative futural narratives—framing them as informed by a deep yearning for something better—and the danger of such futural attachments, manifest in the ways they produce a certain stuckness. This stuckness is precisely what Berlant notes as integral to cruel optimism, insofar as it produces difficulty improvising in the context of an ever-shifting present because of fidelity to a particular cluster of futural promises about what constitutes the good life. A practice of love is proposed, in the place of such hunger, as that which might transform the conditions of the present; Berlant gives this the name of solidarity, which, they write, "comes from the scavenging for survival that absorbs increasingly more people's lives."[43] The most profound love that we witness in Thom's work is that between the trans women who dwell, scavenging for survival, in the Street of Miracles; and it is the practice of love cultivated there that enables each of them to not get stuck in a story, to go "somewhere new." Thom's narrator rejects the scripted futures on offer, choosing instead the sustaining unpredictability of a praxis of love. Thom's work helps us explore the affective structures of trans presents, which are always more nuanced, more variegated, than the Janus-faced structure of conventional narratives of trans futurity would have us believe.

I turn now to the dystopian trans alter-world on offer in the work of Torrey Peters, as it deals directly with questions of negative affect, grappling with the way the everyday is shot through with traumas residual and fresh, which make themselves more or less available within the present depending on conjuncture, chance, affinity, and trigger. Crucially, however, these traumas are positioned not as wounds to be healed, finally sutured in some future-perfect. Rather, the narrative—like Thom's—is resolutely irresolute, refusing to wrap up loose ends, refusing the lure of the palliative gestures of happily-ever-after, yet offering glimmers of possibility for living-otherwise, in and through trauma, and maybe perhaps beyond it. These glimmers are routed through trans-for-trans (t4t) love, affection, and intimacy, presented as simultaneously radically difficult and radically transformative.

The central love story—if one can call it that—in Torrey Peters's novella *Infect Your Friends and Loved Ones* occurs between trans folk, between the narrator and Lexi, another trans woman. This fact alone merits pause. Peters, through this narratological decision, renders a world that actively decenters cis subjectivities, perceptions, and erotic economies of meaning, recognition, and validation. Emphasis is placed on t4t circuits of recognition, attraction, solidarity, and support, and a central animating question emerges: how can trans folk learn to love each other? In exploring the dynamics of t4t intimacy, Peters intentionally performs a radical revision of the meaning of the acronym.

The designation t4t began its life as a category within the personals section of Craigslist (a regionally tailored online version of classified advertisements), one of the handful of options that enabled folks to search through online personals by gender identification. I consider the intimacy elaborated in Peters's work a *détourned* take-up of the t4t acronym. Détournement—a tactic developed by Guy Debord (and affiliated radical French Lettrists) in the 1950s and later taken up by the Situationist International—is most easily understood as the appropriation and repurposing (rerouting, hijacking, derailing) of an existing media artifact in a manner that troubles, subverts, or resists the intended messaging of the original artifact. Understanding the détournement t4t undergoes in Peters's work begins with admitting the obvious transphobic logic that undergirds the initial iteration of t4t: it sequesters trans folks from M's and W's (as in M4M, W4W), partaking of the kind of trans-exclusionary (not to mention cisnormative and homonormative) logic that misconstrues trans as a sexualized gender category unto itself. As Susan Stryker clarifies in her critical rereading of the importance of trans exclusion for the emergence of homonormative political/communal forms:

> As a sexual orientation category, trans appears as a desire, ʾkin to kink and fetish desire, for cross-dressing or (more extremely) genital modification. The "T" in this version of the LGBT community becomes a group of people who are attracted to one another on the basis of enjoying certain sexual practices—in the same way that gay men are attracted to gay men, and lesbians are attracted to lesbians, on the basis of a shared desire for particular sexual practices.[44]

When the digital architectonics of Craigslist partake of this logic, misinterpreting trans identity as kink—and drawing on a long history of such problematic interpretations, ranging from John Money's writing on gynemimetophiles to the work of J. Michael Bailey and beyond—they also deploy "T" as an insulating function, intending to prevent trans-identified individuals from cropping up in the rest of the personals.[45] As Stryker clarifies, "Trans thus conceived of does not trouble the basis of the other categories [M, W, hetero, homo]—indeed, it becomes a containment mechanism for 'gender trouble' of various sorts that works in tandem with assimilative gender-normative tendencies within the sexual identities."[46] It also derealizes the authenticity of trans gender identifications, partaking of the double-bind Talia Mae Bettcher so eloquently parses in "Evil Deceivers and Make-Believers," where trans folk can only be perceived within cisnormative framings as "fooling" cis folks—particularly in intimate/sexual contexts—or "pretending" to be the gender that one is.[47] It is implicit in the structuring logic of Craigslist personals that trans folks are sequestered precisely to guard against cis experiences of ostensible deception.

However, the designers of Craigslist personals also unintentionally produced a kind of proto-trans-separatist space with the invention of t4t, and it is this by-product, this form of alternative usage, that is taken up within contemporary manifestations of the acronym, both as a hashtag and as a descriptor of intimacies extant and desired. The category t4t is a form of contingent, strategic separatism that Chela Sandoval usefully glosses as a mode of oppositional consciousness that is initiated in order "to protect and nurture the differences that define its practitioners through their complete separation from the dominant social order."[48] It is in the tradition of other forms of politicized and eroticized separatism, echoing Marlon Riggs's assertion in *Tongues Untied* that "black men loving black men is *the* revolutionary act," and resonating with the formulation of lesbian separatism as a praxis engaged by "woman-loving women" in order to invent modes of life beyond the stranglehold of interlocking (male, heterosexual, white) supremacies.[49] Importantly, t4t emerges from a recognition that trans subjects, too, might benefit from a severing of ties to cissexist modes of interpellating trans bodies (as failures, fakes, inorganic, inauthentic) and, moreover, that such strategic separatism might be one of the most direct routes toward cultivating self-love, self-regard, and self-care, especially because it confronts and disrupts the assimilationist logics that structure the limiting forms of individuated futural aspiration already discussed. The hope is that, in community with one another, insulated—however temporarily—from cissexist modes of perception, some significant healing might be possible.

Peters's work fleshes out this détourned reinvention of t4t

for the purposes of trans intimacy. She is quite explicit about her reconceptualization of it: the acronym appears on the cover of *Infect Your Friends and Loved Ones,* is spoken as a secret code of care and solidarity at crucial points in the novella, and appears as a stick-and-poke tattoo on Lexi, one of the central characters (the former/maybe future lover and complex frenemy of the narrator). Lexi and the narrator also met through the t4t personals, where the narrator answered Lexi's ad, despite being in a sexless relationship with her current girlfriend (whom she started dating prior to transition) and already involved in clandestine Skype and phone-sex hookups with random men. She wants to meet Lexi, though not necessarily for sex: "Why do I want to meet Lexi? The answer is things I can't say. That I can barely think."[50] The narrator's desire to reach out to another trans woman is opaque, oblique, ineffable—not predetermined, scripted, or prefigured, but an opening to possibilities not yet articulable or even quite imaginable. For me, this admission of unsurety raises several significant questions: What does it mean that the narrator—and perhaps, by extension, many other trans folk—lacks scripts, expectations, and assumptions for t4t intimacy? What possibilities inhere in the space of such unscriptedness? What might t4t intimacy enable in a world less overcoded by forms of genital-centricity that overcode and naturalize linkages between morphology and intimacy?

Peters builds such a world in *Infect Your Friends and Loved Ones* and does this by, first, making everyone trans. Lexi and her trans girl gang concoct a contagious bacteriological infection (derived from agricultural research on pigs) that "causes a body's antibodies to bind to gonadotropin (GnRH)"—as the narrator explains, "the hormone that signals the production of all sex hormones in mammals."[51] This means that the antibodies then attack GnRH, resulting in "a complete cessation of the production of all sex hormones."[52] What this contagion effectively ushers in is a near-global reliance on exogenous hormones—an intensification of what Paul Preciado calls the "pharmacopornographic era" and a quite literal reimagining of Halberstam's early-career assertion that "we are all transsexuals. There are no transsexuals."[53] While we certainly live in a world that is (albeit discontinuously) biomedicalized and in bodies, whether cis or trans, that are deeply imbricated with and reliant on all sorts of exogenous hormones—whether we're on birth control, supplementing ostensibly low T, on hormone replacement therapy to mitigate menopause, or taking hormones to transition—Peters removes the question of agency, establishing a new biological baseline that asks everyone to choose and thus to deal with questions of access, scarcity, and gatekeeping the way trans folk have had to for the last several decades.

In the postcontagion world that Peters constructs, where the body modified by exogenous hormones has become a general ontology, where one's intentional relation to practices of biomolecular modification must be grappled with and there is no recourse to a purportedly "natural" form of biological dimorphism, the phrase "antediluvian trans" comes to mark a difference of identity and agential relation to transition that might otherwise be lost in a world of "auntie-boys" and "T-slabs" (the names Peters gives to folks accessing exogenous estrogen and testosterone postcontagion).[54] The register of trans identity thus shifts, as does the meaning of trans solidarity. What differentiates antediluvian trans folk from others has to do primarily with shared desires and affective orientations rather than access to technologies of transition. In Peters's world, hormones are scarce, subject to a black-market economy, and liable to be tainted with harmful chemicals. Transition-related surgeries have ceased to be available; given that the world is increasingly given over to scarcity and subsistence, the market for such technologies has dried up. Nevertheless, the networks that trans women had formed before contagion persist and are shaped by a t4t praxis of love.

Explicating the meaning of this praxis, Zoey—a member of a trans femme separatist farmhouse on the plains—says, "It's a promise. You just promise to love trans girls above all else. The idea—although maybe not the practice—is that a girl could be your worst enemy, the girl you wouldn't piss on to put out a fire, but if she's trans, you're gonna offer her your bed, you're gonna share your last hormone shot."[55] The narrator responds that this sounds like "some kind of trans girl utopia," to which Zoey laughs and clarifies: "Do you think the words trans women and utopia ever go together in the same sentence? Even when we're not starved for hormones, we're still bitches. Crabs in a barrel. Fucking utopia, my ass."[56] And finally, closing the scene, Zoey drives the point home: "We aim high, trying to love each other and then we take what we can get. We settle for looking out for each other. And even if we don't all love each other, we mostly all respect one another."[57]

In Peters's work, t4t is many things: an ideal, a promise, an identifier, a way of flagging an ethic of being. It is antiutopian, guiding a praxis of solidarity in the interregnum; it is about small acts guided by a commitment to trans love, small acts that make life more livable in and through difficult circumstances. It has no truck with cruel optimism, with the attachment to a toxic present because of a promised future that wears you down and out. It is cynical, skeptical; t4t is set up to fail, about aiming high and taking what one can get. It embraces ethical imperfection and complexity. It dwells in difficulty without the expectation that such difficulties will cease by and through a t4t praxis of love. It is about being with and bearing with; about witnessing one another, being mirrors for one another that avoid some of the not-so-funhouse effects of cisnormative perceptive habits that frame trans folk as too much, not enough, failed or not yet realized. Nevertheless, it doesn't rely on a frictionless and easeful understanding of trans relationality; it hinges on the admittance that trans people often have a very, very difficult time with one another. Appearing together in public might increase the likelihood of being clocked; dwelling in intimate spaces with one another might render one's homeplaces more difficult, rather than less, as trans-related trauma is shared and thus, perhaps, affectively amplified rather than diminished (a phenomenon that is not bad, per se, just complex and—sometimes—tiring). Then there are those other dynamics Zoey obliquely references with the phrase "crabs in a barrel"—the forms of envy, annoyance, jealously, and judgment borne out of survival struggles and economies of scarcity, an emotional ensemble shorthanded by Zoey in one word—"bitches"—a word that is simultaneously an indicator of relational difficulty and a badge of honor, a sign of tenacity, bullheadedness, ambition, and brassiness. Not to mention competing and sometimes incompatible personalities, politics, expectations, and assumptions.

To recall Eve Kosofsky Sedgwick's very first axiom: (trans) people are different from one another.[58] As such, t4t is inevitably a difficult practice of love across difference in the name of coalition and survival, and it thus can't presuppose or predicate such love on identitarian or subjective sameness. Too often, "trans folk/people/communities" gets deployed as an abstract and overcoded monolith, coming to signify for diversely stratified communities. When used monolithically, *trans* coheres in ways that minimize colonial and racial differences and operates as implicitly white and settler, presuming a form of trans belonging sutured through the experience of *trans* as a single-axis form of minoritization. A t4t praxis of love enables and elicits more finely grained attention to differences between and among trans folk, with all the dissonance and difficulty engaging such differences entails. In this movement toward one another, this contingent separatism, space is made to signify and be understood differently, in greater complexity, in excess of reductive cis- and transnormative interpellations of trans subjects. Ultimately, what a t4t praxis of love does is offer a blueprint for surviving lag time, for getting by in the interregnum, which may end up being the only time we have.

Admittedly, this praxis isn't always, or perhaps ever, easy to engage. In the following chapter, I explore what happens when this praxis is hard to put into action, when it's hard to feel or do anything at all. What to make of the way incessant fatigue and anxiety so reliably produce social recessivity, withdrawal, and numbness? I turn to this question next.

2

FUCK FEELINGS

On Numbness, Withdrawal, and Disorientation

The body emerges from [the] history of doing, which is also a history of not doing, of paths not taken, which also involves the loss, impossible to know or even register, of what might have followed from such paths.

—Sara Ahmed, *Queer Phenomenology*

TRANS DISORIENTATION

Disorientation—the feeling of being unmoored, miscalibrated, out of sorts as one tries to learn and relearn the parameters of a world that shifts along with one's shifts in gender—is a fundamental part of trans experience.

In thinking through disorientation, I am accompanied by Sara Ahmed's account of it in *Queer Phenomenology*. She begins with the assertion that experiences of disorientation are "vital"—that is, they bear on questions of livability and survival, on whether or not, and how, we remain sensate and attuned to the milieu on which we interdepend.[1] She writes that experiences of disorientation are "bodily experiences that throw the world up, or throw the body from its ground," that they can range from being unsettling to self-shattering, and that if this feeling of shattering persists, it can "become a crisis."[2] Disorientation, characterized by this affective gradient of unsettling to shattering, might pass, too, and be supplanted by an experience of reorientation, a moment of grounding and settling that enables one to piece the self back together, at least partially and contingently.

Importantly, Ahmed points out that such disorientation can be a routine part of one's daily experience; we can and do shuttle between orientation and disorientation on a regular basis. To illustrate the mundanity of such shuttling, she provides an account of a scene of being interrupted while writing, being called upon while absorbed in the paper on which she writes, an experience that she describes as the inhabitation of a "contourless world" characterized primarily by recession from one's surround.[3] She expounds: "the object—say, the paper, and the thoughts that gather around the paper by gathering as lines on the paper—becomes what it is by losing its contours. The paper becomes worldly, which might even mean you lose sight of the table."[4] Here, writing involves a form of bracketing and withdrawal that means the world beyond the paper recedes, momentarily ceases to be the milieu in which one is orientated. You don't lose yourself in writing, but you strategically minimize the worldly frame until it is constituted primarily, if not exclusively, by the paper upon which you write. This experience is absorptive, but also characterized by a discrete lack of performed emotional expressiveness: the writer appears impassive. Thus, writing is a strategic way of receding from a surround, a way of reducing the impingement of the environment on the sensorium. It might be, then, at least for some of us, a technology of survival—a way of producing some insulating distance from phobic, hostile, and exhausting milieus.

But the recession is momentary. It always comes to end, often by way of intrusion or interruption. The experience of being interrupted while writing can tell us much about how we experience the phenomenon of disorientation. The absorption, our plunge into the "contourless world" of the page is intruded upon by an other or others who force us to suddenly shift dimensions.

These are "moments," Ahmed writes, "in which you lose one perspective, but the 'loss' itself is not empty or waiting; it is an object, thick with presence. . . . You experience the moment as loss, as the making present of something that is now absent (the presence of an absence)."[5] You sense the visceral loss of the world you had been in and struggle to adjust to the shape of the shift in world appearing. It takes a moment—shorter or longer—to reorient. One is literally upset (unsettled, disrupted) by such forcible dis- and reorientation: "You might even feel angry from being dislodged from the world you inhabited as a contourless world. You might even say to the person who addressed you with the frustrated reply of 'What is it?' What is 'it' that makes me lose what is before me?"[6]

What is "it" that makes me lose what is before me? What makes us lose our bearings, our balance? What are our affective responses to being forcibly dislodged from a world? How do we register and respond to the consisting upset of our worlds, the repetitive disorientations that recur? Do we become disoriented when the institutions and social relations we inhabit, and rely upon, fail to hail us and hold us?

I wager that most trans folks can articulate a veritable litany of disorientations: the moments wherein we're referred to by the wrong name, the wrong pronoun, the wrong honorific; the moments when our bodies are referred to with language that registers dissonantly, inaccurately; the moments wherein we are touched in ways that trigger rage, sadness, dysphoria, self-hatred, self-harm, where our bodies are being interacted with as if they were something other than how we understand and inhabit them. In each of these moments, which are so routine as to constitute a trans genre of misrecognition, we experience some form of disorientation. We are forced to ask ourselves whether or not a person or institution means to hail us, forced to wonder whether we are or are not being hailed. This, in turn, prompts us to consider, repetitively and frequently, how we are manifesting in a given room, how are we signifying, how our interpellation and positioning in the world might be clashing with our self-understanding. We are pushed to confront, over and over again, how the world in which we find ourselves is constructed in ways that refuse, exclude, elide, or overwrite our sense of existence.

Here's a story of disorientation from my own backlog, part of my own litany of misrecognition: in the fall of 2018, I was at a meeting, and something happened. It was a typical academic administrative meeting—colleagues, an associate dean, an administrative assistant for the associate dean were present. Why we were meeting might be relevant, or might not be, but I'm going to bracket it out and say simply that the kind of institutional accounting of this thing we call "diversity" was relevant, both to the content of the meeting and to the assembly of bodies in the room. There was a sheet of attendees who had RSVP'd for the meeting; the administrative assistant was accounting for the bodies both present and absent as we filtered into the room, without knowing many of us in an experiential, person-to-person way.

We waited a few minutes past the turn of the hour for folks who might be running late to turn up. Someone suggested we get started. The administrative assistant scanned the list, looked out at the room, and said, "Well, I think we're still waiting on Hilary." My colleagues responded in near-unison, just shy of sounding exasperated, an exasperation I felt indebted to, maybe thankful for: "Hilary's here."

This sort of occurrence is so routine as to feel mundane by this point. My name consistently heralds a body that isn't mine, inaugurates a presence other than the one I'm perceived as bringing to a room. It's worth noting that my name isn't dead to me, though perhaps it would be easier if it were. There are contingencies regarding publication to consider. But more than that, much more than that: this experience of dissonance, this vacillation between assumed presence and the absence of that assumed presence, the kind of stuttering and embarrassment and aggression—often comingled—this dissonance provokes, might very well be the only kind of subjectification that I understand intimately. When a kind of recognition emerges through this crucible of dissonance, it feels almost right, or at least appropriate (as Berlant writes, recognition is the misrecognition you can bear). Pronominal stammering, present absence, absent presence: this is a structure of recognition that is nonbinary. A structure of recognition that feels like it almost encompasses the complex history of living in a trans, intersex body, a kind of body that is consistently related to, as one guide to parenting intersex children has it, as a body that parents "weren't expecting" (the full title of the piece is "What to Expect When You Have the Child You Weren't Expecting").[7] It's not just parents, of course, that weren't expecting this body; no one, no institution, no loose conviviality of folks, seems to expect it. This is resonant, too, with how trans folks are so often interpellated according to an economics of personhood that is always much more and much less, always simultaneously too much and not enough. Extra and failed.

Disorientation is helping me think through how I live this, how we live this, the alternate registers of knownness that make this survivable. How we get through being in a room that we're not recognized as inhabiting, how we make it into and out of spaces, simultaneously material and discursive, that have been deliberately arranged to erase us, to make our presence maybe impossible, but at the very least impracticable. In other words, how we cultivate a tolerance for such repetitive and insistent moments of disorientation; how adept we are forced to become at world-traveling.[8] How we inoculate ourselves against the dizziness and nausea, how we acclimate to the wooziness of being repeatedly unmoored and tossed. When Ahmed writes that "disorientation is unevenly distributed: some bodies more than others have their involvement in the world called into crisis," it's another way of saying that some of us are dizzier, more off-balance, than others, because the shape of the world we're in offers little in the way of stability, little for us to hold on to as we recalibrate and readjust.[9] This is felt as a crisis of motility, as disorientation renders movement queer; the body-in-the-world becomes strange, as we cease to experience ourselves as sovereign in relation to its meaning and movement, as it fails to function as the vehicle for the enactment of our aims and becomes, instead, compromised in its interface with a surround, unable to reach out, make contact, entwine, or transport itself in the usual ways.

How do we deal with such repetitive and incessant experiences of disorientation? In what follows, I theorize how emotional underperformance, social withdrawal, and the selective cultivation of numbness operate as affective means of grappling with the experience of persistent disorientation. I write about the ways in which (some) trans folks inure ourselves to both hostile socialities as well as those shaped by a kind of lukewarm inclusivity. I do this, in part, in order to think through some of the negative affects associated with negotiating trans embodiment in the contexts of sex, eroticism, and intimacy, in order to explore how we feel about fucking (or not fucking, or not wanting to fuck, or how we've been fucked, or how we want to fuck and be fucked). But I'm also attending to the phenomena of numbness, withdrawal, dissociation, and refusal, thinking through the ways in which we distance and detach from different socialities and relationalities that may have once seemed, or continue to seem, alluring (in the sense of luring us) on account of a lack of trust, a divestment from forms of optimism that we've learned, intimately, are too often cruel. In other words, the ways in which we're like, "*Fuck* feelings." My hunch is that trans experiences of embodiment, sexuality, and intimacy are deeply interwoven with these forms of detachment, withdrawal, and numbness, and, further, that these are affective intensities that resonate across different trans experiences, forming what Berlant calls an "affective common that develops through a process of jointly gathered implicitation."[10] Here, "implicitation" means "held but inexplicit knowledge"—what we know but don't articulate, what can be implicitly and nonverbally recognized as a shared affective response or orientation.[11] In this chapter, I explore how flat affect, recession, withdrawal, and numbness circulate as part of an affective commons that informs trans experiences of embodiment, sexuality, and intercorporeality. I argue that they are rooted in, and responsive to, the experience of persistent disorientation.

TRANS GUYS SMOKING

I start with flat affect, a kind of underperformativity that, while articulated in psychological literature as closely allied with schizophrenia and depression and manifesting as verbal monotony, facial inexpressiveness, and generalized apathetic response, has also been richly taken up by Lauren Berlant as a helpful concept in theorizing recent shifts in the ways that emotion is and is not displayed. For Berlant, flat affect is a name for the moments wherein "worlds and events that would have been expected to be captured by expressive suffering—featuring an amplified subjectivity, violent and reparative relationality, and assurance about what makes an event significant—appear with an asterisk of uncertainty."[12] This "asterisk of uncertainty" takes the form of a markedly dialed-down emotive response, as well as what they call a "diffused yet animated gesture"—a modification of affect that splits and spreads, that is more minimal than one might expect, but repeats and recurs like a series of affective aftershocks, low-grade but consistent and insistent, manifesting across a wide range of experience.[13] Imagine a person that reliably shrugs in the face of horrifying news.

This mode of affective underperformance has the effect of loosening the impact of the present, of holding space open, refusing both the emotional solidification and surety that accompany melodramatic response and the distancing, ironizing skepticism that characterizes deadpan response. Flat affect occurs when we don't know how we feel in the midst or aftermath of an encounter, or when we don't have the space or support to feel a certain kind of way, with a certain kind of intensity, or when an encounter might shatter us if we don't impose some kind of distance or cushion between it and ourselves. It might manifest as excessive casualness, the affective equivalent of being, like, "whatever." Underperformance is a way of living in an affective in-between, in the absence of a generalized optimism and in some kind of implicit resistance to a range of affective intensities that may, in themselves, make life more difficult, less livable.

Underperformativity, Berlant writes, "sneaks arounds the codes of sincerity and legibility that make possible normative social trust and trust in the social."[14] It does this through receding from the scene of encounter, withdrawing, refusing the immediate legibility of emotive response. It happens, in large part, when one has no significant reason to invest or trust in the forms of sociality in which they're more or less inescapably embedded, and thus also under an informal injunction to not be affectively disruptive, especially if the cost of such disruption is compromised access to the forms of sociality one depends on for survival.

This point—about sociality, survival, and withdrawal—is the reason why I think there's a particular resonance that flat affect has for trans subjects. Many of us have, of necessity, grown deeply skeptical of the most routine of social encounters, given how the routine remains deeply premised on cisnormative presumptions. The result of this skepticism is, often, social withdrawal or recession. If flat affect (and its variations) is a hallmark of such forms of withdrawal and recession, we might expect it to be a key component of a trans affective commons (spoiler alert: I'm about to argue that it is).

Berlant's cultural archive is definitely cooler, in all its valences, than mine is here; they mention directors like Richard Linklater, Greta Gerwig, Cheryl Dunye, Rose Troche, Todd Haynes, and Gregg Araki, as well as authors and artists like Miranda July, Teju Cole, and Tao Lin. I'm looking, instead, at two documentaries that depict the lives of rural, white, Southern trans men, both of whom, at least at first blush, embrace some of the trappings and affectations we associate with forms of "redneck" or "good ol' boy" types of masculinity. These aren't Gen-X slackers or the auteur-savants of mumblecore. They're dudes who unironically don cowboy boots and listen to country radio, who really like bonfires and barbecues. One—Robert Eads, in *Southern Comfort*—lives in a single-wide trailer on a piece of land he owns in Toccoa, Georgia, on the border of South Carolina where the Piedmont ends and the Blue Ridge begins, a couple of hours from Atlanta.[15] The other, Cole Ray Davis, in *Deep Run*, lives in the eponymous

Deep Run, a town of about three thousand people in Lenoir County, North Carolina, and migrates between a few manufactured homes over the course of the documentary.[16] In *Southern Comfort,* Eads is dying of advanced terminal cancer of the uterus, cervix, and ovaries, for which he was denied treatment by over twenty physicians. In *Deep Run,* Davis—a high schooler when we first meet him—is navigating young love, familial ostracism, and the search for a beloved community (a church that welcomes him and his femme partner) while publicly transitioning and seeking medical transition services (with very little success). Davis struggles to get and maintain gainful employment. Eads isn't working—we infer that he is on disability—and expends what little energy he has caring for his extensive trans chosen family, including his "sons," Max and Cass, and his lover, Lola Cola. The vérité tradition holds firm in these works: they are produced in earnest, dedicated to documenting some of the forms of transphobic discrimination and violence that shape the forms of living and dying that these men experience. Flat affect is, here, less of a deliberate aesthetic choice and more about the shape and frequency of emotional expressivity these men are willing and able to offer both the camera and their communities and, by extension, the shape and frequency of the modes of emotional expressivity they are each able to bear.

Smoking scenes are rife in both of these documentaries; in most of the moments where these men are conversing with the camera, they are accompanied by a lit cigarette (or, sometimes, with Eads, a pipe). An ex-smoker myself, I remain—like most ex-smokers, I think—drawn to the rituals and routines of smoking, mostly because of how they operate as small moments of withdrawal and contemplation, a habit that allows one to recede from the scene of the social, which may be anxiety inducing, overwhelming, a particular form of too-much, in order to find a quiet place and light up, perhaps with one or two other folks who also need this form of reprieve. (How many intimacies form among smokers at parties? It's still always where I find my people; I'll follow folks outside for a cigarette and hang out, breathing in secondhand smoke, secure in the knowledge that they, too, needed a moment.) It's also a self-soothing exercise, chemically mitigating anxiety and rendering tense situations at least a little more bearable. There's a poignancy for me in the fact that each time Eads and Davis interface with their (cis, white, femme) documentarians, they're breathing smoke. Indeed, when we first meet them, they're accompanied by tobacco. Both films open with landscape shots; in *Southern Comfort,* it's a shaky 360° pan of Eads's single-wide and the property it sits on, followed by a shot of him sitting in a plastic chair by his firepit at sunrise, with a diegetic soundscape of roosters crowing and birds chirping, taking long draws from a pipe. In *Deep Run,* it's a series of steady eye-level landscape shots, most featuring some form of evangelical ephemera—a church sign, Jesus statuary, one of those quippy billboards featuring a direct address from God—suggesting the deep interwovenness of the landscape and the particular form of faith that Davis is simultaneously steeped in and estranged from. These shots are intercut with scenes of Davis tugging on a cigarette while a voice-over attests to the difficulties of being trans in the rural South, backed by a droning, shoegazey soundtrack.

During his introductory shot, Eads is quietly, very moderately crying. A single tear stains his cheek as he tells us pensively, with long pauses between sentences, about the medical professionals who refused to treat him:

> It's Easter morning, and it's sunrise. And I wish I could understand why they did what they did, and why they had to feel that way. And I know in a way they've contributed to my dying here. But I can't hate 'em—I don't hate 'em. I feel sorry for 'em. I can't actually say I forgive 'em for what they've done. I think that's more between them and God. But I don't hate 'em. I guess what makes me most sad is that they probably feel like they did the right thing.

He seems to be suppressing what we might expect to be explosive anger at the unnamed "they"—all those parties that refused to treat his cancer—who would, he insinuates at the end, prefer that he died. In the face of a broad-based necropolitical expulsion from the terrain of life and liveliness, Eads holds his pipe and talks quietly about pity and his inability to forgive. Even this is understated, tentative, unsure: "I guess what makes me most sad is that they probably feel like they did the right thing." The hedging language of guessing and probability suggests that Eads has never been directly told the reasons for the many refusals of service he's encountered, or that, minimally, the reasons he's been given stray to the side of the suspected truth: a brutal but unspoken form of transphobia characterized by institutional neglect unto death. No one is talking about it, but it's real—probably, maybe. The indirection that characterizes such neglect makes direct emotional response difficult, perhaps impossible. Instead, we have oblique discrimination matched by a response of mitigated, underperformed sadness. We get, as well, a sense of the very small, protective, and insular world that Eads has cultivated on his land: it's essentially a hermitage, a hideout, a refuge. Even here, in a very small corner of the world where he can exist without harassment, where we might expect a direct statement of outrage, we get, instead, the language of might, maybe.

And then we have Davis, too, with his same recessive smoker's retreat and, in a scene immediately following his introduction, his embrace of his role as a minor league baseball mascot. As we witness him jovially interacting with all manner of game attendees in the suit, he tells us, "The best part about this job is nobody knows who I am. I can just walk around freely." The costume affords forms of social intimacy, regard, and respect that are otherwise routinely withheld. It might be insufferably hot in the suit, but at least people will touch you. In the suit, the ontological stammering that attends and subtends transition and the phenomenon of being perceived as illegibly or liminally gendered is reduced, even erased. This is one of the only spaces in the film wherein we see Davis move with gestural ebullience, one of the only scenes wherein we come to understand why his teenage nickname is Spazz.

The smoking, the costume: I think of both as technologies

of retreat that resonate with flat affect, understood as a way of making some space—to think, to be—in worlds that are unlivable but that one must, nevertheless, persist to exist within; like Davis says, "[Deep Run] is very hostile at times, but it's home." Part of learning to inhabit this home is learning to systematically underperform emotional responsiveness: to quell rage, anger, frustration, sadness, and desire in exchange for a modicum of social belonging, in the absence of a lifeworld that can hold and empathically witness more outsized affective responses. What we see, across both documentaries, is the depiction of trans negotiations with a present that comes to be, as Berlant writes of Gregg Araki's *Mysterious Skin,* "a barometer of pressures inducing people to keep things to themselves."[17] Even the confessional moments come coupled with reticence, underperformance, and a certain anxiety.

In another moment of underperformed affect, Robert Eads discusses the impact of losing contact with his biological family posttransition:

> It comes down to a choice where either you're going to spend your life miserable to make somebody else happy, or you're going to spend your life somewhat happy but having to live with the knowledge that you make people you love miserable. It's a catch-22, it's a no-win. We lose a lot of friends. We lose *a lot* of things—we lose jobs, we lose friends, we lose family. But the hardest of all is family. Because family is the core. Family is the stone. It's what holds everything together. And all of a sudden it's gone. It's like . . . it's like standing out . . . you're out in the middle of the ocean on an iceberg and it all of a sudden melts.

I've been sitting with his metaphor for a while now: "It's like you're out in the middle of the ocean on an iceberg and it all of a sudden melts." What does it mean that Eads describes a closeted trans life as akin to dwelling on an isolated iceberg, one that, although it is selectively peopled, is nevertheless inhospitable, detached, precarious, and surrounded by the likelihood of imminent death should one lose their footing and slip off this terrain that's already quite tenuous to navigate? What does it mean that Eads describes the loss of kin and intimacy that has accompanied his transition as a plunging into icy waters that will, in due time, destroy him? For Eads, the surrounding lifeworld is gauged by degrees of frigidity and numbness, a sensorial dulling informing how one feels while navigating treacherous, frozen ground.

The interesting thing about numbness, though, is that it can be selectively generated to make certain situations more survivable; it can be used in small doses as an antidote or pathway to healing. It might be generated by the surrounding milieu, but it might also be deliberately engineered by a subject to move through the unbearable: a kind of phenomenological muting of the sensorium in the name of survival. Considering these vicissitudes of numbness, I've come to think of it as an affective technology that informs and transforms trans lives. I've become increasingly attuned to the ways in which we curate and control affective responsiveness, the way we sometimes lean on a technics of dulling that generates flat affect, and the calculus of risk and benefit that informs such a practice.

COLD SCENES

It is difficult to talk about dulling without talking about booze, and difficult to talk about risk and reward vis-à-vis this particular form of dulling without talking about alcoholism. Casey Plett's novel *Little Fish* is about many things, but I would hazard to say it is chiefly about numbness.[18] Even the plot enticement on the back cover begins to do the work of situating the reader in a frigid surround, reading: "It's the dead of winter in Winnipeg and Wendy Reimer, a thirty-year-old trans woman, feels like her life is frozen in place." The book explores the phenomenon of stasis, centering on the difficult and plodding slowness of building a future within the grinding repetitions of the transmisogynist daily. It begins in medias res with a meditation on trans temporality, both its multiple valences and characteristic estrangements from straight-cis time, opening with four trans women—Wendy, Raina, Lila, and Sophia—in a booth at a bar:

> It was eleven p.m., and they were all tipsy. Sophie was saying, "Age is completely different for trans people. The way we talk about age is not how cis people talk about age."
>
> "You mean that thing," said Wendy, "where our age is also how long we've been on hormones or whatever?"
>
> "Or do you mean that thing," said Lila, "where we don't age as much. Because we die sooner."
>
> "Both those things, yes!" Sophie said. "But there's more! There's much more. Think of how hormones preserve you. Look—we could all pass for twenty-one if we wanted to."[19]

The conversation continues on this tack, turning from questions of hormone time, necropolitical forms of premature death, and aesthetic preservation to the acquisitive goals and teleologies of a supposedly well-lived life, with Sophie further articulating the complexities of trans time:

> "I don't just mean the difference in how long trans people live. And I don't just mean in the sense that we have two kinds of age. But the difference in transsexual age is what can be expected from you. Cis people have so many benchmarks for a good life that go by age."
>
> "You're talking about the wife, the kids, the dog," Wendy said.
>
> "More than that. And also yes, that. It didn't stop being important," said Sophie. "Cis people always have timelines. I mean, I know not every cis person has that life, but—what are the cis people in my life doing? What are they doing in your life? Versus what the trans people in your life are doing? On a macro level. Ask yourself that."[20]

On a macro level, ask yourself that.

Here's what the trans people in my life are doing, at the level of the anecdotal: selling crafts to save money for top surgery, crowd-sourcing funds to bring trans Latina activists to an academic conference, going through divorces and separations, searching for a job that pays a living wage and comes with trans-inclusive health insurance, asking the internet for advice on how to deal with hostile work and classroom environments, proofreading each other's writing, growing networks of solidarity and support, making gorgeous art about resilience, feeling disappointed by another Scruff hookup, grumbling about the way their clothes are fitting them, struggling to make ends meet after the passage of FOSTA-SESTA made it impossible for them to advertise and screen clients effectively, going to therapy, going to recovery meetings, documenting their experience fostering a child on social media. A quick snapshot. Surely cis folks are doing some, though not all, of these things. At the macro level, though, there are obvious broad-stroke manifestations of poverty, scarcity, insecurity, sickness, fatigue, and anxiety that are so much a part of trans lifeworlds that it's easy not to notice them; this is why Sophia's interrogative is such a necessary and transformative intervention. *Ask yourself that.* What does the comparison turn up?

In *Little Fish,* Plett builds a milieu that is shaped profoundly by the cold. It is set during winter in Winnipeg, where the average low doesn't rise above freezing until May. It is a novel of indoor scenes, of binges and hangovers and bundled-up walks, a world where "pedestrians looked shrunken and soldered into themselves, void blobs of spaceman fabric" walking about in "minus-forty wind chills" where one's best bet is to hole up, buried under blankets, watching "awful reality shows while the wind beat from outside and whistled through the house."[21] The cover of the book is an ink drawing of a winter street scene rendered in blue, black, and gray, with most figures lacking not just facial expressions but faces altogether. They are dressed in the kind of insulating, formless overcoats that obscure embodied particularity beyond the barest of signifiers—the figures are taller or shorter, have longer or shorter hair, but remain nevertheless anonymous, spare, evasive of recognition or identity assignation. They are isolated, mostly solo, folded inward, and occupied with mundane actions that, in periods of extended cold, come to seem like heroic feats: one clutches a cardboard cup of coffee on a stoop, two trudge forward through the snow, grasping packages, one scrapes a car window, one—the only figure in short sleeves—sits perched on a balcony built into a snow-drifted tree, clutching what appears to be a bottle of booze and smoking a cigarette. They're apparently wearing what one of my best friends, in a suggestive and resonant phrase, calls a "booze jacket."

Booze jackets abound in *Little Fish*. The central protagonist, Wendy, is actively grappling with whether or not she's an alcoholic. There are flasks and mickeys of vodka that accompany night walks, liquor in morning coffees, whiskey sours when she's just coming off a bender. Nobody is commenting directly on Wendy's drinking, though—it's obviously normalized and not considered comment-worthy by her intimates. She confesses once to her father Ben, whom she is close with, that she might be an alcoholic; his response is "Fuck off, don't talk like that."[22] He proceeds to tell her that if she's worried, she should count her drinks. The rhythm of the novel is formed by her binges and hangovers; there is a bleariness that spreads across scenes and chapters, with mornings shaped by patchy, piecemeal recollections and evenings bringing with them the routinized cultivation of dullness by drinking, "like slowly clicking down the volume on a TV show."[23]

In his work on emotional absence, philosopher Tom Roberts begins with an account of physical numbness, which he frames as a notable and noticed "discontinuity in how the world is encountered with that [numb] body part: something is felt to be missing from the ordinary order and flow of sensory experience."[24] Physical numbness—when you lose feeling in your fingers after forgetting your gloves on a particularly cold day—is the name for the feeling of noted absence, when your ability to register and be affected by the sensory stimuli you had learned to expect somehow fails or misfires. It's what we call the *absence of what we had expected to feel,* or the failure "to incur the ordinary sensory consequences of transactions at the surface of the skin."[25]

For Roberts, emotional absence—what he calls "feeling noth-ing"—is "the parallel phenomenon in the domain of affectivity: a kind of experience during which one is aware that the world is not having its anticipated emotional impact. . . . What is experienced as absent is the effect of an impingement from outside of the body, where one becomes aware of a failure to be moved by the way the world is, in respect of the bodily disruption that typically characterizes an emotional encounter."[26] *Little Fish* vividly documents the ways in which trans folks, and trans women specifically, cultivate emotional numbness when feeling nothing seems preferable to the impingement of affective response one has learned to expect. The practice of becoming insensate—of slowly turning the volume down on the world, thus minimizing its disruptive capacity—is a risky strategy to pursue in the long term, to be sure, but given the rates of substance abuse that affect trans communities, it's imperative to grapple with our collective relations to numbness: what motivates it, the palliative work that it does or might do, and its continued prominence as a trans technology of survival.

Plett gives us many scenes through which to think the work of numbness. There is a veritable taxonomy of drunkenness offered up, scene by scene. She describes the "childlike" obliterating decadence that makes Wendy feel "hazy and warm, cuddled and soft and beautiful"; the feeling of giving in to a desire to drink that makes her feel "gentle and soft and sleepy and weak, like within was rest"; the quick binge and arrival of dullness following a bout of suicidal ideation, "glug, breathe, glug, breathe, and she did this until she stopped, stopped, stopped, stopped, stopped"; the way "everything in her head was swimming and submerged and operating so slowly and confusing"; how, following an injury, booze enables her pain to ebb as a "fuzzy glow warm[s] her brain."[27] We are given an intimate sense of the affective lure of numbness, the promise of the moment when anxiety, worry, suicidality, and cycles of negative self-talk are eroded by a warm flood of disinhibition, detachment, and fuzziness.

Plett writes of the multiple mornings-after, as well—the late starts, the confusion, the fatigue, the physical pain and recalcitrance of the body (up to and including the shakes), the nearly missed and missed appointments. While she refuses to sugarcoat the physiognomic and practical implications of Wendy's pursuit of numbness, she also, quite pointedly, refuses to frame Wendy as shamed by any of it. Instead, she depicts how Wendy deliberately rejects guilt, shame, and anxiety over what she might have done while drunk: "Annoying people with drink-related guilt just annoyed them more—and anyway, Wendy rarely did anything bad. Drunk guilt was childish, and worrying about it didn't make things better. So she didn't worry about it anymore."[28] Wendy is, above all, a pragmatist when it comes to her drinking. She understands why she's drawn to it: because of its impact on her sensorium, which enables her to cope with an often overwhelming and traumatic transmisogynist surround. She understands that it's an imperfect strategy. She refuses a cycle of repetitive regret in relationship to it.

In a 2018 interview, Plett comments on her decision to write for trans people rather than cis audiences, which enables her to subvert many of the ciscentric tropes that shape the depiction of trans protagonists, from triumphal narratives of rebirth and success to those that frame trans folks as uncommon exemplars of fluidity, shape-shifting, and self-making to hackneyed, victimological accounts of trauma, violence, and discrimination. The trans women in *Little Fish* are articulate, practical, fallible, and complicated, refusing both stereotype and paradigmicity. She frames Wendy's character:

> [She is] part of a larger dialogue where I think that a lot of trans women (myself included) are pretty messed up and I'm interested in exploring that fictionally. I'm also generally disinterested in the trope that trans people are either evil or heroes who do no wrong. That being said, the world is pretty messed up to us (trans women) and that doesn't always make you a better person. Wendy is angry, she's an alcoholic and she can be passive when it comes to her own

life. These were all things I saw reflected in the trans community around me and my own experience, these badass survivors who were also incredibly complicated. I liked exploring Wendy's strength along with all of her clear flaws.[29]

Plett refuses the bifurcated narratives that whittle down the complexities of trans subjects in order to explore the impacts and affects associated with trans arts of survival, implicating herself in this exploration of subjective-communal damage and trauma without making this "messed up"-edness the controlling narrative. She offers us something more than bearing witness and something less than homage: an account of trans living that delves deeply into experiences of negativity to render more resonant characters, attuning the pulse of the women in *Little Fish* to the beat of her own life and experience of trans communality.

Numbness: the absence of a presence. Numbness: what we call touching something that you can't feel. Numbness: what we cultivate in order to be touched without feeling. This is sexual, but not only.

BEARING TRANS INTERCORPOREALITY

Before I turn away from Casey Plett's work, I want to think with and through a complex encounter that occurs near the end of the book. Wendy, already hazily, dreamily tipsy and in bed, receives a text for an outcall—this time, to the exurbs of Winnipeg, far beyond her downtown mise-en-scène, a pricey cab ride away from her home. She takes the job, in large part because the john offers to transfer the price of the cab and half of her fee upfront, and proceeds through the frigid night to a "row of thin, new, cheap-looking townhouses."[30] Once there, she finds a client in the kind of manic, faux-chipper mood induced by coke. He's doing lines and watching porn; she opts, instead, for large, cold bottle of white wine that he has on hand for the occasion.

He had seemed friendly enough during their text exchange. Once there, she's on edge, finding it hard to get a read on the situation at first. He confesses that he loves "shemale porn" and asks her, "Does that make me a faggot?" He hadn't read her ad carefully and wants her to fuck him; she has to explain that she has a "surgical vagina."[31] He wonders aloud if maybe she has any friends that are pre- or non-op; she realizes that she's not hanging out with many trans women that do sex work these days and is immediately triggered, remembering the very recent suicide of her close friend Sophie, who did do sex work, who she could have called if only . . .

She heads into the kitchen to cry, shielding her tears with the faucet on full blast and sucking "at the magnum like it was a water tap."[32] She pulls herself together and returns, having brainstormed a way to satisfy her client. She suggests they watch a short clip she made years ago, prior to having bottom surgery. They do. Wendy thinks to herself that she looked good in this clip from years prior, her hair and nails done perfectly, her regime of beauty maintenance cranked way higher for the camera than she would ever consider in her day-to-day. Her client tells her he likes to wear girl's clothes, asks if maybe she has any extra on her that he could wear while they fuck. She doesn't. He has heels, though, that he wants to wear, so he grabs them and puts them on.

By any stretch of the imagination, this is not a gig that's going well. But the narrative is intercut by italicized moments of recognition and tenderness as it becomes clear to Wendy that her client—young, muscular, ex-military—is more than likely an egg (a trans person who doesn't yet realize they're trans). Spotting a stuffed koala in the otherwise spartan bedroom, she thinks, "*Sweetie.*"[33] She's talking herself through the job, despite being near-blackout drunk. She's simultaneously detached and graciously intimate in this moment, recognizing and validating her clients' desires (to bottom, to wear heels, to be called "faggot"). She's doing her job and doing it well. This seems, in large part, attributable to the simultaneity of numbness and empathy, which produces an affective distantiation that enables forms of recognition and other-identification that might otherwise be unbearably self-shattering. Indeed, we see Wendy approach the brink of this breakdown in the kitchen, with the water running to cover the sound of her crying.

I understand this scene as dramatizing the risks and gifts of trans intercorporeality. Intercorporeality begins with the idea, derived from the phenomenological work of Maurice Merleau-Ponty, that our body schemas are developed through intersensorial relationship with the world in which we're embedded and, by extension, through intercorporeal relations with others.[34] This means, first, that the experience of the body (however united or fragmented that experience may be) is coconstituted, never sovereign or informed by a maximal kind of agency. It is a process, instead, of relation and negotiation. These relations and negotiations may involve compromise and coercion, up to and including outright dehumanization and corporeal violence; but they may also be molded by loving perception, empathic witnessing, and pleasurable forms of intercorporeal intimacy wherein we may even, sometimes, come to feel whole, recognized, rewoven, intact, and provisionally stable. But, no matter what, this sense—what Merleau-Ponty refers to as equilibrium—is temporary, never achieved once and for all. This is because, as feminist philosopher Gail Weiss concisely puts it, the body image is "a dynamic gestalt that is continually being constructed, destructed, and reconstructed in response to changes within one's own body, other people's bodies, and/or the situation as a whole."[35] Our bodies are never solely ours but rather coproduced with and through the bodies of others, and this means that equilibrium is always and only a temporary achievement. Gayle Salamon, building on this feminist engagement with the work of Merleau-Ponty, writes that, within this account, what might be read from the "contours of the body is something less than the truth of that body's sex which cannot be located in an external observation of the body, but exists instead in that relation between the material and the ideal, between the perceiver and the perceived, between the material particularity of any one body and the network of forces and contours that shape the material and the meaning of that body."[36] By *trans intercorporeality*, I refer to the ensembles of touch, connection, embodied intimacy, and identification that circulate between trans subjects. It's a term for thinking what happens when trans bodies meet and intermingle. In Plett's work, there are many, many moments of trans intercorporeality, ranging from the platonic embrace to the deeply erotic. I choose to focus on this moment, however, for what it tells us about the work of numbness in the context of trans sexualities. A superficial reading might suggest that Wendy is inuring herself in order to simply get through the job. However, Wendy's relation with her client deepens throughout her brief time in the apartment, and she engages in an act of gracious topping that enables her client to feel seen, recognized, and deeply erotically satisfied. During their fucking, she asks her client if they have a name: "Wendy massaged, slowly probing and opening him up. 'You got a name for yourself, you little fuckin' girl.' 'Kaitlyn,' he said immediately, 'Kaitlyn. With a K.'"[37] Prior to leaving, and after being asked how she "knew," she gives them information about the clinic through which she accessed support for medical transition, telling them, "You're probably a girl, and that's probably what you need to do."[38]

This is a profound moment in the novel, not least because it so clearly illustrates the ways in which this form of intercorporeal recognition powerfully manifests trans embodiment. This instance of being seen and touched within and as (that is, understood as inhabiting) the name that you understand to hail you is a form of identification "that expand[s] the parameters of body image and accomplish[es] its transition from an introceptive, fragmented experience . . . to a social gestalt."[39] It has the power to make you real, to call you forth, to literally transition you. We might be tempted to understand this interchange as heralding a new beginning for Kaitlyn, as the start of their path toward and through transition. If we make the shift to understanding embodiment as intercorporeal, though, the forms of identification and recognition circulating between Kaitlyn and Wendy make Kaitlyn cohere, make her coherent. Wendy's recognition and relation to Kaitlyn's body conjures it in real time—it is not an aspiration, not a goal, not deferred to the distant arc of an existential horizon. *Kaitlyn is here.* Wendy helps them orient in space and time; together, they produce a world where they can be. This is a gift, too, one that involves forms of generosity that are laborious. During their encounter, Wendy is at the brink of a break, thrown squarely into memories (of her own transition, of the deaths of trans women she loves) that aren't easy to revisit. She draws on numbness to both bear them and participate in the forms of intercorporeal recognition that Kaitlyn desires and needs (even if these needs are only ever obliquely articulated). She numbs herself to move through it.

After disengaging from these intimacies, though, the very same numbness that enabled this gift of recognition nearly results in her death.

She leaves the townhouse and walks toward what she thinks is the main road, planning to call a friend or a cab to come get her. She pulls out her phone and realizes that it's dead. She thinks of returning to Kaitlyn's house to use their phone, but looks back and realizes she, in her drunkenness, has no idea which townhouse is theirs—and that the address is in her phone. She commits to walking toward home and realizes, quickly, that she's underdressed. It's the middle of the night in the exurbs, and she can't very well pound on strangers' doors. "Her legs were numbing and her body was jerking and lurching around she was so fucking drunk *damn it*—she concentrated on her breath and her feet, the muffled crunch her boots made in the snow, actively pressing her brain into pause. She walked. She walked and walked. For a long while."[40]

Time passes. She hails vehicle after vehicle. Some stop, only to leave her after a short interchange. Some swerve entirely around her. Finally, she spots a cab, which picks her up. This moment of reprieve is immediately followed by the approach of a cop car, then a cop, who reports to Wendy that the police have "'gotten two calls now that a tall woman in a black coat has been freaking people out around her. Scaring the bejeezus outta them. Now, that was you, wasn't it?'"[41] The situation unfolds quickly, with the cop asking for her license, repeating her name unbelievingly, and interrogating her as to why she was so far away from home at this time of night. Though no one—not the cop, not the driver—says anything forthrightly transphobic, readers are led to infer that this whole situation—Wendy's interpellation as a threat by the drivers, the unnecessary interrogation, the radical lack of empathy that informs both the cop's engagement with her as well as the driver's (who later extorts cash from her before dropping her off)—is about the risks of being visibly transfeminine in public space, and the dissonance and disorientation this experience entails. It is an instance of "walking while trans," the phrase used to index the disproportionate profiling and harassment encountered by trans women in public space, including the police presumption of involvement in sex work, subjection to commands to disperse, and regular arrest for low-level offenses stemming from suspicion of involvement in sex work.[42] In Wendy's instance, the stakes are life or death. She's directly risking exposure unto the point of hypothermia, though this risk isn't acknowledged by any of the parties that witness her on the street who, in keeping with the phenomenon of walking while trans, overcode her as criminal, illicit, and a threat to public order, in need of police regulation and, possibly, carceral intervention.

I read this as a profound moment of disorientation, not only because Wendy is already, at the level of the biochemical and the affective, intensively disorientated on account of the combination of booze and cold, but because she cannot understand, in this state, why it is that no one stops for her or offers the easy forms of care that would prevent her from literally dying. The routine social mores that would inform how an obviously distressed woman in this situation would typically be treated cease to apply, and Wendy—who is usually savvy and cynical and well-aware of the brutally mundane operations of transmisogyny—cannot, in this moment, believe that this is happening to her.

Reading this scene in the immediate aftermath of her encounter with Kaitlyn, we see quite acutely the high social costs of trans visibility. Kaitlyn is christened, and Plett quickly reminds us that this means she is also an initiate to the multivalent pains and joys of visibility. The moment they share is deeply affirmative, but affirmation is not, alas, celebration. The memories that flood Wendy's consciousness during their encounter speak to transition as coincident with a form of radical vulnerability. She thinks about how, during transition, she never felt like her body truly belonged to her, given her subjection to an endless stream of commentary on each aspect of her shifting physical appearance. She thinks about the forms of necropolitical violence that affect her friends and lovers, about trauma, about suicide. Her concluding commentary, about what Kaitlyn "probably needs to do," is eminently bittersweet. The difficulties that Wendy is so intimate with remain ineffable and unspoken here; it would be a cruelty to allow them to issue forth in such a moment of delicate admittance, vulnerability, and halting recognition. But it is also difficult, when and if one is a trans elder (which has nothing, necessarily, to do with age), to keep them from flooding one's consciousness in such moments.

Sometimes, trans visibility feels like willingly exposing the raw nerve of your self—a self that is always already interdependent, always already reliant on intercorporeal exchanges—to socialities and systems of perception that you know will respond to such exposure with reliably repetitive brutality. We see, in Plett's juxtaposition of a scene of intercorporeal recognition with a scene depicting a fundamental failure of such recognition, how trans experiences of embodiment are crucially molded by such intensively clashing moments of (mis)recognition. Gayle Salamon painstakingly unpacks the ways in which body schema is affected by memory, a condensed consolidation of sense experience where "the wholeness and coherence of the body turns out to be entirely reliant on the operation of memory."[43] Fleshing this out, she writes that the production of body schema "relies for its coherence on a past storehouse of past impressions, sensations, fantasies, and memories" and that "any bodily position only becomes psychically legible (and, thus *physically* legible) within the context of, and based on its resemblance to, its similarity to past physical positions."[44] This is, in part, what we talk about when we talk about triggering. If traumatic and difficult-to-bear scenes of recognition have long informed how your body is both perceived and touched, those forms of perceptive misrecognition become indelibly linked to each new repetition-variant of such a scene. The chain of memory initiated by Kaitlyn's moment of misrecognition—Wendy's brief stint in pornography, the suicide of a close friend, the experience of transition as radical lack of bodily autonomy by way of endless external commentary, evaluation, and judgment—floods in and informs any subsequent interaction they may have, sexual or otherwise. Numbness is an existential pain management strategy that helps Wendy float this flood.

When I write about trans embodiment as profoundly shaped by recurrent disorientation, I mean to gesture at the ways in which we are consistently knocked out of equilibrium, that phenomenological term used to indicate the experience of embodied coherence. For some of us—perhaps most of us, at some point in time—the phenomenological experience of disequilibrium is dominant. An existential archive of disequilibrium is conjured up in each new moment of misrecognition, and we thus learn to inhabit our bodies as fundamentally disruptable, which also means learning to live with a hyperalertness generated by the desire to identify the next threat to our stability, composure, and coherence, which also means living intimately with instability and incoherence. This feels simultaneously exhausting and necessary for survival.

I understand flat affect as a way of making some space when we're not sure how to feel within a moment of misrecognition. I read recession and withdrawal as a means through which we minimize the impact of difficult memories called up by and through intercorporeal moments of misrecognition, and numbness as a means through which we survive such moments by turning down the volume on our sensorium. All of these modes of affective modulation are crucial in coping with disorientation, and none should be stigmatized, dismissed, or easily glossed, especially not as a set of affects that subsides posttransition.

Following Salamon and the phenomenological tradition upon which she draws, all embodiment is (in)formed by memory; if our memories of embodiment are structured fundamentally by disequilibrium, then this intimate familiarity with the difficulties of coherence goes away only very slowly, and only if it is gradually supplanted by consistent and reliable moments of intercorporeal recognition that allow for coherence. This slow supplantation of misrecognition with recognition is a rare privilege for trans folks. Given this, it's no surprise that in the meantime many of us develop strategies to push back, reject, or defer intense affect: to be like, *fuck* feelings. And that we might especially draw on these strategies during—or in order to decline or defer—heightened moments of intercorporeal contact.

It's time, though, to turn away from efforts to dull the sensorium and the impinging force of transantagonism and to turn toward the experience of overwhelming desire, the kind of yearning capable of provoking suffering, a deep and painful want: envy.

3

FOUND WANTING

On Envy

The desire to protect your bro, fuck him, and possess his body is a very transsexual clump of wants, each variously passing as the other (ha ha).

—Charlie Markbreiter, "Peel Slowly and See"

Envy is a tricky topic to broach in relationship to trans experience, in no small part because the desire to transition has been so frequently diminished and dismissed as a kind of envy. To want a gender other than the one you've been assigned is, within essentializing epistemologies of gender, to want something that isn't yours, that doesn't—can't possibly—belong to you. To pursue transition is, within this understanding, to double down on and commit to one's envy, rather than recognizing it as pernicious and doing one's best to quash it.

Lou Sullivan's diaries are full of the slippage between envy and desire, between wanting someone and wanting what they have for yourself. He came of age in the 1970s, negotiating the complexities of becoming a gay, trans man in a moment of rigorously heterosexist medical gatekeeping. He eventually found his way from a Wisconsin suburb to gay liberation–era San Francisco, where he lived until he died of AIDS-related complications in 1991. His journals are a catalog of trans masc longing, an index of icons he wishes to model himself after who are also, so often, the men he wants to love him, the men he wants to fuck. Here's Young Lou at the juncture of envy and desire, routed through a tizzy about the Beatles:

> Mom said I could maybe have a Beatles haircut before the last day of school.
> Paul-Ringo-Paul-Ringo they keep bouncing around my head. Model yourself on them and you'll have no worries. Paul! I love the name. Such a beautiful sound to the ear. Ringo! Such an adorable boy. So sweet and modest. So bouncy. Know that I love you and I'm not crazy. This is a love so strong and real. Oh, love me too, anyone.[1]

Persistent preoccupation. Emulation. Desire. The risk of pathologization that looms over this potent mess of affect ("I'm not crazy"). The fungibility of these men, the roving indiscrimination of the desire to be loved (if not Paul-Ringo then, indeed, "anyone" might do). First the Beatles, then this messiness migrates on to a local celebrity, Richard, front man of a band called the Velvet Whip: "Tonite, I discovered that Richard is everything I ever wanted to be. . . . His wild eyes, his gentle face. . . . I realized he is my heart + mind in a person. I realized I could never be like him because I was a girl and cried. What can I do, Richard? I'd do anything."[2] Then onto lovers he had. Regarding J, an on-again, off-again, inconsistent beau of Lou's prior to, and in the early days of, transition, he writes: "I wish I was J. He's such a lovely male. . . . I want him so passionately."[3] Sullivan provides one of the most lucid accounts of the unpredictable transformation of envy into identification into emulation into desire, though this sequential way of phrasing the transformative circuit of envy isn't quite right. In Sullivan's journals, all of these affective phenomena are copresent: wanting to be and wanting to have and wishing you were and wishing you were wanted by are richly interimplicated feelings that shape much of Sullivan's account of coming into a gay, transmasculine mode of being in the world.

And it's not just Sullivan, of course: trans life writing is full of such complexities. Carter Sickels reflects, in a piece on how the teen heartthrobs of the 1980s led him toward a kind of "tender queer masculinity," on precisely this affective confluence:

> I'm not sure why Ralph Macchio fired me up. Yes, he was cute—young baby face without a wisp of facial hair, pouty lips, puppy dog eyes, and puffy '80s hair. But he didn't radiate the hot masculine bad-boy coolness of, say, Matt Dillon or River Phoenix. Ralph was quieter, plainer, softer. Maybe that's what attracted me—he was dreamy in a safe kind of way. More attainable? Or maybe I saw some other version of myself in him, a boy self, which back then I had no way of articulating.[4]

And let me tell you how my own heart dropped when the boy I loved most in high school, accompanied by a hilarious MIDI instrumental, sang me Peter Cetera's "Glory of Love," which some of you might correctly identify as the romance theme from *The Karate Kid Part II*, starring Ralph Macchio—the adorable doe-eyed boy I wasn't sure whether I wanted to be or be with. Relatedly, when Rocco Kayiatos and Amos Mac describe the genesis of *Original Plumbing (OP)*, their long-running magazine documenting U.S. trans male culture, they are very clear about their source material and sensibility, writing that they were "inspired by zines that spoke to a sometimes underground, often-artsy world, like *BUTT* and *S.T.H. (Straight to Hell)*, and never stopped collecting glossy teen magazines like *Teen Beat* and *Bop*."[5] This mash-up of the soft-focus adolescent pin-up and the explicitly gay erotic deeply informed the playful, beefcake sensibility of *OP* and speaks directly to the sloppy nexus of envy and desire. The eye candy provided by *OP* appealed to a perceived need to see transmasculinity eroticized as both a visual proof of what one might become as well as a prod to desire.

But what, exactly—though inexactitude might be the best

we can hope for with any affective description—is envy? In the Christian tradition, it is a cardinal sin, a capital vice, one of the naughtiest of all passions. In both philosophical and psychological accounts, it is theorized as rooted in lack, insofar as it is an emotion that emerges from a yearning to have what belongs to someone else (Ralph Macchio's eyes, Paul McCartney's shag). As the *Oxford English Dictionary* has it, *envy* refers to "the feeling of mortification and ill-will occasioned by the contemplation of superior advantages possessed by another," though there is also a less utilized, nonmalevolent sense of *envy* as the "desire to equal another in achievement or excellence; emulation."[6] Another, now ostensibly obsolete usage is, simply, "wish, desire, longing, enthusiasm."[7] In this definitional constellation, we can see the slippages and vacillations at work in the operation of envy: there is both ill will and enthusiasm, mortification alongside emulation. Then there is the formal philosophical division between benign and invidious envy, a distinction introduced in order to parse this mess of meanings. Benign envy, in brief, is a form of envy that doesn't come coupled with the wish that the envied subject lose the quality or possession that is envied, while invidious envy hinges on the wish that the envied subject be divested of that which is envied. However, even in instances of benign envy, envy itself is still generally understood as negative. It comes charged with psychic pain. The difference between thinking something or someone is generally excellent and being actively envious of them is precisely this negative affective charge: if the feeling is hard to bear, it's probably envy.

Sianne Ngai, in *Ugly Feelings,* provides the most nuanced and useful account of envy I've come across. She points out, in order to inject some structural and political consciousness into how this emotion is understood, that though envy is most often utilized as a "term describing a *subject* who lacks," it can—and probably should—be understood as a subject's "affective *response* to a perceived inequality."[8] Envy isn't the deleterious response of a maladjusted subject who cannot keep themselves from wanting what isn't theirs, or at least not only. Rather, Ngai suggests that it can index an injustice. Clarifying this point, she writes that the dominant understanding of envy rooted in subjective lack renders and reduces a "particular situation of 'not having' produced by a complex network of social relations" to a "pejorative and morally coded" desire that is understood as a reflection of a "deficient and possibly histrionic selfhood."[9] Her broader point is that, culturally speaking, envy is understood as the province of an irrational, perhaps even hysterical, and very often feminized subject. Though envy most often arises as the result of structural inequities, it is commonly perceived as a personal failing—and an egocentric one, at that. While envy is a fundamentally "other-regarding orientation"—it springs, after all, from close perception of the desirable, possibly emulatable qualities, relations, and possessions of another person—it is frequently spun as a kind of sick obsession that affects those who want more than they deserve, more than their "fair share," someone who simply cannot humble themselves enough to become reconciled to whatever hand it is they've been dealt.[10]

But, when read as a response to inequality, envy might instead be thought of as part of the incipience of revolutionary consciousness. If it is an indicator of structural disenfranchisement, and a reliable record of some of our feelings about deprivation, then it may just be the most bread and roses of affects, for it is the feeling that insists we deserve more than mere subsistence, mere survival. Feminist reinterpretations of that most well-known form of envy—penis envy—point to its radical potential. Philosopher Mari Ruti puts it best: "In a society that rewards the possessor of the penis with obvious political, economic, and cultural benefits, women would have to be a little obtuse not to envy it; they would have to be a little obtuse not to want the social advantages that automatically accrue to the possessor of the penis, particularly if he happens to be white."[11] If the penis is a metonym for power and privilege, why wouldn't those structurally foreclosed from accessing such forms of power and privilege want it, or what it stands for, for themselves? And why wouldn't this wanting also be an index of injustice? Envy might be a name for an awareness of what we have had withheld from us, what seems to come so easily, and be so taken-for-granted, by others. We may, contra popular understandings of envy, actually not be morally deficient on account of wanting something more for ourselves. Rather, demanding access to this "more" can be, at least in some instances, understood as a moral demand. If envy is the name for a burgeoning alertness to the realities of radically unequal divisions of resources, then it is also a prelude to such demands.

While it might be difficult, on the surface, to understand Lou Sullivan's relationship to the Beatles or Carter Sickels's (and my own) relationship to Ralph Macchio as an index of injustice, it becomes clearer if we step back from the most obvious signifiers our respective envy has attached to—haircuts, eyes, a kind of buoyant puppy-dog masculinity—and understand the envy, instead, as grounded in a desire to have that kind of uncomplicated, carefree, rather thoughtless relationship to masculinity (in other words, to be able to be a boy in a kind of simple, unreflexive way; to be a vapid boy; to be a himbo). To have not had to spend years processing whether or not one was a man, or how one could become a man; to have not had to do the hard work of parsing what one's investment in and lure toward masculinity was and whether or not it was problematic (i.e., a product of internalized misogyny, a desire for structurally off-limits forms of patriarchal power). This is not to say that gendered forms of envy don't subtend relationships to masculinity and femininity for cis folks, as well, as they most certainly seem to—I would even go so far as to say that envy and ensuing emulation are part of how all gender is assumed. But I do think that there is a specificity to trans forms of gender envy, because they begin from a place of normative exclusion and entail gender transitivity. The question, for folks like Sullivan (and Sickels, and myself) seems to be, first, whether and how to be a boy, and then, if so, what kind of boy to be. To not have to ask that first question is to have a particular form of cis privilege in the form of (relatively) uncomplicated categorical belonging. Because envy is so intimate, so much about proximate desires that are difficult to translate, opaque, or indiscernible to others, the envy archive in this chapter hews closely to those forms of envy that I understand best: those of (usually feminist and/or queer) transmasculine subjects negotiating their investments in and desires for masculinity while simultaneously attempting to not reproduce the most pernicious aspects of the most typically valorized white, hegemonic, toxic form of it.

For folks who are both feminist and transmasculine there is also, sometimes, intense guilt about such forms of envy. The desire to emulate what some of us understand as a class of oppressors, to transition and thus to come into some (however limited or attenuated) form of belonging in a category shaped by male privilege and the concomitant side effect of such privilege, which is willful, insidious ignorance: this is a tense desire, indeed. The form of envy identified above—the kind that stems from the desire for a less fraught form of becoming and belonging, that himbo yearning—runs headlong into our extant awareness of the violence and vagaries that subtend hegemonic modes of masculinity. To paraphrase the title of an essay by Noah Zazanis that explores precisely this tension: many of us hate men and become one anyway.[12]

The conception of manhood that informs this understanding of the relations between patriarchy, capitalism, and manhood isn't at all nuanced, and it is derived from a definitively nonintersectional understanding of men as belonging to a discrete, unitary sex-class, one wielding power over another, subordinated sex-class: women. A monolithic understanding of manhood rather than a nuanced one, an understanding predicated on the elision of most all axes of difference—race, class, ability, sexuality—that pluralize and complexify what we might mean when we talk about masculinities (plural). Zazanis highlights how this conception of sex-class-based understandings of dominance can actually be, and has been, rendered trans-inclusive. Behind the now-familiar rallying call for trans-inclusive radical feminisms ("trans women are women") lies an understanding of trans women as women on account of being oppressed in the same ways that cis women are. He writes, pithily, that "in the new radical feminism, much like the old, women (including trans women) constitute a class exploited by men (including trans men)."

> This framework puts transmasculine people at a really painful crossroads: Do we transition and self-actualize, with the knowledge that doing so will render us complicit in the oppression of our sisters, the same oppression we've experienced all our lives? Or do we force ourselves to live as women (or else non-men of a different sort, though this ideology leaves little space to conceptualize nonbinariness), repressing the parts of us that call toward a transition away from womanhood and/or into maleness?[13]

In the midst of these deliberations, the appearance of gender envy is troubling: it is an indicator of a verboten and potentially traitorous desire, one that, if acted upon, will lead us into complicity with our oppressors. Though this analysis is leaden in its heavy-handedness, feminist trans men are no stranger to this anxiety, and the decision to transition thus comes coupled with guilt about such assumed traitorousness, such complicity. It's hard to shake these voices, even if you find it fully politically legible to be able to claim that yes, men can be feminist and also yes, transition means grappling with questions of newly attained forms of male privilege that had heretofore been irrelevant (or at least differently relevant) to your daily life. A gender is not the same thing as a politics. And yet, the anxiety persists, because of the stubborn recalcitrance of an antipodal understanding of gender, one where an embrace and inhabitation of masculinity can only ever, at least in the final analysis, be legible in opposition to a rejection (annihilation, even) of the feminine. Cam Awkward-Rich sketches the contours of this dilemma in his essay "Trans, Feminism: Or, Reading Like a Depressed Transsexual."[14] He moves from an account of the TERF (trans exclusionary radical feminist) wars—perhaps the most hackneyed, ham-fisted account of trans antagonisms to feminism, rooted in an entirely dimorphic and oppositional concept of sex-class that figures all trans men as suffering from and duped by a form of patriarchal false consciousness and transitioning as a means of avoiding actually grappling with the harms of sexism, all trans women as fundamentally masculinist aggressors and usurpers of women's psychic and physical space, and all trans forms of life as a threat to the foment of sex equity.

But even if we dismiss the TERF articulation of trans threat, there is still a resonance between this position and those less extreme articulations of the tension between transmasculinity and feminism that we might be more familiar with, usually articulated within the space of feminist theory as well as within lesbian/feminist communal discourse: the idea that transmasculine transitions are political and communal losses and that transmasculine desires signal a flight from a female subject position that hinges on a delegitimization of and antagonism toward the female, feminist subject. To want to become a man is, after all, to not want to be a woman, and this desire (one that might become, might be on its way to becoming, might already be, a decision) is always inevitably a more-than-personal (in other words, a political) desire. What must you think of women to not want to be one? This implicit question crops up repeatedly, motivating commentary from a diverse range of feminist thinkers, from feminist phenomenologist Gayle Salamon—who asks, "If the goal is to achieve a stable and enduring sense of self-identity, is there room for a transmasculine subject to encounter the [female] other's desire without evacuating or annihilating it? Or feeling evacuated or annihilated by it in turn?"—to feminist legal theorist Janet Halley—who asks, "How would feminist resistance to misogyny deal with the yearning of many female [sic] human beings to shed so many of their female attributes?" and, several pages later, explicitly states, "I am assuming that we live in a world where gains for transsexuality might come at the expense of feminism."[15]

BOYS, MEN, DADDIES

There's no easy answer to these questions, which is why they tend to produce contortions among transmasc thinkers who set themselves the task of parsing the relationship between trans-masculinity and womanhood, transmasculinity and feminism. If we, as most feminists do, operate with an analysis of gender as precisely that which isn't determined at birth, and as something beyond a personal, agential preference (in other words, gender as neither side of a determinist/free will binary), we can't just let the subject lie. If gender were merely a personal preference (as the language of "preferred pronouns," hated both by transphobes, because they only dignify assigned sex at birth, and trans people, because we tend to feel much more adamantly about our pronouns than the softened language of "preference" suggests, leads us to believe it might be), we'd be able to say to cis women regarding the inhabitation of a female subject position what we say to other folks when they make decisions that we wouldn't, ourselves, have made: "I *love* that for you." But we can't, for to do so would be to capitulate to the logic of gender-as-mere-preference.

So we position ourselves as "sons of the movement," to cite the title of Bobby Noble's 2006 book on the relation of trans men to feminist and queer cultural landscapes.[16] We interpellate ourselves as the queer kin of feminist foremothers. Or we shift our attention toward the examination and critique of violently toxic forms of masculinity, instead, as Thomas Page McBee has done in his creative nonfiction, including the books *Man Alive* and *Amateur*.[17] Or we articulate and amplify a more nuanced understanding of the relationship between power, privilege, and masculinity, utilizing conceptual tools borrowed from intersectional feminisms to differentiate ourselves from cis men and to clarify the many stratifications of race, class, (dis)ability, and sexuality that differentiate transmasculinities from one another. Noah Zazanis does this in "On Hating Men (and Becoming One Anyway)," writing that "trans men's relationship to gender cannot be understood by adding the privilege of maleness to the oppression of transness; the interaction between these axes substantively transforms both such that it generates an experience qualitatively different from either alone." He goes on to clarify that "this qualitative difference is particularly salient for Black trans men and transmasculine people, whose experiences at the intersection of race, gender, and trans status are especially ill-captured by a sex-class approach."[18]

As I write this, in the midst of the Covid-19 pandemic, I hear my partner teaching a lesson in their Introduction to Women's Studies course through the closed door of their office. It's early in the semester, so they're tackling common myths about feminism. They ask their students, "What about the idea that feminists really just want to be men?" The specter of the gender traitor looms large. We seek to prove, over and again in its shadow, that we are still feminist, not misogynist, not victims of patriarchal false consciousness, and of use to feminist movements. But there are psychic costs that attend combatting the assumption that to transition is to denigrate womanhood, and one of them is the inculcation of guilt vis-à-vis envy: feeling bad about what you want to be.

One way to sidestep such guilt is to make our objects of envy boys rather than men. There is a definitive boyishness to the litany of masc aspirational figures I opened this chapter with, and it's not at all incidental. They are all safe boys to love: nonthreatening, gentle, empathic, features that are amplified by the nexus of youth and whiteness. This is, indeed, what makes them popularly palatable teen heartthrobs, and what makes transmasc cathexes to them ones that don't threaten to devour. Awkward-Rich, in a brilliant criticism of what he calls "the boys of queer trans theory," suspects that the figure of the boy (as theorized in the work of Jack Halberstam, Bobby Noble, and others) emerges as central to these strains of transmasculine theorizing because he stands for a kind of "masculinity without phallic power" that "fashions masculinity for the [feminist] movement."[19] In Halberstam's work, the boy—and, specifically, the paradigmatic boy that is Peter Pan—signals a refusal to grow up and into the staid gender stereotypes associated with heteronormative adulthood.[20] The boy who refuses to grow up as queer, transmasc idol is a deeply familiar trope. Sassafras Lowrey has even refashioned the Peter Pan narrative as a trans/queer punk fable in hir novel *Lost Boi*. It begins, tellingly, like so: "All bois, except one, become grownups. They go to college or work in construction. They sign domestic partnership, civil union, or even marriage certificates. Some bois become artificially inseminated, have top surgery, or work in an office or as PE teachers. They go to law school or work in non-profits. Growing up happens to the best of us, even when we said it wouldn't."[21] The boy is the antinormative figure par excellence, and this holds, here, for a variety of normativities: hetero-, homo-, and trans-.

Awkward-Rich points out that these motivated reworkings of boyhood persistently sideline the figure of the girl, who becomes not much more than witness to and fodder for these revisions of masculinity. He writes that "the boy's story is yet another story of her displacement," that "the boy gets all the attention while the girl misses out on all the fun."[22] As a case in point, just look toward Paul Preciado's deployment of VD—the autotheoretical proxy of Virginie Despentes, the French feminist writer and filmmaker affiliated with the postporn movement and author of the feminist rape revenge classic *Baise-Moi*[23]—in *Testo Junkie*. He entitles a chapter "In Which the Body of VD Becomes an Element in an Experimental Context." The "experimental context" seems to be fucking; specifically, a transmasc fucking someone who newly identifies as lesbian. At its core, though, the chapter is about Preciado's relationship to masculinity. We find out that the psychoanalyst he visited as a teenager called him megalomaniacal because of his "desire to fuck only those at the top of the femininity pyramid, the alpha bitches, the supersluts." Preciado is convinced that the analyst would have told a cis man this just meant he had "self-esteem."[24] We find out that since childhood, he's had "a fantastical construction worker's cock" that reacts to "every piece of ass that moves."[25] We find out, in keeping with this macho laborer fantasy, that his experience of fucking VD is "harder than factory work, harder than driving a truck loaded with nitroglycerine in a cowboy film."[26]

It's not surprising that the reception of *Testo Junkie* has spent much more time tarrying with Preciado's coining of the biopolitical-zeitgeist-naming concept of "pharmacopornography" than it has with his extensive meditations on his own sex life. Pharmacopornography—which refers to the intertwined contemporary processes of "biomolecular (pharmaco) and semiotic-technical (pornographic) government of sexual subjectivity"[27]—enables readers to abstract from the visceral and intimate details of the text, wherein Preciado makes his own newly-on-testosterone experience the central case study of the book (it opens with him filming himself shaving his head and crotch, gluing on a mustache composed of the shorn hair, and fucking himself—all framed as an homage to his recently deceased friend, the gay French writer of autofiction and polarizing advocate of barebacking, Guillaume Dustan). In part, I suspect that this is because some of the admissions that readers encounter are hard to read if one's reading is motivated by the desire to recuperate masculinity for feminism, a vision of masculinity without phallic power, for phallic power is, or at least seems to be, precisely what Preciado craves. The desires Preciado describes—to fuck only the most powerful women, and to fuck like the banal yet persistent fantasy of the hypersexualized, deeply macho, working-class stud, a kind of queer punk resignification of Lady Chatterley's lover—are almost embarrassingly familiar (to readers of heterosexual erotica, to anyone who has encountered gay clone culture, to anyone who has ever fantasized about being, or having, a macho service top). They tend to dominate the libidinal economies that many of us dwell within.

But even though Preciado renders, in vivid detail, his obsession with this virile, powerful figure—let's call him Daddy, for short—he tries to make clear that his aspirational embodiment of such a man has nothing in common with that of cishet guys. He's very clear that he's not like the other boys, or at least not *those* other boys. Revisiting his bourgeois, suburban Spanish hometown, and reencountering the "supersluts" he wanted (and sometimes had) as a teenager, he describes these women unflatteringly: "They've already lived the best years of their heterosexual life and are preparing to reach forty, with only the hope of a rejuvenation technique. Some are happy about having children or are justifying not having had them; others seem indifferent; some are still in love with their husbands, or pretend to be. But in a certain way, within a temporary rift, they are still my little girls, my bitches. They still have time for the revolution."[28] These women are forever his; his dick (however incorporeal it may have been) irrevocably changed them.

I'm interested in the phrase "temporary rift" here, and what it refers to: a kind of tear in the spacetime of heteronormative reproductive futurity that returns them to a world absented from the domineering gaze and desire of cisheteromasculinity; a recursive return to a world wherein they still belonged to Preciado, who makes clear that his adolescent affairs with these women are primary, fundamental. "Before they'd even had the time to cross the street and meet the boys at the secondary school opposite," he writes, "they'd already put their tongues in my mouth. They're mine."[29] In Preciado's imagining of these women, their eroticization of a queer, trans form of masculinity is the prelude to a decades-long commitment to cisheteronormativity, inverting the normative mimetic logic that would make transmasculinity a bad/fake copy of the cismasculine real. This originary desire displaces the Law of the Father; the girls' school becomes a space before and beyond the stranglehold of an erotics informed by misogynist logics. This is, I suppose, why Preciado can call these women his bitches, can repeat, as a refrain throughout this chapter, that they belong to him. In the libidinal economy Preciado envisages here, one that precedes the supposedly staid and circumscribed lives these women come to live, girls are not the property of men, and *bitch* is a pejorative that is always already reclaimed. If these women, as adults, could just find their way back to that temporary rift, they'd be fit for the (queer-trans-feminist) revolution.

As far as just-so stories go, this one is pretty appealing. This is, I suspect, mainly because Preciado rejects the trope of transmasculine longing, the long years spent imagining what kind of guy you might want to be, as well as the forms of envy that come along with such longing. Preciado doesn't just want a "fantastical construction worker's cock"; rather, he's had one all along. There is no deferral of desire to a timespace ostensibly posttransition; rather, there is a consistency from his childhood on through to his present: he's always wanted girls at the top of the femininity pyramid, he's always wanted to fuck anything that moves, he's always been the kind of boy he is, though the epiphenomena of embodiment may have only recently changed, biochemically speaking. This is part of what makes his theorization of gender so brash, braggadocious, self-assured. He's not suspicious of his own investment in masculinity; it operates almost prereflexively here, and shamelessly. Which is, from the perspective of a transmasculine person with a deep and abiding suspicion of my own relationship to masculinity (Am I enthralled by, in thrall to, phallic power? Do I, or do I not, or do we all, have penis envy?), kind of enviable. And also kind of unbelievable.

Considering this, we are thrown straight into the gulf that stretches between the argument that trans guys are just like other guys and the argument that trans guys are, as a gender-class, distinct on account of their past as coercively assigned female. Most of us have to learn to float in the indeterminacy, and navigate the tidal shifts of, this gulf—to cultivate rhetorical strategies to sidestep the bifurcated logic that shapes the shore, to sometimes claim sameness with cisness and to, other times, insist on difference. If I were Derridean, maybe I would use *différance* to index this strategy, with the meaning of the transmasc experiential forever deferred on account of its inevitable routing through limited and limiting conceptions of gender that it, nevertheless, relies on for its own sense. But I'd rather just defer to Jordy Rosenberg who, in his essay "The Daddy Dialectic," comments that, for transmasc folks, certain words—he, they, Daddy— "cast a language shadow. This shadow is cast over the body itself, awakening organs that flex only in the presence of certain fantasies, certain shared lexica. This shadow and what it awakens function in complex collective counterpoint to (and through) the Law of the Father and all its symbolic violence, and so it (and all its refutation of self-enclosure as 'reason') is as much a part of our resistance to the oppressive forces of the present as any-thing else."[30] It's the ineffable felt response to certain words—the "language shadow . . . cast over the body itself"—where trans and queer resistance to the overcoded determinations of gender lies, where demimondes of meaningful sense experience can be found. These affective experiences inevitably fail to be easily con-verted into language. This is why, when writing of the pleasure of being called a *certain* word by a *certain* person, Rosenberg circum-vents this translational dilemma, writing, "If you grapple with your Father-figure desires through a queer lens, then you know that the private alchemies that exist to make our pleasures pos-sible are not to be divulged in mixed company. I will say, though, that there exists a species of intimate adult relation in which the exchange of one particular word—addressed to you as an adult from another adult and with no child present—produces a kind of ease and excitement at once."[31] His use of "private alchemy" here goes beyond even the concept of argot in its refusal to trans-late: all he says is that you do not divulge such pleasures in "mixed company" (comprised, assumingly, of faithless witnesses, clue-less interlocuters—other times, elsewhere, these people might be called cishet). But, even if it cannot be spoken of directly, there is nevertheless a certain transubstantiation that occurs when the elements are in place, when the vibe is right. In this space, "daddy" is able to exceed the determinations of the Law of the Father and the dyad of sameness and difference vis-à-vis masculinity that produces so much tension, so much anxiety, in the lives of (some, though certainly not all) trans guys.

Sometimes, envy can be a form of reprieve from this anxiety: to be lost in a certain yearning for what other men have is a way of sidestepping some other bad feelings. Envy is anticipatory, comprised of the future tense imaginings of "what if," "if only," "one day," and also "maybe impossible," "maybe never." It reso-nates with the temporality of becoming, which has a privileged status as the concept most deployed in trans translations of ex-perience, in iterations both Deleuzian and quotidian, utilized as both a progressive verb and a noun. From Jamison Green's classic *Becoming a Visible Man* (which Jennifer Finney Boylan, reviewing it for the *New York Times,* describes as "the first great memoir from a trans man") to the decidedly less-great documentary *Becoming Chaz,* about Chaz Bono's transition, to numerous essays in trans studies, becoming is deployed over and again, most amenable to shorthanding the transformations that transition entails.[32] As trans scholar T. Garner writes in hir synopsis of the term in the very first issue of *TSQ—Transgender Studies Quarterly,* becoming "is a highly productive concept in transgender studies and in theoretical perspectives on the body in general because of its capacity to provide a way of reconsidering the nature of the body and body modification. In particular, it has the potential to undermine the accusation that trans bodies are unnatural or constructed."[33] A body that is becoming is webbed, networked, intra-active, and engaged in the ever-ongoing process of transmutation, rather than a fixed, stable, static thing. Deleuze and Guattari, in their articulation of the concept in *A Thousand Plateaus,* are very clear that individuals are never in control of processes of becoming, asserting that "becoming produces nothing other than itself. We fall into a false alternative if we say that you either imitate or you are. . . . This is the point to clarify: that a becoming lacks a subject distinct from itself; but also that it has no term, since its term in turn exists only as taken up in another becoming of which it is the subject, and which coexists, forms a block, with the first."[34]

If envy can be experienced as a reprieve, it is because it's possible for it to be a reverie of becoming, a fantasy space of what might be. Prereflexive, perhaps unrealistic, but still a kind of daydream-codex of future gender, one that is introjected, incorporated into the self. "We fall into a false alternative if we say that you either imitate or you are." This assertion of Deleuze and Guattari's is strikingly similar to Ngai's understanding of envy as closer to emulation (a desire to become) than identification. Envy is not about recognizing oneself in another subject but about desiring part-objects for oneself (Paul McCartney's hair, Ralph Macchio's eyes, Peter Pan's ability to never grow up).

And, as anyone who has ever actively envied (so, all of us) understands, it's not without antagonism.

"THIS IDEALIZED OBJECT PERSECUTES ME": TRANS ANNOYANCE AND HORIZONTAL HOSTILITY

Years ago, I was at an academic feminist conference, having a between-panel conversation with a beloved friend. It was long before I went on testosterone, which is an important piece of information for this story. We were both on the academic job market, both scouting positions, both suffering through the attendant frustrations that come along with this. They—a nonbinary transfeminine person—leaned in and half-whispered, conspiratorially, about "all these good-looking, young trans guys" getting interviews. They were talking directly about "the boys of queer trans theory," in precisely the moment when Halberstam was valorizing Peter Pan stories, when Gayle Salamon was speculating about annihilating transmasculine desires, when *Original Plumbing* was publishing its first issues. Trans men were becoming more visibly present as interlocuters within academic feminist spaces, particularly those that leaned heavily toward queer theory. They were also being actively eroticized, sometimes fetishized, by some folks in these spaces. We were jealous. I was also more than a little envious of these trans men who were early entrants into the supposed security of an academic tenure-track post (though in reality this was, and remains, only a very, very small minority of guys, to say nothing of the radical dearth of trans women in the academy). This envy, like others, was rooted in structural disadvantages, a whole webbed network of them, though two in particular stand out: the post-2008 recession and its coincident paucity of academic posts was combining forces with the economic and geographic lack of availability of transition-related technologies that kept me, and many, many others, from medically transitioning. I was happy for these guys:

they were brilliant and hot and seemed well-adjusted and re-spected. I was pleased that at least a few of us had gotten a foot in the door, but also, ugh. They had what I wanted, in a situation heavily shaped by imposed austerity and scarcity. As Ngai points out, building on the work of psychoanalyst Melanie Klein in her classic essay "Envy and Gratitude," envy "enables the subject to formulate the assertion *This idealized object persecutes me.*"[35]

For Klein, the idealized object stems "predominately from persecutory anxiety" derived from "excessive envy," and the folks who suffer from such forms of persecutory anxiety and exces-sive envy most intensively are those who have experienced forms of fundamental deprivation.[36] Such idealizations are inevitably disappointed, as no one can live up to expectations predicated on idealization. When this inevitable disappointment comes to pass, "the former idealized person is often felt as a persecutor (which shows the origin of idealization as a counterpart to perse-cution), and into him [sic] is projected the subject's envious and critical attitude."[37] In other words, deprivation breeds idealiza-tion, which then breeds envy and criticism.

Although a full grappling with the implications of Klein's work is beyond the scope of this text, there is something about her analysis of the operation of envy that rings true, especially insofar as it helps name and describe dynamics within trans com-munities that manifest as horizontal hostility or intracommunal antagonism. Fault lines tend to open up around questions of relative privilege and transnormativity and take multiple forms: arguments between transmedicalists and those who believe one can identify as trans without experiencing gender dysphoria or undergoing medical transition, between stealth and out trans people, between cis-passing and non-cis-passing folks, between binary trans folks and nonbinary trans folks, between those with relatively uncomplicated access to medical transition and those who encounter much more rigorous gatekeeping (whether eco-nomic, racial, ableist, geographic, or some or all of these at the same time). Envy undergirds these antagonisms, and it cuts both ways. The most obvious manifestations, though, are directed toward those folks understood as embodying and benefitting from the privileges that attend normative gender presentation, unclockable forms of embodiment, and easy access to medical transition. What we envy may differ—for some, it might be easier-to-afford surgery, for others, it might be the ability to be selectively stealth, for still others, it might be the cultural legibility afforded to transnormative subjects. But however they manifest, these desires can be experienced as, and often are, shaped by deprivation: the result of an unfairly stacked deck, directly stemming from entrenched structural inequalities. Sometimes, such envy is rooted in forms of microfascism or internalized oppression—for instance, internalizing the notion that passing as cis is and should be the transition goal of all trans folks and that not attaining such passability is a personal failing. Even though we may be consciously against this expectation, which is also a logic that produces hierarchies of trans validity, authenticity, and legitimacy, it is still consistently reinforced at macro-, meso-, and microlevels, from mainstream trans representations to everyday encounters with colleagues, neighbors, acquaintances, and intimates. It's hard to outrun it, hard to work against its reinforcement. But it's easy to be envious of those whose lives don't seem to be determined by such struggles. And, as for envy cutting in the other direction: who wouldn't be envious of someone who feels able to lay claim to a trans identity without being interpellated and vetted by the medical industrial complex, with someone who seems wholly disinvested from the politics of trans authenticity, with someone who has stopped utilizing and being invested in cisnormative barometers of legibility, with someone who disidentifies with the gender binary and perhaps has an abolitionist stance toward gender, full stop. Depending on the vantage point, these are all enviable positions. Each one is prone to idealization—and to disappointment.

My aim here is not to weigh in on either ostensible "side" of the debates surrounding transmedicalists and "transtrenders," nor on what *trans* does or doesn't, should or shouldn't encompass, nor where to draw the line(s) between transgender, transsexual, and nonbinary. I want, instead, to point to what I understand as a motor of those debates: the operations of envy in the everyday lives of trans people, especially as it is or becomes directed toward other trans folks. To even frame these debates as comprised of neat and bifurcated sides undermines the extent to which the animus that operates within them emerges out of the fuzzy nexus of envy, emulation, identification, and desire that so often shapes forms of horizontal hostility within marginalized (and traumatized) communities. Felt dis/similarity tends to breed such animus, which is why it so often cleaves along fine-grained identitarian lines. Marginalized peoples tend to put each other through tests of legitimacy and authenticity in order to determine belonging, as well as access to the practical, emotional, and psychological supports that come along with a sense of belonging. Trans folks are no different, though this form of gatekeeping remains radically undertheorized, while the forms of medical gatekeeping that negatively affect trans subjects and communities has a robust and continually growing literature. The forms of gatekeeping that circulate intracommunally are much more difficult, and much riskier, to address.

This is why, when decolonial feminist philosopher María Lugones drafted her meditation on the operations of horizontal hostility within communities of color, she included the phrase "ginger reflections" in the subtitle.[38] To treat a topic gingerly is to treat it with care, with a deep awareness of the fragility and importance of the topic so handled. I intend to be ginger here, as well, and to draw on some of Lugones's insights in order to frame how it is that horizontal hostility is always tied up not just with questions of normativity and privilege but also with questions of belonging and homeplace. Her essay is concerned with the conflicts that arise between folks of color who have a strong, "solid . . . core, easygoing" sense of their "identity of color" with "sense of faking it or of being perceived as a fake not in one's experience" and those folks of color who are more misfit with regard to communal belonging: "green-eyed Blacks, never-been-taught-my-culture Asian Americans and U.S. Latinos, émigrés, immigrants, and migrants."[39] While I'm writing about a quite different set of identities and communal forms of belonging, she was my most important mentor and teacher, and her hard-won wisdom on the emergence of horizontal hostility in marginalized communities, as a queer, Latinx, feminist intellectual who persistently felt like she never quite fit in the communities and movements she was with/in guides me.

She writes that folks with a solid, core, relatively untroubled sense of belonging to a minoritized community sometimes "administer legitimacy tests" to determine belonging and adjudicate acceptance. I think the anxiety that some folks experience surrounding being "trans enough" stems from the administration of (or fear of administration of) such legitimacy tests. While this practice is indissolubly intertwined with and informed by legacies of medical gatekeeping, it now operates independently in the spaces of trans-centered social media, where arguments between trans influencers often circulate around the nexus of who is, and who isn't, really trans. Such arguments are exacerbated by the fact that, unlike the "solid, core" folks Lugones writes of, trans folks—even the most "solid, core" ones—are raised in relative isolation and disconnection from one another; the commonalities that undergird a sense of shared history, culture, and sense of self are inevitably mediated by distance and technological prosthesis, and it's more common for our avatars to be interpellated and (mis)recognized than our material bodyminds. This means that the litmus tests for authenticity and belonging are grounded in something other than shared history, mores, and ways of being in the world. It's not surprising, then, that the locus of legitimacy tests, the gauging of authenticity, tends to hinge on the desire for and telos of transition.

Lugones writes of resistant communities as "seeing circles," asking, "Where do you go to be seen? To be seen as something other than a more or less monstrous imitation, an imaginary being?"[40] That is, to whom do you turn to recover from dominant modes of perception that construe you as fake, deluded, imaginary, unreal, unwell, illegible, illegitimate? A bad copy of the real thing? Where do we turn to heal from cis-dominant modes of perceiving trans bodies, trans selfhood? And what happens when we do? Some of us find more or less seamless acceptance, and the seeing circle becomes an "anchor . . . that gives one substance."[41] The seeing circle confirms legibility, authenticity, and a sense of sameness, a sense of resonant experience. But it also threatens loss; if the seeing circle confers and confirms a sense of not being overcoded by dominant logics, the transformation or expansion of that circle can prompt a loss of communal, and thus subjective, coherency. She writes that "going from less to more encompassing circles born from the need to form a politics of resistance means the loss of some degrees of assurance in one's solidity, unless one can succeed in asserting one's values over the larger circle."[42]

This struggle to assert one's values over the larger circle is precisely what I think of when I watch self-proclaimed "tranpa" (trans grandpa), trans porn star and entrepreneur Buck Angel, excoriate an eighteen-year-old YouTuber for his understanding of transness as encompassing trans subjects who don't experience dysphoria or desire medical transition.[43] It is what I think of when I read essays by transmedicalists arguing that the legibility and legitimacy of trans subjects in dominant culture hinges on the diagnosis of dysphoria, or when I see the excoriation of transmedicalists discussed out of context, without attention to the politics or traumatic impact of legacies of medical gatekeeping, discontinuous access to technologies of transition, and institutional transphobia.

There is a desperate desire for there to be a there there, some grounding commonality that unites trans experience, that could serve as constitutive criteria for belonging, something that causes the seeing circle to cohere, that makes witness possible. But as the seeing circle expands, whatever this constitutive criteria might be becomes more troubled, more desiccated, less legible, so that even the lines between cis and trans are fuzzy, permeable, interpenetrating. As A. Finn Enke points out, insisting on a neat division between cis and trans "effectively asserts the naturalness of medico-juridical determinations of and control over trans existence" while, "at the same time, cis further distances from trans by establishing its own relative normativity."[44] Going further, Enke argues that "the compulsion to identify or even to posit a cis/trans binary is an effect of neoliberal politics in which identity categories are crafted to maximize a share of normative privilege."[45] To bring Enke and Lugones together, we might say that the effort to control the terms of the seeing circle—to "assert one's values over the larger circle"—is rooted in a fear of loss of the (however meager) forms of privilege those doing the asserting have been able to attain. This fear is, indeed, at the root of transmedicalist discourse: utilizing the diagnosis of dysphoria alongside desire for and attainment of medical transition places a crucible of suffering at the center of trans experiences, and enduring such suffering becomes the price of trans inclusion. Within this logic, medical transition is only ever ameliorative and curative, and the difficult battles waged and partially won—collectively and individually—to garner access to such technologies are the gauntlet through which one must pass to garner mutual recognition as "really" (authentically, legitimately) trans. Perhaps more importantly, though, prioritizing dysphoria places the experience of discomfort and distress at the center of debates about trans authenticity. To be trans is to feel bad enough that you must transition, by whatever means at hand.

The locus becomes how we feel about what we aren't rather than what we desire. Furthermore, how we feel about what we aren't is framed in firmly delimited and limiting affective terms: discomfort, distress. I would never argue that these feels aren't integral to many trans experiences, but they certainly don't exhaust the affective range of trans feelings about transness, transition, being a bodymind in the world. What about ambivalence? What about euphoria? What about exhaustion? Anger? Pleasure? Cynicism? Curiosity? Experimentation? Is there room in the concept of dysphoria for affective lability, variation, vacillation? In other words, what do we lose—what can't we think—when we render dysphoria the constitutive criteria of transness? And a bigger question: what can't we think when we insist that there must be some kind of constitutive criteria that unifies transness to begin with?

I find envy far more politically and conceptually interesting than dysphoria because it is fundamentally relational, about yearning, desire, and becoming. Envy is an indicator of what we want, of what might be possible, as much as it is an indicator of real, material forms of deprivation. It is certainly part of the affective complex that attends dysphoria, as dysphoric distress and discomfort are produced, at least in part, by yearning for that which is hard to obtain. To think envy is to train our focus on that yearning rather than the wretchedness it sometimes produces; it is to claim that envy isn't a sin, or an indicator of pathology, but rather a barometer of desire and disenfranchisement. Envy is idiosyncratic, complex, messy, while dysphoria is a conceptually tidy name for the felt impacts of inhabiting transphobic social worlds; we might even call it an epiphenomenal byproduct of such inhabitations. Dysphoria is individuating—about how we feel, on our own, in our bodies and about our being in the world. Envy takes us beyond the self (though not without difficulty), as it is motivated by desires that we are too often shamed for, desires that are too often compromised or foreclosed. To grant trans envy its power is to admit that it's okay to want what we want: a different kind of embodiment, another gendered modality of being in the world, at least some measure of comfort in the dwelling-place of our enfleshed and carnal selves.

The next chapter traces what happens in the aftermath of such admissions, as one manifests what such admissions make possible as they move in the world. It explores trans rage: what happens when we are routinely and exorbitantly punished for such wanting.

4

TOUGH BREAKS

Trans Rage and the Cultivation of Resilience

Rage
gives me back my body
as its own fluid medium.

—Susan Stryker, "My Words to Victor Frankenstein above
the Village of Chamounix"

Rage is equated by dominators with hysteria or insanity.

—María Lugones, "Hard-to-Handle Anger"

THE PRODUCTIVITY OF RAGE: THE WORK OF THE BREAK

Pop psychology would have us believe that anger is only a mask for sadness, a carapace protecting us from feeling the effects of a much deeper woundedness. It has been analyzed within psychotherapeutic literature as a form of "problem anger" and countless strategies have been developed in order to help folks therapeutically "manage" it.[1] It tends to be analyzed in highly individuated terms, as a problem endemic to individuals, to be resolved—typically through a therapeutic relationship—at the level of the individual. The few social scientific analyses that theorize rage as a social phenomenon tend to focus on the way it shapes majoritarian, hegemonic forms of subjectivity—that is, they analyze the rage of the privileged, the forms of rage driven by entitlement and characterized by intersections of xenophobia, racism, sexism, transphobia, and homophobia.[2]

Anger is, within these readings, that which protects the subject from experiencing the full psychic impact of trauma; it is a dissimulating mask that deflects attention away from profound hurt, that supports an idea of the subject as inviolable, impenetrable. It is a defense reaction that stands in the way of "true" healing, a roadblock on the way to recovery. We are told that one of the unfortunate aspects of anger is that it's too often coupled with a conviction of moral righteousness, a righteousness that can be utilized to justify all manner of belligerent violence, all kinds of acting out and acting up. Anger is almost exclusively understood as a negative, deleterious emotion that is best worked through and then discarded; the possible resurgence of anger must be guarded against; if it does reemerge, it should be prevented, contained.

I turn away from such culturally dominant articulations of rage and toward feminist philosophical reevaluations of supposed negative affect because I seek a different way of interpreting anger, a different mode of understanding the phenomenon of rage. I think, contra popular understandings of the effects of rage, that it offers a critical resource for minoritized subjects. Engaging the work of women of color feminist theorists and trans scholars, artists, and activists, this chapter examines how rage is key to the survival of minoritized subjects; it is an energy that propels us toward more possible futures, an energy that encourages us to break those relationships that do not sustain us, that do not support our flourishing. Placing the artistic production of Cassils, a transmasculine, nonbinary durational performance artist, and the literary production of trans movement leader, intersectional feminist, and prison abolitionist CeCe McDonald into dialogue with feminist philosophies of anger, I explore how rage is transformative and worldbuilding, not merely a negative affective force that compromises flourishing and impedes the cultivation of resilience.

Rage is an orienting affect.[3] It moves us. It is a repellant affect, meaning it scares away certain others and, in doing so, propels us as well. It is our vest of porcupine quills, that which makes us prickly, that which prevents proximity, deters the closeness of threatening forces. It is a kind of armor, shielding us from that which seeks to harm. It can form a force field; it is a radiating affect that distances. This distancing can produce a small modicum of space for being that is less subject to trespass, less likely to be violated. Rage can make us seem unfriendly, unapproachable—it can deter less-than-welcome approaches. Being perceived as unfriendly can be an important mode of self-preservation, a way to inure ourselves in relation to hostile publics, a way to inoculate ourselves against the emotional toxicity that is directed our way.

Rage happens. It happens to you. Is it welling up from within? Is it visited upon you, an exterior force you must grapple with? It feels overwhelming, excessive, too much. It leaves us short of breath. It leaves our rational capacities short-circuited. It is difficult to articulate. As María Lugones reminds is, it is hard to handle.[4] It happens when you sense the situation you inhabit is, in some significant way, inimical to your self-preservation, hostile to your survival. Minoritized subjects are so angry, it is said. So often angry. Why are we so upset? So depressed? So unhappy?

Sara Ahmed painstakingly unpacks the normative cultural and political work these accusations of negative feeling do. They serve as a prelude to a lament about our failure to be pleased with the worldly conditions we encounter; we are told that others "just want us to be happy," that our unhappiness is making them unhappy, that our anger is eroding the social and familial ties that bind. Ahmed calls this process "affective conversion," and it is how minoritized subjects are made into killjoys.[5] Bad feelings stick to us; once stuck, we become "affect aliens"—those beings not made happy by conventional happiness causes, those beings who deviate from normativities, and in so deviating, pervert the normal, disturb the customs, rituals, and habits that shape dominant modes of sociality.[6] This is how we become "unhappiness causes": we convert "good feelings into bad."[7] We tell our uncle his joke is racist. We leave the family table when we're consistently gendered incorrectly. We ask our loved ones to stop deadnaming us. We tell a transphobic street harasser to fuck off. We refuse eye contact with the stranger aggressively ogling us. We make eye contact with the stranger aggressively ogling us and sneer. We trouble others; we make trouble for others.

Rage helps us come unstuck, helps us find an exit from these troubling relations. Ahmed writes, throughout her oeuvre, of breaking points, limit points, moments of outspokenness and reaction that sever bonds, that transform—and often end—relationships. In her meditation on bearable lives—a reworking of Butler's theorization of livable lives[8]—she writes:

> A bearable life is a life that can hold up, which can keep its shape or direction, in the face of what it is asked to endure. . . . An unbearable life is a life which cannot be tolerated or endured, held up, held onto. The unbearable life "breaks" or "shatters" under the "too much" of what is being borne. . . . When "it" is too much, things break, you reach a breaking point.[9]

Rage is what happens, sometimes, when "it"—the institutional, political, and interpersonal modes of relationality that shape your present—is too much. A moment of shattering, a moment of breaking.

A break can be a moment of mental "instability" (as in a psychotic break), what I would prefer, rather, to understand as a moment of intense cognitive divergence. It can be a desirable reprieve from our quotidian reality ("I could really use a break") or an invective that names a statement or situation unrealistic, absurd, ridiculous ("Give me a fucking break"). Importantly, a break can also be all three (or, perhaps, the three are not as distinct as we may tend to believe). Can we understand breaking as a phenomenon that partakes of each of these inflections of meaning without necessarily imposing hard separations of sense between them?

Rage breaks things. Rage signals a break. Breaking leads us beyond rage. Rage enables a break.

Why do we break? I turn to Judith Butler's critical reappraisal of the Spinozan concept of the conatus as a way into thinking the why of the break. Spinoza uses the term *conatus* to name the desire to persist or persevere in one's being—in other words, the desire to keep on living. The conatus is not a uniquely human trait but one common to all things. Butler, too, has dealt throughout her career with questions of survival, particularly with the question of what makes life livable. Her interrogation of livability leads her to approach the conatus asking what conditions need to be met in order to desire to persist in existing.

Put differently: when we desire to live, what is it that we desire?

Butler argues that, for Spinoza (as for her), selfhood is never self-contained, never ends at the border of the skin. Additionally, the fact that the conatus is driven by a desire for self-preservation means that it is always a more-than-individual matter: "the desire to live implicates desire in a matrix of life that may well, at least partially, deconstitute the 'I' who endeavors to live."[10] Clarifying, she writes that "to live means to participate in life, and life itself will be a term that equivocates between the 'me' and the 'you,' taking up both of us in its sweep and dispersion. Desiring life produces an *ek-stasis* in the midst of desire, a dependence on an externalization, something that is palpably not me, without which no perseverance is possible."[11] Self-preservation is fundamentally reliant on others. Survival is always collective. The desire to persist in one's being is dependent on conditions that are in many ways external to the self. "The problematic of life," she writes, "binds us to others in ways that turn out to be constitutive of who each of us singly is. . . . [However], that singularity is never fully subsumed by that vexed form of sociality."[12]

I focus on self-preservation because I think it is at the heart of the matter when we're considering trans rage. We feel rage and are transformed by rage whenever we sense, or are reminded, that the networks we rely on for survival are inimical to such survival. This sense precipitates loneliness, the feeling of being ontologically adrift, unmoored, homeless; it also, for many of us, produces suicidality or precedes suicide. Considerable social science research has been undertaken in order to track the prevalence of suicidal ideation and attempts among trans populations; a recent review of such studies reports ideation rates ranging from 9.2 percent to as high as 84 percent.[13] However the numbers are crunched, it is clear that trans subjects engage in suicidal ideation and attempt suicide at rates that far outstrip cisgender populations, including cis lesbian, gay, and bisexual populations. It is also apparent that such high rates are significantly related to interpersonal, institutional, and systemic forms of discrimination, with "forced sex or rape, gender discrimination (being discriminated against due to one's gender identity/presentation), and physical gender victimization (being beaten or physically abused due to one's gender identity/presentation)" all operating as independent predictors of attempted suicide.[14] Correlatively, insulation from such forms of interpersonal and institutional violence—in the form of strong social support systems and the existence of "reasons for living"—is understood as a protective factor that mitigates such high rates of suicidality.[15]

This research resonates with Butler's claim that the problem of suicidality arises not from within but when the singularity that one is finds extremely limited support within the "vexed form of sociality" one inhabits. It is not an individuated pathology, not the product of individual mental sickness. Rather, suicide—the phenomenon that seems, on the face of it, to fundamentally trouble the concept of the conatus—actually works to uphold this Spinozan/Butlerian understanding of the self as simultaneously singular and radically interdependent. If one's desire to persist involves a form of subjectivity that is unintelligible, persecuted, or condemned—though it causes no deleterious effect to others, though it does not actively intervene in the flourishing of others—one finds themselves simultaneously desiring to live and lacking the necessary supports to persist in doing so. This is how lives are rendered unlivable. This feeling, of life being or becoming impossible, is often, if not always, what produces suicidality. Sometimes, a break is followed by a suicide; but often, a break is a moment that enables a more livable life to be realized. We associate instability with breaks precisely because of this radical differential of possible aftermaths, precisely because of these high stakes. Breaks scare us, and others, for that reason. But our survival is radically dependent on these others; what happens during and after a break depends on the communal uptake such breaks receive, how they are witnessed and understood. If one breaks—if one keeps breaking—and is met only with criticism, pathology, censure, isolation, or institutionalization, the specter of suicide looms larger and larger.

The desire to live, Butler argues, is commensurable with the desire to live well. The conatus seeks augmentation, an expansion of potential (what Spinoza refers to as *potentia,* an increase in ability or capacity). It can be diminished in potential, as well, when it finds itself encumbered by sad passions, which also travel under the name of negative affect. Butler glosses Spinoza on this topic: "The *conatus* is augmented or diminished depending on whether one feels hatred or love, whether one lives with those with whom agreement is possible, or whether one lives with those with whom agreement is difficult, if not impossible."[16]

Which brings us back to the break.

We break to keep on living. We break when engulfed by sad passions, when living among entities intent on minimizing our capacities. To paraphrase Deleuze, it is always in the interest of authority to produce sad passions; sometimes, the institutions we are reliant upon—and family is always one of these institutions, whether chosen or blood, kith or kin—precipitate our breaking.[17] One final quote from Butler:

> It might be that the constituting relations have a certain pattern of breakage in them, that they actually constitute

and break us at the same time. This makes for a tentative or more definitive form of madness, to be sure. What does it mean to require what breaks you? If the dependency on those others was once a matter of survival and now continues to function psychically as a condition of survival (recalling and reinstituting that primary condition), then certain kinds of breaks will raise the question of whether the "I" can survive. Matters become more complex if one makes the break precisely in order to survive (breaking with what breaks you). In such situations, the "I" may undergo radically conflicting responses: as a consequence of its rupture with those formative relations, it will not survive; only with such a rupture does it now stand a chance to survive.[18]

Butler references survival quite literally here. Trans folks—youth, particularly, as well as those of us who are multiply marginalized— intimately understand the high price of severance from communities of origin, the slow death precipitated by our social and institutional illegibility and estrangement. So often, we must rely on relationships with people and institutions that interpret us as subhuman, or at the very least misrecognize us so profoundly that the "I" conjured in interaction barely resembles the "I" we understand ourselves to be. So many of us have faced this dilemma Butler references: we must break to survive, yet in that breaking our survival becomes compromised. Breaking with what breaks you is a risky matter; it puts one's existence on the line. One might not survive the break, as one might lose the fundamental social and institutional supports that make life possible, yet one cannot survive without such a break if one's interdependencies are embedded within socialities shaped by interpersonal and institutional transmisogyny and transphobia.

Rage often accompanies the break; importantly, it can operate both as a sense-making tool and an affective response that places one on the outer boundaries of sense. How rage is understood depends on the interpretive community of witnesses. Are there witnesses? Do they empathize with our rage? Does it resonate with them, produce what Teresa Brennan identifies as an "affective transfer," what Claudia Card calls "emotional echoing"?[19] Or does our rage appear to these witnesses as outsized, unfathomable, overreactive? Is it illegible? Does it make a claim to authority to respect us? Does it demonstrate to a community of similarly marginalized folks that their experiences of rage are shared, legible, and legitimate?

Butler contends that the relational quandary produced by being both constituted and sustained (however poorly) by relations that break us produces a "tentative or more definitive form of madness, to be sure." I don't believe Butler is seeking to pathologize the concept of madness here, but I want to press a little harder on the status of madness in relation to the break, accompanied by the work of María Lugones. In "Hard-to-Handle Anger," a deeply self-reflexive essay committed to exploring the role of anger in the lives and work of women of color, she develops what I think of as a nonce taxonomy of anger. Nonce taxonomies, as Eve Kosofsky Sedgwick conceives of them in *Epistemology of the Closet*, are tactically developed from the lived experience of oppression as a means of "mapping out the possibilities, dangers, and stimulations" that shape the "human social landscape" of marginalized peoples.[20] They are forms of categorization that are essential to our survival, though they are not necessarily intelligible or perceptible to dominant culture. Nonce taxonomies are also, often, stealth taxonomies. You understand them only if you need to understand them, only if your experience necessitates deviant and intricate forms of uncommon sense.

Theorizing from her felt experiences of anger and the wide range of responses it receives, Lugones produces a useful set of classifications that parse anger in relationship to its potential for politically resistant use. At the outset of this essay, she renders vivid a multiplicity of angers:

> There is anger that is a transformation of fear; explosive anger that pushes or recognizes the limits of one's possibilities in resistance to oppression; controlled anger that is

measured because of one's intent to communicate within the official world of sense; anger addressed to one's peers in resistance; anger addressed to one's peers in self-hatred; anger that isolates the resistant self in germination; anger that judges and demands respect; anger that challenges respectability.[21]

We see, then, that anger is much more than an undesirable loss of control, an irrational form of overreaction. It can be productive; it can transform selves and situations in ways that are not exclusively negative. Anger, for Lugones, is not merely a symptom of pathology or an exclusively isolating phenomenon; it is often a sign of injustice, a semaphore that communicates effects of systemic and interpersonal maltreatment. In and through communication, it transforms social relations. In transforming social relations, it transforms us. Sometimes, as Stryker notes in her germinal "My Words to Victor Frankenstein," it gives us back our bodies and lives, steals them back and recuperates them from dominant systems of sense where they are illegible, dehumanized, and significantly maltreated; dominant systems of sense where we are understood as mad, insane, hysterical (importantly, dominant systems of sense operate in such a way that these terms carry a negative valence—they are not signs of cognitive divergence but rather operate as indicators of pathology that become cause for scapegoating and shunning).[22]

How anger communicates is, as I mentioned above, contingent on the interpretive community that bears witness. There is anger that is a bid for respectability within official modes of sense; this anger is usually tamed, a means of communicating displeasure to someone with more institutional power than you. There is anger that is displaced, that occurs within peer groups of similarly marginalized peoples—the externalization of internalized oppression, the transmutation of self-hatred into excoriation or judgment of others. There is anger that produces a rejection of others, that supports the desire to be alone—the kind of anger that pushes folks away, often to protect what

Lugones, following Gloria Anzaldúa, understands as a "resistant self in germination."[23] A kind of cocooning anger. This is a form of transformative anger—it enables one to take a break, institutes some distancing between oneself and harmful relationships that gives one the chance of healing but also the possibility for becoming otherwise, for flourishing once one departs from abusive situations.

Another manifestation of transformative anger is "anger that challenges respectability."[24] This anger rejects official worlds of sense wherein one's being is pathologized, dehumanized, understood as dysfunctional, malformed, undesirable, wrong. This is a defiant anger, an anger that provides resources for working through internalized oppressions that manifest as self-hatred and self-abuse. When collectivized, such anger becomes protest. In order to become collectivized, this anger must resonate, must transfer affectively from one being to another. We witness it, we hear it out, and we feel it; we affirm it. We sometimes say, in these moments, in the spark of recognition that occurs when affect is made manifest in a way that meshes with one's own, perhaps yet-to-be-articulated experiences, "I feel you."

This is a casual way in which we index what Teresa Brennan conceptualizes as the "transmission of affect," which she understands as a process whereby "the emotions or affects of one person, and the enhancing or depressing energies these affects entail, can enter into another."[25] The transmission of affect troubles understandings of subjects as bounded and impermeable. If affect transmits through, travels between, and influences other bodies, it means that our embodied, feeling selves are always coconstituted, cocorporeal. The transmission of anger between bodies in the form of the collectivization and sharing of a sense of rage—so often pathologized and criminalized—can be crucial to survival. It can help, to return to Butler, one move through the difficult process of "breaking with what breaks you," demonstrating that one has company, that there are others who grasp the logic, significance, and impact of such ruptural moments.

Philosopher John Protevi reminds us that these transmissions of affect can also work to form what he calls "bodies politic." He develops this term in order to "capture the emergent—that is, embodied and embedded—character of subjectivity: the production, bypassing, and surpassing of subjectivity in the imbrications of somatic and social systems."[26] "Bodies politic" refers to the affects that pass transversally between subjects, out of which political collectivities emerge. This occurs through the coordination of autonomous affective reactions, and this coordination is shaped by the "approving or disapproving reaction of others," which subsequently "form patterns of acculturation by which we are gendered and racialized as well as attuned to gender, race, and other politically relevant categories."[27] What I'd like to suggest is that the kind of affective transfer that occurs when "anger that challenges respectability" resonates and travels between similarly minoritized subjects enables transformative worldmaking according to different, emergent patterns of acculturation. It is one way that minoritized subjects can become otherwise. When this kind of anger is collectively mobilized, it becomes a movement. Movement: that which shifts the horizon of possibility for minoritized subjects, that which makes other worlds, other ways of being, more possible. I am primarily concerned with manifestations of transformative anger and the role it plays in trans artistic and intellectual expression.

Transformative anger is often misinterpreted by dominant culture as illogical, irrational, "mad," "insane." Lugones highlights how accusations of madness work as a means of stigmatizing rage: a form of oppressive logic that interprets rage as madness, hysteria, or insanity. Lugones notes how this contributes to the mythologization of the anger of women of color as an "attitude" or "sickness."[28] This failure to understand anger as a legitimate, rational, and productive response to discrimination further entrenches the essentialized stereotype of the always-hostile woman of color—the angry Black woman, the fiery Latina, the Dragon Lady.

Trans and gender nonconforming folks are, similarly, often accused of illness, pathology, unnaturalness, abnormality, and monstrosity for merely being open about ourselves. Any public display of negative affect—anger, rage, hostility, unwillingness— exacerbates these associations, and those of us who are multiply marginalized experience this even more intensely. A 2017 joint report of the Human Rights Campaign and the Trans People of Color Coalition, entitled *A Time to Act,* details that there were upward of twenty-five trans homicides in 2017 and that "84% of them were people of color and 80% identified as women."[29] These statistics make exceedingly clear the fact that when racialized feminine typologies merge with transphobic understandings of non-cis embodiment, the specter of death is brought near.

TOWARD AN INFRAPOLITICAL ETHICS OF CARE

CeCe McDonald's prison letters, edited by Omise'eke Natasha Tinsley for publication in *Transgender Studies Quarterly,* illuminate the high cost of rage for Black trans women. McDonald was imprisoned for twenty-six months in the Hennepin County Jail Stillwater and Saint Cloud facilities in Minnesota, following an act of self-defense where she fought off a transphobic attacker, emerging with her life intact. Her letters, written from within what she calls the "concrete chaos" of prison life, speak to us of the genesis of Black trans rage but also of the resilience and love that both motivates such rage and emerges in its wake.[30]

In these letters, McDonald uses her story as an opportunity to reflect on the failure of the carceral state to address violence against women—all women, but especially trans women and women of color. She discusses the assumption of the police that the group of Black queer and trans youth were the aggressors in the attack, writing, "Surely, for them, it had to have been the group of Black kids who started all this drama."[31] This is not at all surprising; as Lugones reminds us, the racist, sexist typology of the irrationally angry Black woman runs deep in official worlds of sense. In the imaginary of the arresting officers, we can safely assume it was compounded by assumptions about the supposedly endemic aggression and violence of Black urban youth. McDonald's conclusion, drawn from a lifetime of violence, shunning, and scapegoating, with no viable institutional or legal means to redress this abuse, is this: given her status as a trans woman of color, she would be foolish to believe that the state will protect her. The people who will save her life, who will make her life livable, are herself and her friends. In this environment, rage is a resource—it quite literally saves lives. Embracing her learned willingness to protect herself in the context of repeated bashings (which she recounts, in detail, in her letters), she reflects:

> Street violence and transwomen go hand in hand, and I'm sure that if asked any transwoman can agree that most of her conflicts occurred outside of her dwelling. For me, all of the incidents that I've experienced were outside of the home. I, and most transwomen, have to deal with violence more often and at a higher rate than any cissexual person, so every day is a harder struggle, and the everyday things that a cissexual person can do with ease are a constant risk, even something as simple as taking public transportation. Street violence has affected me drastically, and I think—no, I know—that *if I never learned to assert myself that I would've never gained the courage to defend myself against those who have no respect or gratitude towards others in the world, I would have met my demise years ago.*[32]

In situations of abuse, particularly those wherein calling the police only redoubles violence and injustice, an infrapolitical ethics of care is called for. By "infrapolitical ethics of care," I mean a reliance on a community of friends to protect and defend one from violence, to witness and mirror each other's rage, in empathy, and to support one another during and after the breaking that accompanies rage. *Infrapolitics,* a concept developed by James C. Scott in *Domination and the Arts of Resistance,* names the forms of resistance enacted by subordinate groups that don't tend to register on the radar of oppressors. It indexes "the circumspect struggles waged daily" that are, "like infrared rays, beyond the visible end of the spectrum."[33] Infrapolitics takes many forms, very few of which register as conventional forms of political resistance. It is shaped by an attention to the forms of care that enable coconstituted, interdependent subjects to repair, rebuild, and cultivate resilience, whether that is housing someone after they've been ousted from the dwelling of their family of origin, cooking for someone in a moment where healing might be needed (post-surgical transition, in the context of an emotional crisis, or because someone is in danger of activist burnout), defending one's beloveds in the face of multivalent forms of violence, or simply empathically listening to someone describe such forms of violence.

Crucially, Scott contends that infrapolitics "provides much of the cultural and structural underpinning of . . . more visible forms of political action."[34] By conjoining the term *infrapolitics* to *ethics of care,* I explicitly position care ethics—the embodied, person-to-person practices of assistance and support that foster capacities for personal and communal flourishing—as integral to political movement in a way that disrupts any rending of the private (the ostensible realm of care) from the public (the ostensible realm of political action). In doing so, I build on the work of feminist care ethicists like Nel Noddings and Fiona Robinson, who argue for the necessity of understanding care as a fundamental component not just of kin relations but of public policy and international relations, thus disrupting the assumption that an ethic of care is limited to the domestic sphere.[35] Somewhat differently, an infrapolitical ethics of care is located in excess of this binary. Rather, it is a form of care that circulates among a beloved community that enables both political resistance and intracommunal survival and resilience. It moves us beyond (sometimes troublingly neoliberal) understandings of self-care and into a terrain shaped by the recognition that caring, in the context of structural marginalization and systemic violence, must always be collective. An infrapolitical ethics of care is comprised of all of those phenomena that enable one to piece themselves together in the aftermath of a break, all those forms of caring labor, from attending to basic survival needs to generating, supporting, and coelaborating continued reasons for living.

We see this ethic throughout trans and queer histories, from Stonewall to the uprising at Compton's Cafeteria to the activism of Bash Back! and pink-bloc antifascist protestors. Maintaining one's life sometimes comes down to the ability of a squad, crew, or clique to counteract street violence. We also see an infrapolitical ethics of care at work in the experiences of the New Jersey 4, the group the *New York Post* indicted as a "Lesbian Wolf Pack," who were imprisoned for self-defense when they fought back against a homophobic street attacker.[36] We see it again in the phenomenon of the queer/trans D.C. gang documented in the film *Check It*.[37] While certain actions undertaken in the name of this ethics might open the door to imprisonment and other forms of institutional abuse, particularly if one is racialized as nonwhite and thus subject to intensified forms of state, carceral, and administrative violence, they do make it more possible to emerge with one's life. To put this differently: one of the central aspects of an infrapolitical ethics of care is to support vulnerable and traumatized persons in the context of a break—to witness, hold space for, and, when appropriate, amplify and intensify their anger, especially if this amplification serves the greater purpose of keeping each other alive. This is the precise opposite of shunning, wherein a break brought on by trauma is met with communal criticism and rejection, and especially distinct from the practice of calling the police in the hopes that they, or some other state actor, might successfully manage or mitigate a break. Sarah Schulman, in *Conflict Is Not Abuse*, expounds on importance of such practices of empathic witnessing, writing that "nothing disrupts dehumanization more quickly than inviting someone over, looking into their eyes, hearing their voice, and listening."[38] She positions this form of infrapolitical care as a communal responsibility shared between and among marginalized subjects, calling it the "duty of repair."[39]

Repair is essential to an infrapolitical ethics of care. It is crucial that we support practices of healing and accountability as we move through and beyond breaks and aid one another in the process of envisioning and inhabiting more livable lives. Situating ethics infrapolitically and collectively, as something that happens between friends and parallel to, outside of, or beyond institutions, means that we assume responsibility for each other's lives. It means that our support in the context of a break should remain present in the aftermath of one; that we do our best to recognize, simultaneously, the possibilities that breaks enable and the vulnerability and precarity that is often exaggerated in their aftermath.

My thinking about this ethics is derived from Butler's writing on "ethics under pressure," which is a form of ethics that takes as central the idea that each one of us desires life, which means desiring the endless renegotiation of the social and political conditions that enable life.[40] Within an ethics under pressure, bodies "incite one another to live."[41] It would seem, on the face of it, that rage has no place in an ethics under pressure, but rage is, I think, a manifestation of dealing with pressure and responding to trauma. Rage is what must be grappled with to come to a place wherein we incite one another to live; it is a manifestation of the conatus, of the drive to keep living, in and through conditions that seem inimical to our survival. Put differently, the desire to live well, to lead a life under conditions that support resilience and flourishing, sometimes manifests as rage. If we understand rage to be an extroverted response to forms of trauma that, when internalized, manifest as depression, this means that rage is closely allied to desire. Rage is a legitimate response to significant existential impediments, to roadblocks that minimize, circumscribe, and reduce one's possibilities, and it is a response that seeks to transform, and destroy, such impediments.

It is instructive to revisit Audre Lorde's writings on the anger experienced by women of color in response to the racism of white feminists, as what she says about anger illuminates the ties between rage and desire. This commentary resonates, as well, with Schulman's discussion of the duty to repair insofar as processing and working with anger is central to negotiating infrapolitical support, even—perhaps especially—in moments of conflict, dissension, and affective and communicative difficulty. Lorde situates her meditation on anger by highlighting that minoritized subjects engaged in social justice movements are "working in a context of opposition and threat, the cause of which is certainly not the angers which lie between us, but rather that virulent hatred leveled . . . against all of us who are seeking to examine the particulars of our lives as we resist our oppressions, moving toward coalition and effective action."[42] For Lorde, it is necessary to dignify and learn from both forms of anger—the anger generated by the violence of dominant culture(s), of which all marginalized subjects have a "well-stocked arsenal," as well as anger that occurs between and among differently marginalized subjects.[43] Lorde writes of the infrapolitical imperative to attend to these angers, to voice them and listen to them, reporting that "anger has eaten clefts into [her] living only when it remained unspoken, useless to anyone."[44] She unpacks the transformative significance of such voicings and hearings, writing, "it is not the anger of other women that will destroy us but our refusals to stand still, to listen to its rhythms, to learn within it, to move beyond the manner of presentation to the substance, to tap that anger as an important source of empowerment," and, further, that "anger between peers births change, not destruction, and the discomfort and sense of loss it often causes is not fatal, but a sign of growth."[45] Anger is a sign of our desire for transformation; infrapolitical engagement with anger is an integral form of repair that supports transformative and visionary worldmaking, a crucial way in which minoritized subjects can incite one another to live.

Although rage enables breaking, it is not an affect that can be sustained indefinitely. There is a phenomenology of rage indicated by the physiognomic impacts associated with it, which are difficult to endure—the shaking, the cold sweat, the inarticulate brain fog, the adrenaline dump. It may recur, but it does its best work if coupled substantially with periods of recovery or repair. I hesitate to use those words, as they signify a return to a former state, while I'm arguing that rage transmutes subjectivity in such a way that makes becoming—not a return to a static self—possible. Perhaps a better way to think of it would be as a denouement, an impermanent subsidence, a gradual tapering off. Rage changes us, yes, and it changes us through the impact wrought by enduring it. It teaches us about survival and endurance; it teaches us how to become resilient by leaving us with options: remain undone, in the space of breaking enabled by rage, or reterritorialize, attach differently, in a way that enables living well, that enlarges our capacity and potential. Experiencing rage prompts one to consider how best to move through it and encourages the seeking out and invention of spaces and subjects who might make experiences of rage easier to survive and recover from. Considering literature on the cultivation of resilience among trans and queer subjects, it is quickly apparent that all indicators of resilience— for instance, ability to access safer spaces, opportunity to narrativize experiences of pain and trauma, the support of kith and kin who understand, dignify, and respect the complexities of queer and trans experiences, the ability to enact agency than can reach beyond protective forms of closeting, and the cultivation of forms of political and infrapolitical communal healing—rely on navigating negative affect in ways that enable living differently. Learning to live with and through ostensibly negative affects drives the coproduction of trans- and queer-affirming connections and spaces; again, anger is a transformative energy. Kenta Asakura, a professor of social work specializing in queer and trans community-based research, calls this "paving pathways through pain," and his phrasing suggests that paving such pathways is less about restoring the self to an unharmed state and more about utilizing negative affect to drive worldmaking projects.[46] Resilience is thus not about bouncing back, or about moving forward, but rather a communal alchemical mutation of pain into possibility.

It might also be that our ability to process rage, to use it in transformative ways, depends on a pedagogy of rage. By this, I mean access to performances of rage that work in multivalent ways: that demonstrate rage as shared and common, that articulate rage as a justified response to situations of injustice, that amplify rage in such a way that it becomes a mobilizing political affect, capable of transforming a body and a body politic. When considering the archive of trans rage, performed rage emerges as integral. Susan Stryker, in "My Words to Victor Frankenstein," comments on the transformative pedagogy inherent in performances of trans rage:

> Transgender rage is a queer fury, an emotional response to conditions in which it becomes imperative to take up, for the sake of one's own continued survival as a subject, a set of practices that precipitates one's exclusion from a naturalized order of existence that seeks to maintain itself as the only possible basis for being a subject. However, by mobilizing gendered identities and rendering them provisional, open to strategic development and occupation, this rage enables the establishment of subjects in new modes, regulated by different codes of intelligibility.[47]

Rage produces estrangement and exclusion from official worlds of sense and ways of being and, through this exclusion and estrangement, becomes central to trans forms of becoming. Trans rage is productive and enabling, as it addresses ciscentric conceptions of trans embodiment as impossible or inauthentic with a call to become monstrous, to reject the logics of embodiment and personhood that make your life unlivable. As Harlan Weaver writes, commenting on Stryker's essay, "her words reach towards us so that we too might become like her in kind, so that we might also be transformed by affect."[48] Trans rage as affective contagion.

Performances of trans rage, while seeming excessive, outsize, or hysterical to majoritarian witnesses, signal ways out to those witnesses who see their own rage mirrored. This dynamic between performer and empathic witness is a form of communication that validates an understanding of rage as essential to survival and transformation. As Kelly Oliver writes regarding the importance of empathic forms of bearing witness, "our experience is meaningful for us only if we can imagine that it is meaningful for others."[49] For trans folk, performed trans rage demonstrates that another way of being is possible, and rage is the generative, propulsive force that helps us get there. It illuminates that rage is much more than an affective phenomena that merely possesses us; rather, it undoes us so that we may transform.

In the following section, I examine the relation between trans militancy and performed rage, as articulated through the writing of CeCe McDonald and the durational performance art of Cassils.

TRANS MILITANCY, PERFORMED RAGE, AND THE CULTIVATION OF RESILIENCE

McDonald, reflecting on the importance of Trans Day of Remembrance and her new mantle as a community leader and spokesperson for multiple, intersecting marginalized communities, writes:

> Of course it is more than important to recognize and pay homage to our fallen, but we also need to put our feet down and start being real leaders and making this stand. And personally speaking, if it's true that this is my personal journey as a leader, I want to lead my troops to victory. I can't continue to say "how bad" that another brother, sister, mother, father, partner, friend is gone from blind-hatred. From ignorance and discrimination.[50]

"I want to lead my troops to victory." In the long and vibrant tradition of Black, queer, and trans radicalism, loss becomes militancy; the memory of the dead becomes a call to arms. Collective trauma transmutes and becomes collective strength. This happens when we deindividuate trauma, when we no longer believe we are suffering independently, or have somehow called trauma upon us through our nonnormativity or through our difficulties navigating life conditions that operate as an adversely stacked deck. When we have a beloved community to witness trauma, to hold us through it, to open up possibilities for life otherwise, we can fight together. We can incite ourselves and others to live.

Toward the end of *Living a Feminist Life,* after a long meditation on the ways in which trans-exclusionary radical feminists quite literally dehumanize trans women through recourse to what she calls "gender fatalism," Sara Ahmed echoes this militancy.[51] She sharply articulates the ways in which an antitrans stance is an antifeminist stance and writes about this form of transphobia:

> [It is] against the feminist project of creating worlds to support those for whom gender fatalism (boys will be boys, girls will be girls) is fatal; a sentencing to death. We have to hear that fatalism as a punishment and instruction: it is the story of the rod, of how those who have wayward wills or who will waywardly (boys who will not be boys, girls who will not be girls) are beaten. We need to drown these anti-trans voices out, raising the sound of our own. Our voices need to become our arms: rise up; rise up. . . . Intersectionality is army.[52]

Both Ahmed and McDonald offer accounts of the hope that trauma can be transformed into militancy. They offer testimonies of the productivity of collective rage. Militant rage is a central phenomenon of analysis for Ahmed; she centers *Living a Feminist Life* around the visual rhetoric of the raised fist, a transnational symbol of minoritarian political outrage. She writes of arms raised and turned into fists; of the transformation of bodies punished in the name of docility, obedience, and subservience into corporeal vehicles for the elaboration of anger; of a multiplicity of arms—"laboring arms," "striking arms," "broken arms," arms that deviate from the "narrow idea of how a female arm should appear"—that, together, become an intersectional "army."[53] She does not shy away from metaphors of militancy; neither does McDonald. I cite them because, for an infrapolitical ethics of care, the relation to militancy is important. Vets share their traumatic experiences with other vets; the telling of war stories is always the telling of stories of violence, harm, and coercion. These painful stories are sometimes masked, albeit very thinly, by bravado or braggadocio, but their sharing happens most powerfully among those who have similar experiences. In terms of recounting trauma, and developing resilience in the aftermath of trauma, it is necessary to access folks who share a similar crucible: this is your squad (or your consciousness-raising group, your crew, your clique, your support system).

Army stories are stories of embodied resistance indissolubly linked to trauma—stories of resistance and resilience emerging from a space of rage, of anger, of hard-to-handle affect.

Another army story, one that speaks to the importance of performances of trans rage, is the story of the genesis of trans-identified performance artist Cassils's recent project *Becoming an Image*. In 2013, Cassils—known for their history of gender-transgressive body modification through weight lifting and intense physical training, as well as their durational performance art that focuses on pushing the physical limits of the body—conceived a site-specific performance piece for the ONE Archives in Los Angeles, the oldest active LGBTQ archive in the United States. The premise of the piece is simple: in a dark room, there is a two-thousand-pound block of clay. Spectators are brought into this darkness, along with a blindfolded photographer. Cassils, their highly muscled physique clad only in nude underwear and tape gloves to protect their hands, begins attacking the clay, kicking and punching it, gradually transforming it through their pummeling. No one—not Cassils, not the photographer, not the audience—can see. Cassils fights the clay for nearly half an hour in total darkness. Their enemy is (mostly) invisible but haptically tangible; it exerts a weighty presence. It is heavy. Recalcitrant. Difficult to transform. Any modulation of the clay effects a modulation in the body of Cassils. Our tendency is to think of the clay as inert, nonlively, but the performance makes its animacy obvious. In interrelation, Cassils and clay transform one another. Cassils attacks; the clay fights back with its stolidity, its resistance to transformation. At random intervals, a photographer's flash illuminates the darkness, capturing a small slice of action and burning it into the retina of the viewer. This strategy elongates the temporality of embodied rage; a flicker, an instant, becomes durative, lingers longer afterward than one expects.

(Rage is like this; it has many afterlives.)

Cassils, in the trailer released for the performance, describes it as a meditation on the relation between documentation, memory, and visibility. They intone calmly, as we watch blackness interspersed with brief moments of illuminated action from the performance, that "the act of photographing is the only way in which the performance is made visible. . . . Performed in the gutted room of an archive and inspired by the oldest active LGBTQ organization in the United States, *Becoming an Image* points to the Ts and Qs often missing from historical records. It calls into question the roles of the witness, the aggressor, and the documenter."[54] In place of an archive, a battle between two very distinct opponents: one spry, muscly, mobile, human, actively engaged in trying to transform something, the other malleable, but also heavy, recalcitrant on account of its mass.

Could there be a more vivid dramatization of the force of official, sedimented histories? The superpower of these histories, the superpower of the institutions shaped by these histories: they resist struggle by just being there, dense, heavy, hard to move. Cassils does more than point to the trans and queer folk absented from the historical record—they fight as one of them. The battle is witnessed only ephemerally, but they leave traces that mold and mutate that which they attack. What is fought takes the form given by the battle marks, though the opponent, after the fight, is no longer present. Given Cassils's positioning of the piece as a meditation on the historical erasure of trans and queer subjects from supposedly official gay and lesbian histories, we're forced to ask after the tangible marks left by the struggle of those left out. One implication: trans rage leaves material traces. There is a material history to rage. The material history of trans rage is manifest even in those places where we are absent, where there is only a very minimal record of our once having been present.

How does our exclusion, erasure, and absence manifest? In the shape institutions have taken. The shape institutions take is the shape of our absence, but also the shape of our struggle against them.

Trans rage is forceful. The greater the force, the greater the material shift effected. *Becoming an Image* makes clear the immense resources—physical, emotional, psychical—necessary for us to make even the slightest institutional or historical dent. Cassils, with all their years of training, with all their meticulous preparation for a durational performance like this, can last less than half an hour in battle. A question then arises: How do we strategize to make greater impact? How do we take care of selves and bodies so that they can fight, rest, and repair in order to fight again? In other words, how do we sustain the transformative effects of rage? How do we marshal resources to make sure the traces of our rage and the impact it has wrought are made visible, documented, remembered, memorialized, turned source material for transforming our presents and making possible less violently oppressive futures?

There is a polysemy to this performance, however, and other suggestive readings are certainly possible. Cassils may also be inhabiting the position of a queer/transphobic agent of violence; the animation clay they attack might very well be representative of trans and queer communities adapting and persisting in the face of a near-constant onslaught of violence, absorbing the blows, reconfiguring and mutating as they do so, but still present. No matter lost, just shape-shifted from the multivalent impacts of violence. It is this latter reading that Cassils elaborates in the extension of the performance entitled *Monument Push*.

For *Monument Push,* Cassils had the clay from a performance of *Becoming an Image* cast in bronze and named it *Resilience of the 20%.* "The 20%" is a reference to a 2012 report that indicated a 20 percent rise in the murders of trans folk from the previous year. The piece becomes a monumental memorial to monumental struggle; a representation of the resilience of those trans and gender nonconforming folks whom we've lost. *Monument Push* is, put simply, a performance piece where *Resilience of the 20%* is pushed by a loose collective of LGBTQIA folks through the streets, past spots of note to trans and queer communities. The first—and, to date, only—performance of *Monument Push* took place in 2017 in Omaha, Nebraska, over the course of four hours on a dreary, early spring day. At six different spots, the procession participating in pushing the sculpture paused for a moment of silence or a brief rally. They stopped at a spot where a gay-related hate crime had taken place, as well as at a correctional center where one of the featured speakers—Dominique Morgan, a queer community advocate, R & B vocalist, recent recipient of an NAACP Freedom Fighter award and founder of Queer People of Color Nebraska—had been incarcerated for eight years, for writing bad checks while seventeen and homeless in the aftermath of being kicked out of her childhood home and then living with, and subsequently leaving, an abusive partner.[55] At the correctional facility, she sang. Art historian Karen Emenhiser Harris, writing up the performance for *Hyperallergic*, recounts this moment: "When [she] raised [her] voice for the refrain, it echoed off the walls of the center, amplifying [her] personal pain and trauma," a moment of aural and affective resonance that speaks to the work of empathic witnessing and the reparative work done through such infrapolitical sharing of pain.[56]

Monument Push highlights the fragility of trans and queer existence and marks the ways that our personal rage, the intensity of our effort to fight, is sometimes not enough to keep us alive, and can often make us targets. We see this with McDonald's unjust arrest and imprisonment: fighting back, defending oneself and one's beloveds, opens one up to intensified racist, transphobic interpersonal and state violence, particularly if one is multiply marginalized. Cassils's work suggests that collectivizing and amplifying negative affect—rage, pain, trauma—is integral to developing resilient strategies for survival and flourishing. The disparate life chances that Cassils and McDonald encounter, with Cassils being an internationally recognized, grant-winning artist and McDonald still struggling to attain basic subsistence needs, speaks further to the racialized differentials in how rage is met, addressed, and punished (or not).

McDonald and Cassils demonstrate the hard process of transmuting rage into resilience, illustrating that trans activists, artists, and thinkers specialize, as Susan Stryker reminded us at the opening of the first international trans studies conference, in "deep and substantive change."[57] We are deeply learned in the art of transmutation; experts at learning how to take something—flesh, affect, circumstance—and render it elsewise. The work of McDonald and Cassils demonstrates the ways in which trans rage is a powerful force for becoming, a manifestation of the conatus that has an integral role in making life in adverse circumstances more possible. Trans rage is an affective response to the cumulative effects of (racist, heterosexist) manifestations of transphobia across multiple domains of power relations and carries significant force when it is collectivized, when it is able to amplify, resonate, and echo. What their work highlights is how the sharing of rage among communities of empathic witnesses—whether through the publication of prison letters or through the collective pushing of something far too heavy for one person to bear—can actually transform rage, can render it a source of communal resilience. Documenting, demonstrating, and sharing the anger it takes to keep on living, or the anger elicited through the ongoingness of our practices of living, helps us not only survive but invent projects that enable a communal ethic of flourishing. When rage is collective, it is that much harder to scapegoat, punish, Other, demonize, or dismiss the bodies, persons, and communities so affected. Sharing army stories helps us develop and learn the tactics that we can utilize against transphobic apparatuses in order to ensure our survival.

The work of survival and the cultivation of communal flourishing is essential, ongoing . . . and tiring. This next chapter is about precisely this kind of existential exhaustion: the experience of being trans and being deeply burned out.

5

BEYOND BURNOUT

On the Limits of Care and Cure

I don't need to know the name of why I feel so run down.
—Lou Sullivan, *We Both Laughed in Pleasure*

These next pages home in on burnout, the beyond of being tired. Focused on the burnout experienced by trans folks in their interface with medical professionals specializing in transition-related services, the chapter is grounded in analysis of the archives of the Harry Benjamin International Gender Dysphoria Association (HBIGDA), housed in the Kinsey Institute for Research in Sex, Gender, and Reproduction at Indiana University. HBIGDA was the very first consortium of trans medical specialists, established in 1979 (later rebranding itself as the World Professional Association for Transgender Health, or WPATH) for the purpose of developing a unified and comprehensive standard of care for trans subjects, attempting to regularize the terrain of trans biomedicine at a moment of rapid proliferation of services and service providers. Recognizing that the only way to consolidate their authority and expertise was to recruit key trans community leaders as mouthpieces and boosters, members of HBIGDA began to actively enlist their assistance. Here, I look at the archived correspondence of trans medical professionals with one another, prospective patients, and community advocates, mapping how this strategic turn recruits the care labor of trans subjects, positioning them as stakeholders and experts (rather than merely prospective or current patients) while simultaneously asking them to deploy such (unpaid or underpaid) labor and expertise in the service of consolidating forms of deeply hierarchical biomedical authority that render cis medical and sexological professionals, rather than trans subjects, experts on trans lives. I read these letters alongside written work and testimonial from trans activist and therapist Rupert Raj, as well as selections from early issues of *Chrysalis: The Journal of Transgressive Gender Identities*, a print periodical published by the American Educational Gender Information Service (AEGIS) from the mid-1990s through the early 2000s that explicitly coaches trans subjects on how to navigate medical and social transition.

This archive is rife with reports of burnout, which come coupled with testimonials of frustration, annoyance, and mistrust from trans subjects, directed at both medical professionals and one another. I position trans burnout as generated explicitly by the economies of scarcity that inform the politics of access to medical transition, economies of scarcity that relentlessly recruit the care labor of trans subjects while doing little to address rampant institutional transantagonism. But before parsing how burnout affects trans subjects and communities, I want to detail the emergence of the concept itself, which has more to do with mutual aid in the service of social justice than one might think.

BURNOUT: A BRIEF GENEALOGY

Journalist Anne Helen Petersen, in her best-selling book on millennial burnout, *Can't Even,* pinpoints the emergence of the term *burnout* in the year 1974, in the work of psychologist Herbert Freudenberger.[1] Petersen describes burnout as the beyond of exhaustion, writing that "exhaustion means going to the point where you can't go any further; burnout means reaching that point and pushing yourself to keep going, whether for days or weeks or years."[2] For her, burnout means becoming acclimatized to exhaustion as your physiognomic and psychological baseline. Living with burnout is a trial of fatigue endurance wherein one is never able to rest, reset, or recover. It has come to be understood as an extreme and extremely common form of work-related stress. As neoliberal capitalist forms of labor extraction evolve in ways that come close to fully subsuming the entirety of one's waking hours in the tasks of productive and reproductive labor, while social and financial safety nets erode and debt intensifies, burnout becomes the predominant affective milieu for an entire generation.

But when Freudenberger first coined the term in the early 1970s, it meant something quite different: it referred specifically to a phenomenon experienced by folks who volunteered at free clinics. The term emerged from Freudenberger's experience at the first free clinic in the United States, the Haight Ashbury Free Clinic, in 1968, and from his later founding of the St. Mark's Free Clinic in the East Village of New York City in 1970. The Haight Ashbury Free Clinic was established in order to provide medical, dental, and psychological care to the hippie counterculture of San Francisco, and it became a model for a number of other free clinics that popped up in metropolitan centers throughout the 1970s. The free clinic movement in the United States can be best understood as an antidote and ameliorative to the mainstream medical industrial complex and is premised on the now familiar (and frequently reiterated) leftist principle that health care is a right, not a privilege. Participants in the movement resisted moralizing judgment, especially around sexual practices and drug use, and the Haight Ashbury Free Clinic pioneered a form of treatment for bad trips—psychedelic adventures gone awry. Physician David E. Smith, the founder of the Haight Ashbury Free Clinic, attests to this in a 1976 retrospective essay on the first ten years of the free clinic movement, writing, "In the drug subculture of the Haight, I observed non-physicians experienced with psychedelic drugs, treating their friends without the use of medication in a non-medical environment that emphasized positive set and setting. To my surprise, their non-medical talkdown produced much better short and long-term results with bad LSD trips than the traditional method had, something we were not told about in medical school."[3]

At this moment in the late 1960s, standard medical treatment for bad trips involved heavy-duty pharmaceutical tranquilization with a substantial side of derogation. Smith founded that first free clinic because he realized that the forms of stigma and treatment options encountered by marginalized communities in mainstream medical facilities often caused more harm than good. He believed that effective medical and psychiatric care needed to be grounded in community knowledge and values in order to be responsive to community need. The free clinic movement is rooted in a commitment to destigmatization and an awareness that expert knowledges of care proliferate well beyond the bounds of the traditional medical establishment. Because of this, it quickly took off, adopted and adapted by urban communities of color and, later, by urban gay and lesbian communities. In some ways, the LGBTQIA+ community clinics that serve trans populations in metropolitan areas today are direct descendants of the Haight Ashbury Free Clinic.

In the first free clinic, many workers were volunteers, often without medical credentials, and also fellow members of the counterculture, interested in helping folks with issues similar to their own. Science historian Matthew Hoffarth, in an account of the conceptual emergence of burnout, highlights how this made "the lines between professional, volunteer, client and patient . . . quite blurry."[4] The clinics were an attempt to fulfill some of the fundamental health care needs otherwise inaccessible to participants of drop-out culture, who often lacked steady jobs, insurance, funds for pay-out-of-pocket services, and access to the forms of basic caretaking labor usually fulfilled by family members, as they lived in alternative domestic/kinship configurations that may or may not have provided such care. The workers at the free clinic were encouraged to live in the same neighborhoods as the communities they served, in order to deepen connections across patient/provider boundaries and thus undo the hierarchical power dynamics that structured such relationships in mainstream medical settings. Folks laboring in the free clinics tended to understand their work as resistant and transformative; they weren't just serving their patients, but working to transform health-care services in more just ways. But they were also being deleteriously impacted by the fuzzy boundaries, emotional investments, and deep need of the folks they served. Because the people drawn to such work were generally altruistic, empathetic, and concerned with socially just transformations of health care, because they were intimately involved with the communities in which they labored, because the work was poorly paid or unpaid, and because the emotional and physical demands of the work were intense, these workers began to suffer from a particularly toxic combination of exhaustion, irritability, and cynicism.

Freudenberger called this "burnout," borrowing the term from the lexicon of the counterculture he served. *Burnout*, prior to entering diagnostic language, referred to both the affective complex that followed a long period of chronic drug use and the subject suffering from it. It was used as both an adjective and a noun: one could be burned-out or be a burnout. Not only that, however, *burnout* was also the term used to describe urban areas of economic and infrastructural abandonment; it was used recurrently to describe areas affected by white flight to the suburbs and neighborhood repopulation by poor communities of color, where government and real estate investment had slowed or ceased. It was a synonym for so-called urban decay. Hoffarth points out that, given this etymology, *burnout* points "not only to the pathologies of emotional interaction, but also the pathologies of environment."[5] Free clinics, in other words, were often populated by burnouts in burned-out neighborhoods, which produced burnout among the folks who worked in them.

In its initial iteration as a pathology of emotional interaction and environment, burnout was articulated as both situational and structurally produced. Furthermore, it emerged most acutely in the context of what we might now call social justice work—that is, labor engaged on behalf of marginalized and resistant communities by similarly marginalized and resistant subjects. Such work was exhausting not simply because it was work but because those who undertook such labor were already in situations of structural precarity and were invested in changing the political and economic landscape that produced such precarity.

But by the time the term became popular in the 1980s, in large part thanks to the work of psychologist Christina Maslach, it was used as part of a self-help discourse that shifted responsibility for dealing with burnout onto individual workers. It came to be used not just in the context of social justice work but with reference to all "helping professions"—nurses, social workers, service workers—and rather quickly came to be indiscriminately applied to all forms of employment: anyone, in any occupation, could suffer from burnout. And while it is still understood as structurally produced, the "cure" for burnout lies not in a reorganization of work itself but rather in the cultivation of what Maslach calls "detached concern"—the ability to separate oneself from the people (increasingly understood as "clients" rather than community constituents) one serves. *Detached concern* refers to an affective disposition that blends "closeness and distance," where one delicately maintains an equilibrium between the poles of interest and disinvestment, care and coldness, without being "pulled toward one or the other of these apparently antithetical poles."[6] Burnout happens when one allows themselves to care too much, which is a prelude to being, in effect, used up, depleted, and exhausted by servicing the needs of others. It is not, on Maslach's account, overwork that is the problem; rather, it is the affective responses and defense reactions that workers cultivate in order to survive overwork: emotional exhaustion, depersonalization, and a sense of failure, inadequacy, and reduced personal accomplishment. The reason that burnout rates are higher in certain helping professions has to do with the fact that these occupations serve primarily "traumatized" or "troubled" clients, which intensifies compassion fatigue and produces vicarious, or secondary, trauma. It's a labor-specific variant of Hell as other people, a rendering of folks in need on account of structural precarity as energy succubi, emotional vampires out to take all they can from a too-trusting, too-caring, too-empathetic worker.

In tracing this transformation of the concept of burnout from 1970 to the early 1980s, I'm highlighting how the cure for burnout shifted from large-scale social transformation (of health care, the workplace, and networks of social and institutional support) to individualized techniques of self-governance (specifically, the cultivation of detached concern). It's no surprise that this transformation coincides with the emergent dominance of neoliberal economic policies and their attendant subjective logics. The power of unions is eroded, labor is casualized, job insecurity heightens, already inadequate social security supports are eviscerated, the precariat comes into being, labor protections are loosened, pensions disappear, the workday overflows until much of one's daily life is subsumed by it, and the solution? Grab a self-help book and learn how to care less. Forget structural transformation. Forget solidarity. Forget coalition-building and prefigurative politics. Forget resistance.

BIOMEDICALIZATION AND BURNOUT: ON THE RECRUITMENT OF TRANS CARE LABOR

In this decade-long moment wherein burnout slowly transforms from a symptom of social justice work best solved by social transformation to a more generalized symptom of overwork best managed by deeply individualized techniques of self-governance, trans health care also undergoes significant transformation. The era of the university-run trans medical clinic comes to an end and trans health care becomes increasingly privatized, which expands access to technologies of transition, but primarily only for those able to pay high out-of-pocket costs.

The late 1960s had witnessed the establishment of a significant handful of university-based clinics that specialized in trans medical care—Johns Hopkins in 1966, Northwestern in 1967, Stanford in 1968, and more to follow. Historian Joanne Meyerowitz calls this the "Big Science" period of trans medicine and estimates that "by the end of the 1970s, more than a thousand transsexuals had undergone surgery at the hands of doctors based at American universities, and fifteen to twenty 'major centers' conducted transsexual surgery in the United States."[7] But by the early 1980s, she remarks that "a number of private doctors discovered a lucrative practice in transsexual surgery and began to specialize in sex-change operations. With surgery more readily available, the number of people obtaining medical treatment increased."[8] Alongside this increase in availability were efforts to coordinate trans surgical care at the national level in order to both establish standards of care and cement the reputations of specialists in trans medicine. Conferences on trans health care were held in the United States from the early 1970s onward with the hopes of laying the groundwork necessary in order to establish a national trans health organization, and the Harry Benjamin International Gender Dysphoria Association emerged from this collaborative network of physicians, therapists, and researchers in 1979. "Transsexualism" was added to the *Diagnostic and Statistical Manual* the following year. This consolidation of trans medicine in the United States coincided with the temporary waning of (always already tenuously) organized trans activism and heralded the deep institutionalization and entrenchment of a system of rigorous medical gatekeeping. For some time afterward (and still), medical professionals would become the arbiters of trans authenticity and legitimacy. The forms of U.S. trans activism that would emerge in the 1980s and 1990s would take aim at precisely this consolidation of medical power.

In the years that intervene between the dissolution of the first wave of university gender clinics and our present moment, the ensemble of biomedical services marketed to trans patient-consumers has multiplied, and the framing of trans subjects primarily as consumers of medical services has intensified in ways that map neatly onto the account of the transformation of medicalization to biomedicalization offered by Adele Clarke, Laura Mamo, Jennifer Ruth Fosket, Jennifer Fishman, and Janet Shim. They write that whereas "medicalization practices typically emphasize exercising control over medical phenomena—diseases, illnesses, injuries, bodily malfunctions . . . biomedicalization practices emphasize *transformations of* such medical phenomena and bodies, largely through sooner-rather-than-later technoscientific interventions not only for treatment but also increasingly for enhancement."[9] There are many features of the movement toward biomedicalization that are relevant to understanding the recent history of transformations in trans health care. Chief among these is the privatization of medical services and the concomitant spread of pay-out-of-pocket services that strategically enhance bodies rather than merely "curing" already extant conditions. Clarke et al. outline this shift in brief, noting that "as healthcare costs and competitive pressures for personnel and revenues escalated, many [public/not-for-profit] facilities closed or were bought out and consolidated by for-profit corporations."[10] The shuttering of the first wave of gender clinics was part of this process of privatization. Alongside privatization, we also witnessed the heightened commodification of biomedical procedures and the emergence of a patient-consumer model of health-care access. The spread of private practices specializing in transition-related services, the proliferation of such transition-related medical procedures, and the framing of trans subjects as primarily consumers of these services (rather than patients in need of a cure, an intensively pathological understanding of trans identity put forth in the spaces of mid-twentieth-century sexology) all testify to the transformations wrought by biomedicalization.

So by the time Christina Maslach was popularizing individualized solutions to burnout in the early 1980s, the newly consolidated trans medical industrial complex had begun to actively recruit trans subjects. This was, in part, in order to grow the private practices of trans medical specialists, creating a closed loop between trans community support groups and the offices of therapists and surgeons. Take, for instance, Alice Webb, who would in the late 1990s become president-elect of HBIGDA. Throughout the 1980s, she ran a therapy practice in Galveston, Texas, as well as a support group for folks exploring trans identities. Some of her files have made their way into the HBIGDA archives housed at the Kinsey Institute at Indiana University, and they are full of correspondence with prospective patients. These patients typically reach out to Webb to find out about the process of diagnosis and the path toward hormones and gender reassignment surgery; nearly all are trans women or on the transfeminine spectrum. Her responses are pro forma; the following excerpt is a paradigmatic example. A prospective patient writes Webb in order to find out if she does therapy by mail, being too geographically distant, too time-strapped, and too broke to be able to afford regular trips to Webb's office. She responds with the following:

> I'm sorry to have to tell you that I really can't do therapy by mail. I understand that you are very confused about your desire to cross dress and want some kind of explanation or cure for it. As for the operation to make a vagina, yes there is such an operation but it would only be done after a long period of the person living full time, 24 hours a day, as a woman. This would include working as a female. The surgery itself is very expensive and that isn't always the solution for everyone. Perhaps you would be interested in coming to one of my group meetings, which are held on the first Saturday of the month. . . . Let me know if you would like to attend. There is no fee for the meetings and they are at night, so you wouldn't have to miss work.[11]

What I find most striking—and also, unfortunately, most predictable—about this response is the primacy Webb places on questions of labor and economics. In her role as medical gatekeeper, she accentuates both the high cost of surgery and the necessity of engaging in the so-called real-life test, a core component of the standards of care developed by HBIGDA at the dawn of the 1980s, which stipulated that one must live in their chosen gender 24/7 for a period of up to two years before they would be granted access to hormones or transition-related surgery. This was incorporated into the initial standards of care despite there being no actual empirical evidence as to whether or not it provided an effective litmus of potential patient regret or effectively parsed "true" transsexuals from cross-dressers, transvestites, and other folks with gender-transitive desires who, nevertheless, didn't desire to be, or couldn't feasibly be, "full-time."

Her patient letters effectively vet patients by warning them about the high costs of medical transition, which far exceed the costs of surgery. Due to the imposition of the real-life test, trans subjects were forced to transition on the job—as Webb stipulates, "this would include working as a female"—prior to accessing affirming hormones and surgical procedures. This demand comes at a historical moment wherein corporate restructuring and downsizing is becoming de rigueur, when there is a radical dearth of employment protections for trans laborers, and within a cultural and political milieu that is deeply transphobic, broadly speaking, as well as intensively transmisogynistic. In other words, it demands that one transition publicly, and maintain or obtain the kinds of well-remunerated employment that the high cost of transition necessitates, in a moment wherein only a very privileged few would be able to do so. And while her group meetings are free and held after the close of traditional business hours, her preface to this invitation has a chilling effect on those who may otherwise be interested. After all, what's the point of beginning to explore a process—transition—that is actively made structurally impossible (or, at the very least, impracticable) for poor and working-class folks, as well as tenuously middle-class folks who stand to lose employment if they're out on the job?

Webb is very clear, in another letter, about the function of the group that she runs, what it is and isn't. She writes that it is "a peer support group for gender dysphoric persons. . . . These meetings are not meant to be [a] place where people look for dates or sexual liaisons. I am not against such activities, but my group meetings are not the place for them."[12] While, superficially, this reads as a kind of "no chasers allowed" caveat, I think that her clarification actually exceeds those parameters, especially given that she's responding to a prospective patient who has written to her to inquire after psychotherapy and referrals for hormones and surgery, not a trans fetishist. When she stipulates that the space of the peer support group is not a romantic or sexual space, I take her to mean that it is not a space for cultivating trans intimacies that exceed the traumatological. Peer support groups are spaces where trans folks (or maybe-trans folks) go to find out about routes to transition, to share tips about navigating the process of transition, to tap the insider knowledge of other trans folks, as well as medical professionals like Webb, in order to ease the existential difficulties that accompany transition. The peer support group, in this iteration, is effectively a skill-share focused on how best to negotiate the newly consolidated trans medical industrial complex. Other concerns, other connections, other intimacies must be left at the door. It is meant to bring trans folks together in order to recruit—in the name of support and community-building—the expertise and savvy of folks who have been out, or in the process of transition, longer.

This echoes what David Valentine found while undertaking ethnographic research among trans peer support groups over a decade later in New York City. Though the book that emerged from this research, *Imagining Transgender: An Ethnography of a Category,* is centrally concerned with the genealogy of the identity marker "transgender" and its attendant exclusions, his fieldwork is grounded in and uniquely enabled by a "staff position in the Gender Identity Project (GIP) at what was then called the Lesbian and Gay Community Services Center in Manhattan. . . . The GIP operated out of cramped offices on the third floor as a part of the Center's Mental Health and Social Services program, with a staff of a director . . . and a number of hardworking *volunteer* peer counselors and outreach workers."[13] In *Imagining Transgender,* he reproduces a flyer for a twelve-week series of group sessions at the GIP emphasizing health and wellness for HIV-positive trans folks that makes plain the logic and rhetoric deployed in recruiting unremunerated trans care labor. It demands: "We need you to share your experience, strength, and hope with others while healing yourself." It exhorts: "You deserve this time to take care of yourself."[14] The invitation trades in what Miranda Joseph terms "the romance of community," the positing of community involvement as an antidote to the anomie, alienation, isolation, individualization, and exhaustion endemic to capitalist modes of production. The community, in the romantic view that she outlines, becomes a supplement to capital, a collective wherein one rediscovers the forms of connectivity, belonging, and trust in a group of like-minded individuals that have been lost on account of the hyperindividuating impacts of work and the organization of domestic life under capitalism. A certain nostalgia undergirds this understanding of community; as Joseph points out, it tends to be "invoked for the sake of a contrast between a problematic 'modern' present and a 'premodern' past that is generally articulated as a Golden Age of community."[15]

If the loss of communality is a general condition of life in a post-Fordist capitalist economic order, it is intensified for trans folks, particular those multiply marginalized folks most significantly interpellated by this GIP invitation: HIV-positive transfeminine folks of color. What does it mean to proffer this kind of trade, to ask that they share "experience, strength, and hope with others" in order to heal themselves? In this vision of trans community, voluntary trans care labor isn't further exhausting, traumatizing, or depleting—it can only heal, and the promise of healing, of recuperation, is the lure that is used to pull in volunteers. The peer support group offers physical space that is decentered and trans-dominant, and this alone is seen to be enough to recruit the care labor of trans folks already grappling with a daily grind constituted by unemployment and underemployment, difficulties in accessing and affording health care, financial strife, and the cumulative impacts of economic disenfranchisement, racism, transphobia, transmisogyny, and transmisogynoir.[16] It is imperative to note that, in his fieldwork, Valentine follows these subjects to spaces radically distinct from the peer support group—balls, bars, protests, spaces where they perform sex work—that don't engage in recruitment on the basis of the romance of community; these spaces are sites of communality less informed by the intentional recruitment of unremunerated care work, and may indeed be more healing and thus more integral to the cultivation of communal flourishing and resistance precisely on that count.

Dean Spade, in his essential 2004 essay on the limits of medical understandings of transness, "Resisting Medicine, Re/modeling Gender," engages in an extended meditation on the role of the trans peer support group. I want to quote this at length, in part because it is an enduring testimonial to the ways in which trans subjects do indeed engage in crucial care labor in order to ease one another's navigations of the medical industrial complex, but also because it's important to point out that Spade stops just shy of theorizing the peer support group as a deliberate and necessary supplement to the consolidation of trans medicine. He writes:

> After attending only three discussion group meetings with other trans people, I am struck by the naiveté with which I approached the search for counseling to get my surgery-authorizing letters. No one at these groups seems to see therapy as the place where they voice their doubts about their transitions, where they wrestle with the political implications of their changes, where they speak about fears of losing membership in various communities or in their families. No one trusts the doctors as the place to work things out. When I mention the places I've gone for help, places that are supposed to support queer and trans people, everyone nods knowingly, having heard countless stories like mine about these very places before. Some have suggestions of therapists who are better, but none cost less than $50/hr. Mostly, though, people suggest different ways to get around the requirements. I get names of surgeons who do not always ask for the letters. I have these great, sad, conversations with these people who know all about

what it means to lie and cheat their way through the medical roadblocks to get the opportunity to occupy their bodies in the way they want.[17]

Spade's comments make clear that trans elders in peer support groups are operating as translators, or even transition doulas (or doulos, or doulxs)—making transition possible, tenable, easier to navigate, utilizing their accumulated expertise about specific procedures, specific clinics, specific practitioners in order to demystify the transition process and lower the threshold of (in)accessibility. They're also, quite obviously, doing therapeutic work, discussing trans familial abandonment, having complex conversations about the way transphobia works across differently marginalized communities. Thinking about Spade's comment in connection to Valentine's research in the Gender Identity Project and considering Webb's group as an immediate historical precursor to the solicitation of voluntary trans care labor, we can hazard a guess that such solicitations are actually structurally endemic to the late twentieth-century consolidation, privatization, and biomedicalization of trans medicine. This matters when it comes to thinking about trans experiences of burnout—and, indeed, reconsidering whether or not "burnout" is the most accurate way to describe this phenomenon of what we might better call the unremunerated appropriation of trans expertise and the exploitation of the desire for community, conviviality, and t4t connection.

"VOLUNTARY GENDER WORKERS": BEYOND BURNOUT

To flesh these connections out, I turn to two figures whose work was absolutely integral to the transformation of trans access to technologies of transition in North America: Rupert Raj, based in Canada, and Dallas Denny, based in the southeastern United States. Both of these trans elders were deeply active liaisons between the burgeoning trans medical industry and actually existing trans subjects and communities throughout the 1980s and 1990s (and deep into the following decades, as well).

Rupert Raj has been doing trans care work since 1971—the year he began to transition, at age nineteen. At the 2016 Moving Trans History Forward conference, Raj participated on a "Founders" panel as one of a handful of trans movement and advocacy lifers. He summarized his experience with a not-so-brief timeline, schematizing the bulk of his life's work as such:

> From 1971 until 2002, I was a voluntary gender worker (or professional transsexual), now known as a "trans activist," providing information, referrals, education, counseling, and peer support to transsexuals and cross-dressers and their partners and families across Canada, the US, and abroad. I also offered free education, doing training workshops, offering newsletter and magazine subscriptions on transsexualism, gender dysphoria, and gender reassignment to psychiatrists, psychologists, psychotherapists, social workers, physicians, and nurses, as well as researchers, academics, educators, students, lawyers, policy makers, and politicians.[18]

I was struck by the occupational equivalences with which he began this description and the temporal dimension he assigned to them—his movement from "voluntary gender worker" to "professional transsexual" to "trans activist." He claims the term *voluntary gender worker* for himself, and it's likely that he coined it. He started a consultancy group that he dubbed Gender Worker in 1988 and ran a short-lived newsletter for gender workers called *Gender NetWorker* around the same time. Though the newsletter only lasted for two issues, the impulse behind it—to produce a resource for trans folk who found themselves doing mostly unremunerated advocacy work—speaks both to the absolutely common and widespread phenomenon of voluntary gender work (anecdotally, I don't know any trans people who don't do this work) and to the dearth of communal, institutional, and social support for such work, which makes such labor ultimately unsustainable and typically deleterious in the long-term.

It's not surprising, then, that he began his talk with a frank admission that he'd recently taken a leave from his job as a psychotherapist at Sherbourne Health in Toronto, where he counseled trans, nonbinary, two-spirit, intersex, and gender-nonconforming folks as part of Sherbourne's comprehensive trans health program. In his own words: "I've been on an indefinite medical leave since last May due to, ah, work-related stress, an unhealthy workplace culture, chronic burnout, vicarious traumatization, clinical depression and generalized anxiety requiring psychotropic medication and ongoing psychotherapy." This allied set of causes, symptoms, and manifestations, however, is not at all unfamiliar to him. Back in 1987, in an issue of *Metamorphosis*—a bimonthly magazine for trans men that ran from 1982 to 1988—he penned a feature editorial entitled "BURN-OUT: Unsung Heroes and Heroines in the Transgender World," which offers up a list of fourteen trans men and women who, after many years of unpaid advocacy work, left their posts or ceased to do such work. He concludes this list with a discussion of his own experience: "I have been serving the transgender community in a variety of capacities (administrator, educator, researcher, counselor, peer supporter, local convener, public relations/liaison officer, networker, editor, writer, chairman of the Board—you name it, I've been it) for the past 15 1/2 years without any form of monetary remuneration whatsoever."[19]

What Raj describes is something more intense and insidious than burnout, at least Maslach's popular account of it. This literature, as articulated at the outset of this chapter, is primarily concerned with decreased rates of job satisfaction and declining workplace productivity, especially in response to the chronic emotional strain of dealing extensively with other human beings, particularly when they are troubled or having problems—a common enough occurrence in the so-called helping professions. It's one type of job stress. Although it has some of the same deleterious effects as other stress responses, what is unique about burnout is that the stress arises from the social interaction between helper and recipient. There are a number of founding assumptions worth troubling in this articulation of burnout. The first is that burnout is, specifically, a stress related to employment and thus a problem for both employers and employees to recognize and attempt to manage. Another is that it is characterized by a fundamentally bifurcated and unequal energetic exchange, where the roles of helper and recipient are clearly demarcated, hierarchical, nonfungible, and nonreciprocal—the relationships that produce burnout are not horizontal or nonhierarchical, peer-to-peer. As an extension of this logic, burnout is conceptualized as a personal—individualized—rather than a communal issue, one that affects, in particular, those in the (often feminized) helping professions. Another extension of this logic is that the cause of burnout is rooted, most often, in working with traumatized or troubled recipients of care and that burnout is, thus, a kind of "compassion fatigue" or vicarious trauma—not necessarily complicated by the helper's own troubles or traumas.

Let me return, then, to thinking about whether or not burnout is the most accurate way to think about the kind of fatigue Raj describes, a fatigue that is deeply familiar to anyone who has been a voluntary gender worker for a significant amount of time. Historically, this kind of work is unpaid. We're only just beginning to inhabit, for better or worse, more formalized nonprofit and institutional structures that variously—and unevenly—remunerate such labor, and the trans folks who inhabit these kinds of positions often come into them after years of unpaid hustle. Raj is a case in point, here: he got his credentials as a psychotherapist in 2001 and only then was able to make a living doing the kind of work he'd already been doing for decades, by finally legibly inserting himself within the diagnostic and treatment apparatus he'd worked for years to help build, particularly as the founder of the Foundation for the Advancement of Canadian Transsexuals (FACT, formed in 1978) and, for years, through his magazines, newsletters, consultations and trainings, and public advocacy. His experience of burnout occurs within the context of unwaged, "voluntary" labor, but what can *voluntary* possibly mean in a context like the one Raj transitioned within, with no formal workplace protections, without a streamlined process to access technologies of transition or to modify gender documentation to make one's legal identity consistent, and with the constant risk of being outed in transphobic workplaces? It is not just a problem of long hours, emotionally extractive labor, underpayment, and underappreciation—though it is, of course, most of those things. It is experiencing all of this in the absence of wages and having to engage in this kind of unwaged labor to build an ever-so-slightly habitable world for trans folks. I'll let Raj tell it:

> In fact, my preoccupation with the welfare of the transgender community is the reason why today I am without a paying career or steady source of income. Don't get me wrong, this was my choice and mine alone (my mission or calling in life) to serve this neglected, misunderstood and, even today, stigmatized class of people—rare victims of what Kim Stuart has so aptly termed "the uninvited dilemma" [of gender dysphoria]. After all, I am a post-op F-M TS [female-to-male transsexual] myself and I guess I want to "take care of my own."[20]

When Raj dedicated himself to networking, organizing, and advocacy on the part of trans communities, he made a decision quite counter to the standard, hegemonic medical advice given to trans folks in the 1970s, which was to go stealth, blend in, and live as normatively as possible. This was a choice, yes, but certainly not an unconstrained one. When reality is so markedly discriminatory, the advice that one should go stealth and proceed with life as if the fact that one is trans were irrelevant radically underdetermines the extent to which being trans continues to matter, even "post" transition.

In a situation of unwaged affective labor as a voluntary gender worker, what tools does one have to deal with burnout? There is no vacation time or flextime and often a scarce support network that could take over one's responsibilities while one takes time out for self-care and healing. In the nascent days of trans advocacy and activism, it is very possible—indeed, likely—that there was no one waiting in the wings to take on the forms of unwaged labor so necessary to securing access to transition-related procedures. Who was lining up to take the reins of *Metamorphosis* or *Gender NetWorker*? Who was ready and willing to step in and become the coordinator of FACT? Given the wide geographic dispersal and extensive closeting of trans folks in the 1970s and 1980s (testified to by the fact that so many communicated through a robust network of newsletters and periodicals, punctuated by the occasional regional meetup if one was lucky enough to live in or adjacent to a metropole), who had the time, emotional bandwidth, and energy to do this kind of work? I imagine the list was quite short.

Being a voluntary gender worker means you are, as Raj says, taking care of your own. This is doubly so if you are experiencing the social death and natal alienation so common to trans experiences. The boundaries between who is a carer and who is a recipient of care are pretty radically blurred in such a situation; any act of caring is simultaneously an act of maintaining those minimal networks of support that sustain you. Trans collectives and communities are deeply interwoven and interdependent, enmeshed in a way that makes distinguishing between the roles of carer and recipient difficult—they're rotating, interchangeable, and reciprocal.

The language of *compassion fatigue* or *vicarious trauma*—used often in the pop psychological literature on burnout—becomes challenging here. Compassion—the experience of deep sorrow or sympathy for the suffering of another—is an inadequate affective accounting of what transpires when a community or collective is involved in acts of caring and being cared for that are informed by similar and mutually resonating forms of traumatization. Other terms utilized within the psychological literature for this phenomenon are secondary traumatization or *secondary traumatic stress,* which enumerate a hierarchy of traumatization that can't possibly, in its ordinal logic, do justice to the kinds of mutual traumatic resonance that circulate between trans subjects involved in acts of caring.

The framework offered by burnout posits a discrete subject or subjects as the source of the carer's fatigue, stress, and trauma. It encourages the person suffering burnout to causally transfer these allied negative affects to an other or others, who then become the source of the burnout that affects the subject. This denies the very basic facts of interdependency, mutuality, and the interwovenness of one another's lives and life chances and encourages us to instead minimize the complexity of the affective interchanges at work when marginalized subjects engage in the work of making each other's lives more possible. How can we think beyond burnout? How can we do justice to the fact that we are often triggered by one another in the act of caring but nevertheless need one another, in both specific and abstract ways, to get by? How do we deal with the forms of infrapolitical hostility that such situations inevitably produce? How do we mobilize the frustration that attends such work in order to effect change?

"IF THEY DON'T ADAPT THEY WON'T SURVIVE": MOBILIZING TRANS FRUSTRATION

When I think about mobilizing trans communal frustration, I think about Dallas Denny and the Harry Benjamin International Gender Dysphoria Association.

Dallas Denny is responsible for starting both the American Educational Gender Information Service (which was originally the Atlanta Educational Gender Information Service, before its national rebranding) and *Chrysalis Quarterly,* which she describes in the very first issue, circa 1991, as a "magazine which explores in depth issues of gender and gender expression in American life . . . [focused] primarily on issues of importance to transgenderal and transsexual persons."[21] Her position as a liaison between the trans medical industrial complex and trans communities came about on account of intense communal contestation of the real-life test, which seemed designed explicitly to invite intensified harassment, potential job loss, and the overall reduction of life chances, all in the name of proving one's commitment to transition to a risk-averse medical establishment. Though Denny was already doing significant trans care labor, it wasn't until debates about the HBIGDA-established Standards of Care threatened to compromise the newly won authority of that association that Denny stepped into prominence as a trans community leader, taking on the role of disseminating accessible information about the process of medical transition (just before the internet would partially democratize access to such information) while simultaneously arguing with HBIGDA about the inadequacy of extant trans medical care.

Piecing together a narrative from internal communications within the organization, conference proceedings, executive board summaries, and correspondence between doctors, prospective patients, and trans community members and activists, I realized that the HBIGDA of the 1990s is an organization in crisis, grappling with the new forms of criticism being levied by trans communities regarding the medicalization of transition, desperately trying to drum up organizational membership and influence, struggling to figure out how to incorporate actually existing trans people within organizational membership, and learning how to coordinate and codify the proliferation of transition-related procedures within the Standards of Care developed by the organization without running roughshod over the concerns about treatment accessibility and livability being articulated within the spaces of trans activism. The archives attest to a collective realization that in order to move forward and do justice to these historical mutations, they may need to reconfigure the vision, reach, and mission of the organization. *Chrysalis Quarterly,* AEGIS, and Dallas Denny emerge as key figures within this reconfiguration.

Rumblings of communal criticism are scattered throughout the HBIGDA archives and manifest acutely in correspondence between executive board members throughout the 1990s. Take, for instance, the Xeroxed photocopy of an introductory update to the January 1995 edition of the *FTM International* newsletter sent to then-director of HBIGDA Alice Webb, recounting a visit she paid to the collective that ran *FTM International* (which included Rupert Raj). It begins with the news that HBIGDA is in the midst of revising the Standards of Care and desires community input, and goes on to report:

> A number of people in attendance took advantage of the opportunity to criticize HBIGDA for wielding too much power over us, or for providing therapists with a tool (the Standards) to keep us under their thumbs. Ms. Webb tried to explain that HBIGDA has no official power, and that the standards were developed to protect consumers (us) from unscrupulous providers, based on the assumption that a provider's status as a member of HBIGDA would assure us that the provider had knowledge of gender issues and had a network of resources to rely on to obtain the best possible care for us. As we know, it hasn't always worked that way.[22]

A few months prior, in the fall of 1994, a letter to the editors of *TV/TS Tapestry*—another journal integral to trans communal formation—plainly asserts that "grief arises from the tyranny of HBIGDA, which controls the treatment of transsexuals."[23] This, too, had been photocopied and sent to Alice Webb by another medical practitioner, in order to signal the rising tide of trans discontent.

Sometimes, the signs of discontent with the Standards of Care—and the shoddy, piecemeal implementation of them—are more harrowing. Sharon Satterfield, a psychiatrist who served as secretary-treasurer of HBIGDA in the mid-1990s and worked in the Program in Human Sexuality at the University of Minnesota, writes to Alice Webb on December 15, 1994, opening with apologies for her recent lack of communication and explaining that she's been "totally stressed out." She goes on to explain the circumstances producing this stress:

Our Department of Human Services has been delaying and manipulating our transsexuals. One was approved for surgery, postponed innumerable times, and then the day before surgery, cancelled. She hopped a plane anyway, went to Pittsburgh, and tried to cut her penis off in the Plastic Surgery Clinic. The day she came back, I saw a TS who had just arrived from Chicago. After I told her about the political problems [ostensibly with the Department of Human Services], she blew her brains out. Then later in the same week, a patient tried to strangle me and no one responded to the panic button. The next week our new SRS surgeon was kicked out of the hospital for sexual harassment, and now I get thirty phone calls per day from frantic patients. Therefore, I have a temporary (hopefully) case of telephone phobia.[24]

The extent of ethical malfeasance suggested here is staggering. ꓵ the politicized waffling of the Department of Human Services charged with the task of coordinating SRS, to the insinuation of Satterfield's unwillingness to answer patient inquiries regarding their access to and eligibility for SRS, to the disturbing note about the surgeon dismissed for sexual harassment, it is clear that the implementation of transition-related health care is failing on multiple levels. Chains of communication are malfunctioning at every juncture: care coordination between psychiatrists and surgeons is being obstructed, the professionals who are ostensible advocates for trans patients are overburdened and refusing dialogue with said patients, and patients themselves are panicking, resorting to desperate measures in order to demonstrate the dire affective and existential consequences of such poor medical care. As the (casually, and brutally—or perhaps cynically—detached) mention of suicidality makes clear, these failures of medical access and case management are directly rendering trans lives unlivable. HBIGDA, having positioned itself as the primary arbiter of relations between the medical establishment and trans communities, finds itself the target of intense criticism for its history of restrictive, unrealistic, hard-to-attain Standards of Care. They are also simultaneously struggling to reform the poor medical care and, more broadly, the insidious forms of transphobic administrative violence that delay, deter, and prevent access to such care. Trans folks are rapidly losing faith in the efficacy of the organization and are increasingly organizing for an end to bureaucratized medical gatekeeping and for self-determination of ostensible fitness for gender transition.

Enter Dallas Denny, *Chrysalis Quarterly,* and AEGIS, the organization that Denny ran in order to connect trans persons with comprehensive information regarding medical, legal, occupational, and interpersonal aspects of transition. Denny, AEGIS, and the magazine had been on the radar of HBIGDA for quite some time, having become the subject of considerable organizational controversy in 1994 on account of an August 9 letter to Rupert Raj wherein she stated that HBIGDA was nothing more than "a dinghy in a world full of iron clads," ineffectual when it came to actually reforming trans medical services. She followed this up by stating that "if they don't adapt they won't survive. In fact, I intend for AEGIS to be the organization which replaces them if they don't change with the times. But the way to approach them is not through emotion, it's through data."[25]

This letter made its way into the hands of HBIGDA organizational leadership, who were, in a word, upset by it (a dinghy, capsizing). Their commentary vacillated between chastising Denny for being ungenerous and overblown, admitting that they needed Denny as a liaison, and brainstorming ways in which they could bring a greater number of trans folks into organizational consultation and decision-making. Importantly, Denny herself is suggesting, through her commentary on the necessity of data, that trans advocacy organizations become more intensively involved in research. Her call is prescient in relation to our contemporary moment, where trans-specific research is increasingly performed by folks who identify as trans, where the interdisciplinary field of trans studies is flourishing, and where many trans-run organizations are actively intervening in health-care delivery systems, at the level of public health advocacy as well as through interventions in and reformations of clinical protocol.

Shortly after the dinghy debacle, Walter Bockting, another member of the executive board, suggests the formation of a trans consultancy group in order to address this loss of faith, writing to Alice Webb on January 30, 1995:

> I believe that a response from HBIGDA to this growing controversy is called for. As a part of this response, I suggest you consider forming *a consumer group* of transgendered individuals (that includes representatives from transgender community organizations) to provide a forum for dialogue about such issues as the Standards of Care. I believe that such a group can aid the revision and continuing support of the Standards of Care, and beyond that would provide a forum for exchange and mutual support to enhance quality of care and research.[26]

The terms of this suggested interpellation of trans people into deliberations over trans health-care protocol are worth noting: they are understood not as activists or as concerned constituents of a community that HBIGDA is ethically responsive to; rather, they are brought into the fold as consumers. Without their economic support, the small handful of medical and psychiatric specialists that specialize in transition-related services that comprise HBIGDA would have significantly economically compromised practices.

We witness, in this instance, how the power of trans communities to transform medical practice becomes linked explicitly, and exclusively, to their consumption of biomedical services. *Chrysalis* is enlisted in the project of marshaling communal support for HBIGDA Standards of Care and approved biomedical practices while simultaneously mobilizing trans communal criticism of medical protocols of transition, but its critique is effective only to the extent that cis medical practitioners understand and interpellate trans people as dissatisfied consumers. I understand *Chrysalis Quarterly* as a crucial part of a broader contestatory trans "healthscape," a term coined by Adele Clarke to mark a "way of grasping, through words, images, and material cultural objects, patterned changes that have occurred in the many and varied sites where health and medicine are performed, who is involved, sciences and technologies in use, media coverage, political and economic elements, and changing ideological and cultural framings of health, illness, healthcare, and medicine."[27] Healthscapes are assemblages that speak to complex transformations in the conceptualization of health and health care.

Chrysalis Quarterly began publication at a moment that would prove critical, in multiple senses, to the transformation of trans health care and attests to the multifaceted work of trans community members to reform a medical industry that refuses to understand that work as work, that refuses to understand us as affected by gatekeeping beyond our role as disgruntled customers. To be merely a consumer of medical services is to be in debt—both literally and metaphorically—to the medical industry. If trans folks are indebted to medical specialists, it becomes very improbable that those specialists can grasp the extent of expertise and the high degree of epistemic authority trans subjects bring to bear in their critiques. The hierarchy of need and debt that structures the patient-consumer relation renders such recognition deeply unlikely. The burnout that trans subjects experience in such a milieu is hardly recognizable as such—after all, how can consumption produce burnout when burnout is supposed to be brought on by unjust labor conditions and consumption is perennially understood as the flipside of labor, as a site of pleasure and enjoyment uniquely enabled by, and counterposed to, work? Being an exploited worker is very different from being an unhappy consumer. But I want to insist, again, on understanding the act of organizing and mobilizing critique—and caring for one another in and through the midst of such organizing—as work: work that occurs in deeply stratified and unjust situations, work that isn't even dignified as such.

(FAILING TO) BECOME "GOOD CONSUMERS OF GENDER SERVICES": DALLAS DENNY AND THE CIRCUITS OF TRANS ANNOYANCE

The first few issues of *Chrysalis Quarterly* are overwhelmingly concerned with coaching trans subjects through the process of medical transition. The very first issue is dedicated to the topic of "Health and Transition," and the cover features a simple line drawing of a long-haired woman lying prone in a gurney, hooked up to an IV, with her face turned away from the viewer. The sac of fluid that the IV is attached to is labelled "Premarin ® conjugated estrogens for injection." Beneath this image are the words "Premiere Issue." On the second page, we encounter a shield logo and a description of the mission of AEGIS: "The word AEGIS means, variously, shield, protection, and sponsorship. We will strive to live up to our acronym by at all times maintaining confidentiality and by helping transgendered persons make reasoned and informed decisions about the ways in which they will live their lives."[28]

We see, immediately, the entanglement of trans health with biomedicalization. The "premiere" is not just of the journal but also, ostensibly, of the woman in the hospital bed (strongly connoting a postsurgical moment) hooked up to a consistent drip of conjugated estrogens (rather than the pain medication we might expect in a postsurgical scene). This heavily medicalized image belies the diversity of perspectives present in this premiere issue, however, which variously details the experiences of non-hormonally transitioned trans women and folks with disabilities or contraindications that render hormonal or surgical transition too risky, as well as folks who are forthrightly skeptical about the high price tag attached to both medical and legal transition. For instance, the issue includes a short poem called "The Take," which is an all-too-common lament about the high cost of transitioning, filtered through the lens of a trans person considering legal assistance with the process of gender-marker changes. It begins, "They start by being very nice," and shifts tone quickly, detailing the lawyer's request of a $10,000 legal fee in order to merely "file some papers with the courts." The poem concludes with an emphatic all-caps direct address of the lawyer in question: "ALL YOU WANT IS YOUR TAKE!"[29]

Amplifying this sense of skepticism and anger about exploitation, the following page bears the headline "BEWARE!" and warns readers of the activities of a "Doctor" (the journal intentionally utilizes scare quotes) named Philip Salem. Denny writes:

> Salem is a west-coast based charlatan who exploits transgendered persons. He reportedly sells very low-potency hormone tablets through the mails for high prices, runs a transie prostitution ring, and does other illegal and questionable things to separate T-people from their money. He should be avoided at all costs. Those who associate with Philip Salem or speak highly of him are also suspect. Be especially aware of offers for "reassignment surgery" in which you are expected to fly the "surgeon" to your hometown.[30]

These excerpts are just a sampling from the first few pages of the inaugural issue of *Chrysalis Quarterly*. What to make of the fact that the magazine is primarily occupied with detailing the ways in which transfeminine populations have been systematically targeted for financial exploitation by medical charlatans and legal professionals alike? Denny and her contributors are developing an emergent critique of medical and legal exploitation that frames the mission and work of the journal, as well as AEGIS. They aim to protect trans folk from such exploitative practices while providing tools that enable us to navigate the byzantine systems of medical and legal transition.

The second issue of *Chrysalis* continues this tack. Entitled "Being a Good Consumer of Gender Services," it opens with an AEGIS-sponsored warning about "non-sterile, non-medical grade" silicone injections offered to trans women as a less-expensive, easier-to-access alternative to plastic surgery. The public service announcement concludes: "Sometimes the price of beauty can be too high. If you desire surgical augmentation, see a plastic surgeon." The issue features articles on "How to Shop for a Service Provider," an account of the history of and rationale for the Standards of Care developed by HBIGDA ("to safeguard service providers, and transsexual men and women"), and a lengthy article on hair removal.[31]

What is most striking about this issue, to me, is the way in which becoming a "good consumer of gender services" is explicitly linked to being a "good" trans person. The commentary provided in the opening "From the Publisher" letter, penned by Denny, warns against the dangers of approaching transition-related services in a less-than-systematic manner, coaching readers on ostensible best practices and strategies:

> Transsexual people should plan for transition just as for any other major life change—education, career, or marriage. They should not "closet" themselves for years and then expect to blossom overnight. Nor should they stop in mid-transition, accepting deviant lifestyles because they have found some acceptance as she-males, drag queens, or street hustlers. Unfortunately, the haphazard and slipshod manners and lifestyles of many transsexual persons lead them into continual difficulty throughout the transition process, and eventually land them in the gender twilight zone.[32]

Especially striking here is the hierarchy of trans authenticity at work. Within this hierarchy, stealth trans women are framed as the apotheosis of trans being, and those subjects who find "some acceptance as she-males, drag queens, or street hustlers" are condemned to a "gender twilight zone," an unsavory demimonde brought on by an embrace of "deviant lifestyles" and caused by what Denny refers to as a tendency "to face the reality of their inner selves through a haze of doubt, guilt, insecurity, and ignorance," a tendency that is "compounded by the apathy, distrust, prejudice, and ignorance of the general public and, unfortunately, sometimes of service providers."[33] Here, the "apathy, distrust, prejudice, and ignorance" of the public and, selectively, the medical establishment, is framed as an intensifier of the negative affect already operative within trans subjects—that "haze of doubt, guilt, insecurity, and ignorance"; the relation between such negative affect and the negotiation of social and institutional milieus that so heavily stigmatize, censure, and punish trans women is significantly underthought.

This letter, in exhorting trans subjects to become good consumers of gender services, frames the failure to do so as a primarily individual phenomenon, eliding the many reasons why trans women—particularly those who labor as drag queens or street hustlers, working primarily in economies of service and sex—may not be able to become good consumers. Further, this logic understands those subjects who may not embrace the hierarchy of authenticity at work here as failures—the decision to live as something other than stealth must be, within this account, the product of some cocktail comprised of an embrace of deviant lifestyle, lack of self-knowledge, and internalized transphobia. The letter goes on to detail the misfortunes of trans subjects who fail to become good consumers, intensifying the individuated logic of failure at work in this coaching attempt:

> The mistakes made by some transsexual people are legion. I worry about those who have sent large amounts of money though the mails to purchase illegal hormones; who have prematurely dismantled their lives—before there was any reasonable chance of passing in the gender of choice— leaving them with inadequate support systems; who have tried to transition or even have surgery before beginning electrolysis or before they have let the hormones do their work; who needlessly reveal their transsexual status at an early stage; who have had trouble giving up their transsexual status for that of a "real" man or woman, ending up in gender limbo; who have expected hormones (or surgery) to turn them into men or women overnight; who have been "pumped" with illegal silicone until they look like caricatures of women and men; who have taken inappropriate

dosages of hormones or who have taken hormones in inappropriate ways; who have denied they needed therapy (yet who obviously did); who have come on great guns, and then disappeared into the closet. Others have calmly and methodically gone about the business of turning themselves into men and women. I have no doubt that the latter individuals will make it. I have my doubts about the others.[34]

There is a teleology of transition at work here, a path to embodying one's gender in the "right" ways that seems to bear quite grim consequences if one deviates in the slightest; the failure to "make it" is commensurable with consignment to "gender limbo," a purgatorial state that isn't quite fleshed out here but is framed, quite simply, as terrifying. Again, there is no address of all of the myriad reasons why trans subjects may deviate from this path—they may not be able to access trans-competent clinical practitioners in their corner of the world, they may not be able to afford plastic surgery, they may actually want to inhabit hyperbolic or intensified versions of femininity or masculinity, rejecting aesthetic ideals of gendered "naturalness."

My aim here is not to excoriate an orientation to transition that is undergirded by such teleological understandings; rather, I want to point out whom it excludes, the hierarchies of value and authenticity it introduces, the ways in which it relies on individuated patient-consumer models of medical access, and the ways it tends to elide intersectional, compounding forms of structural discrimination and administrative violence that deeply structure access to transition-related services. More specifically, though, I want to suggest that the hierarchies of authenticity, of trans "goodness," that circulate among trans subjects engaged in voluntary gender work produce annoyance—the kind of low-grade gnawing irritation that so often accompanies the forms of exhaustion and depletion that we associate with burnout. It's important to consider this commentary as a manifestation of depersonalization that instantiates distance between Denny and less privileged trans subjects. Denny, in her position as community liaison and transition doula, has engaged in a significant amount of care work aimed specifically at easing the path to and through medical transition and is well aware of the many structural barriers that produce the forms of deviation from medically approved routes that she critiques. However, her attention to these structural barriers languishes at precisely the moment one might hope it intensifies. Instead, the failure to abide by the protocol Denny advocates is heavily individuated, and the subjects who do so are utilized as a cautionary tale about what happens when one doesn't heed the advice offered by Denny and other key community liaisons. Her annoyance is palpable throughout these accounts and seems to be fueling her repeated exhortations to do transition the "right" way, but it's quite clear that her annoyance is also fueling the arguments she has with trans medical specialists. She's in an impossible position, caught between a gatekeeping organization that exploits her connections and knowledge while refusing to dignify her as an actual expert on trans health care, on the one hand, and community constituents that are often structurally unable to actually follow the reams of advice and practical support she's offering, on the other. She's at an impasse; we might even say she's in the impasse.

Lauren Berlant writes of what they call the "impasse of the present," and their theorization of this concept is integral to parsing the kind of existential and affective situations that produce burnout.[35] It is especially useful to think through the forms of burnout I describe throughout this chapter, forms of burnout that are truer to the original meaning of the term, used to indicate the radical exhaustion, depletion, and depersonalization that affects folks working for social justice on behalf of the communities and collectives they belong to. As the genealogy of burnout demonstrates, before it came to be used as a synonym for overwork, it referred to the cumulative negative impact experienced by folks working for the realization of better life chances—and the very material redistributions of wealth and resources that would enable this—while deeply and negatively affected by inequities and maldistributions of resources for survival.

The impasse of the present refers to a sense of the present as "a holding station that doesn't hold securely but opens out into anxiety," characterized by the feeling of "dogpaddling around a space whose contours remain obscure."[36] Berlant points out that the word *impasse* was invented to replace "*cul-de-sac*, with its untoward implications in French," and as such, it names a space-time wherein one keeps moving but never seems to get anywhere new, anywhere else.[37] In an impasse, one acts, but in the absence of narrative genre that can somehow make sense of that action; this activity "can produce impacts and events, but one does not know where they are leading."[38] Dogpaddling: treading water in the absence of a refined technique to get one somewhere, doing what one can to stay afloat, with no particular destination and no definite goal, save merely keeping oneself from going under. When we talk about the loss of meaning and interpersonal connection that characterizes burnout, we're talking about how folks feel when they're navigating the impasse of the present, a present wherein there's no guarantee of a better tomorrow, no concrete or practicable plan for transforming the structural conditions that make life feel like an exercise in deterring sinking. Burnout is a name for the feeling of dwelling—or being trapped in—situations that "don't hold securely" but instead "open out into anxiety," when the present is precarious, the undertow is strong, and there's no narrative of hope you can latch onto that might quell your nerves. The impasse of the present names a space of transition, but one unmoored from a telos, a promised future, a narrative of what's to come and how this moment may lead to that. Burnout is a name for how it feels to inhabit such a space of indeterminacy, such a holding pattern, for days, weeks, months, years. To labor as voluntary gender workers and yet to not be recognized as actually working in such a role. To be called on as token representatives again and again, while not being understood as credible interlocuters and advocates whose expertise is integral to transforming systems of health-care access and delivery. To experience rigorous gatekeeping at the hands of medical and social support systems that render many trans lives difficult, untenable, perhaps even unlivable, while being actively recruited and encouraged to become literally indebted to those self-same systems.

So much of trans living takes place in an impasse. No wonder so many of us are burned out.

6

AFTER NEGATIVITY?

On Whiteness and Healing

*"The ego functions to create a barrier of me versus not me.
The ego functions to keep us different," says Alexander Belser,
co-investigator at Yale University, where he works to develop
affirmative psychotherapies for LGBTQ people. "Psychedelic
medicine allows us to experience ego-loosening experiences.
The philosopher and psychologist William James said the
confining selfhood begins to melt down." Belser says that psychedelics can accelerate the process of healing, which requires
understanding our identity as an experience, deconstructing it,
and regrowing it in a way that feels less encumbered by cohe-
sive powers that told us stories about who we should be.*

—Nicolle Hodges, "How Psychedelics Help with Gender
Identity and Transition"

Fatigue, numbness, envy, rage, burnout: thus far, this book has
toggled between these five phenomena with the hopes that tarrying with them might provide some deeper sense of the difficulties that motivate trans arts of living and some of the more
challenging affective textures that shape trans lives at the most
quotidian levels. In varying ways, each of these feelings work to

distantiate a person from the surrounding milieu. Fatigue names a form of existential exhaustion, a wearing-away that situations of continual deferral produce; its hallmark is a radical slowing of reactivity. Numbness is a means of muffling the sensorium in order to dull the impingements of the milieu you find yourself in, so that you feel less intensely, so that you might find it hard to feel much at all. Envy names the absorption of one's attention in the act of wanting that which the present conjuncture lacks. Rage, theorized here in the form of the break, is both a caesura and a kind of possession, an affective swell that overwhelms, capable of drowning out the present—or, put alternately, capable of absorbing the entirety of the present. Its temporality is that of a time out of time. Burnout is characterized by an abiding sense of futility and persistent, recalcitrant apathy.

In the preceding pages, I have tried to illuminate the myriad reasons why some—I would argue many—trans subjects live in ways shaped deeply by the conjunction of such affects. There's valuable information there. Tarrying with negativity makes one skeptical of too-simple palliative suggestions. Throughout this book, my strategy has been to point to how such affects are structurally produced; this means that the address and amelioration of them must be rooted in structural change as well (all the self-help in the world could not convince me otherwise). At the same time, we need—and, indeed, have cultivated—strategies for survival and resistance, and have done so through the crucible formed by these allied affective phenomena. I follow the thinking of Ann Cvetkovich here, who, in the introduction to her book *Depression: A Public Feeling*, writes that she's been looking "for forms of testimony that can mediate between the personal and the social, that can explain why we live in a culture whose violence takes the form of systematically making us feel bad," while admitting that "saying that capitalism (or colonialism, or racism) is the problem" does not help her get up in the morning.[1] Her hunch—and it is one that I share—is that spending time with such nuanced testimonies might "offer some clues about how to survive these conditions and even change them."[2] But even if they don't, they still move us beyond the level of the individual and the symptomatic. Narrativizing and amplifying such negative affects is a means of testifying to their widespread commonality, a way to make sure they're rendered public and conceived structurally. This book is full of such testimonies. They demonstrate, over and over again, that thinking of any of these affective states as exclusively deleterious elides their nuance, especially the ways in which they birth creative practices of survival (rage), tune us into the degree of our exhaustion and exploitation (burnout), trouble our investment in cruelly optimistic teleologies of transition (fatigue), help us cope with the relentless everyday impingements of transphobia, transmisogyny, and transmisogynoir (numbness), and serve as a codex of both desire and injustice (envy).

After years of thinking about the work of such affective phenomena in trans lives, I found myself turning increasingly toward practices engaged by trans subjects that are understood to be explicitly healing, reparative, and transformative: group therapy, meditation, bodywork, breathwork, psychedelics, and other forms of integrative medicine. I think of these as the verso face of the ostensibly negative affective states I've been absorbed by over these last years and, like those states, which do much more than merely whittle away at the conatus, these practices do much more than heal: they also appropriate, exclude, and propagate ideals of self-transformation underwritten by the racial logic of neocolonial neoliberalism. Just as dwelling with the negative cultivates an attunement to the more than deleterious effects of such states, a deep dive into the work of healing teases out the less than ameliorative impacts of such practices.

In this concluding chapter, I turn a critical lens on trans discourses of spirituality, healing, wholeness, and becoming, analyzing a handful of historical traces of trans engagements with psychedelia and New Age spirituality, from Harry Benjamin's correspondence with LSD researchers in the 1960s and 1970s to the quarterly publication of *GenderQuest,* a periodical concerned with trans spirituality, "shamanism," and healing ritual, in the late 1990s and early 2000s. Certain trans subjects—most famously, millionaire philanthropist and activist Reed Erickson—have turned to psychedelics as a means of experiencing and exploring alternative realities, often on account of understanding themselves as in excess of or alien to hegemonic forms of sociality and institutional life. We even find the phrase *psychonaut*—an explorer of "inner space" through the use of psychedelic comestibles—détourned in the title of Monika Treut's 1999 experimental documentary *Gendernauts: A Journey through Shifting Identities*. The late twentieth-century trans archive is replete with connections—sometimes literal, sometimes metaphoric—between psychedelic experiences and experiences of gender liminality, transition, and transformation. In the 1960s and 1970s, this manifested in trans engagements with the human potential/New Age movement, while in our contemporary moment it operates through tarrying with the promises and visions associated with transhumanism and posthumanism, in quotidian engagements with rituals and practices we sometimes colloquially refer to under the banner of "woo," and in the resurgence of academic and medical research into the therapeutic uses of psychedelics in relation to trauma.

In order to more fully understand trans involvement with psychedelics, New Age spirituality, and the utopian future visions these practices so often inform, I investigate how such engagements are underwritten by a conflation of trans embodiment with forms of plasticity and mobility that are deeply informed by whiteness, steeped in racial privilege and cultural appropriation, and that rhyme with prevailing Eurocentric biomedical discourse on trans embodiment. I dwell on this nexus of healing and trans experience in order to point out the ways in which heavily individualist neoliberal logics conspire with racial capitalism even in those spaces where subjects are seeking out alternative ways of being. I'm curious about how strategies for deindividuation and cultivating interconnectedness remain stubbornly limited by mechanisms of racial exclusion and the concomitant exoticization and appropriation of non-Western spiritual practices, and about what that might mean for collective trans healing.

But first, a detour through Harry Benjamin's archives.

THE RACIAL LOGIC OF "HUMAN POTENTIAL"

I traveled to the Kinsey Institute archives in the spring of 2018 in order to look at materials associated with the Harry Benjamin International Gender Dysphoria Association (HBIGDA). As discussed in the prior chapter, HBIGDA, the organization that was to become the World Professional Association for Transgender Health (WPATH), formed in the late 1970s and was comprised primarily of sexologists, surgeons, and other medical and psychiatric clinicians working in the areas of transsexuality and transvestism. They specifically resisted the tactic of psychotherapeutic normalization and instead advocated for a model of surgical and hormonal gender transition. The formation of HBIGDA helped consolidate the authority and sway of this approach, drawing what historian Joanne Meyerowitz calls the "medical turf war" between psychologists and surgical and endocrinological specialists to a close.[3] The association took Harry Benjamin's name by way of homage, as he was elderly, nearing the end of his long career, and had been a key figure responsible for legitimizing gender transition in the United States. When I arrived at the Kinsey, it turned out that the HBIGDA materials were at an auxiliary storage site and wouldn't be delivered to the reading room until much later that day. Shawn Wilson, associate director of library and special collections at the Kinsey, suggested that I might spend some time with Harry Benjamin's archive while I waited. So I did.

It's often the case with archival work that you find things you don't expect, items that divert or entirely reroute your research itinerary. I think that folks who do archival work have a particular predilection for this feeling of being knocked off course, surprised by what the archive offers up. The challenge is to develop framings and concepts that do justice to the complexities of what surfaces, and this necessitates epistemic humility, a willingness to be wrong, and a loose hold on whatever historical or political narrative you might have at the beginning of such encounters. This form of epistemic humility rests on a willingness to be transformed by archival encounters, to grapple with worlds of discourse and sense that don't necessarily cohere with hegemonic narratives, or that resist narrativization itself. I think about this relation to archival work as a kind of world-traveling, one that tarries with ghosts, traces, and hauntings of various sorts; one that disrupts temporalities, particularly teleological narratives of progress.

I had gone to the Kinsey with the aim of mapping the formation of HBIGDA, interested in the strategies the organization used to consolidate medical authority, particularly in transnational contexts. I wanted to understand how HBIGDA became the World Professional Association for Transgender Health, the widely recognized authority on best practices for medical forms of transition, an organization with great international influence and sway. I was attempting to document the ways in which the development of WPATH mirrored colonial cartographies of knowledge and power, abiding by a distinction between the "West and the rest" where medical knowledge and know-how, as well as the etiologies, pathologies, and ontologies that undergird such knowledges, are transferred from North American and Western European research sites to clinics in other areas of the world. The growth trajectory of WPATH certainly attests to this; the archives contain a breakdown of member institutions and practitioners for each year by nationality and, unsurprisingly, the vast majority of the members of this ostensibly global organization are from North America and Western Europe. This is a pattern that has held steady since the formation of HBIGDA.

What I wasn't prepared to encounter, and wouldn't have encountered without the delay of the HBIGDA materials, was the quite explicitly racist correspondence between Harry Benjamin and one Robert Masters, who in the 1960s cofounded (along with his wife, Jean Houston) the New York City–based Foundation for Mind Research. Masters built a career by writing on sexual taboos and minoritized sexual subcultures, authoring the 1962 volume *The Homosexual Revolution* on the homophile movement (a book *Kirkus Reviews* describes as "not quite as flamboyant or militant as the title would lead you to believe"), the 1963

Forbidden Sexual Behavior and Morality, the 1964 *Prostitution and Morality,* and the 1966 *Sex-Driven People.*[4] The year 1966 witnessed his turn toward psychedelics and LSD research; that year he released, riffing on William James's hallmark text on mystical experience, the coauthored volume *The Varieties of Psychedelic Experience.* The book's subtitle announces the historical significance of the text: it brands itself as "the first comprehensive guide to the effects of LSD on the human personality." He began corresponding with Benjamin in 1961, seeking an authorizing foreword from him for *Prostitution and Morality* and *Forbidden Sexual Behavior and Morality,* ostensibly on account of Benjamin's ascendant sexological reputation and his destigmatizing approach to issues of gender and supposed sexual deviance. In these early letters, he requests a draft of Benjamin's book on transsexuality (probably referring to Benjamin's 1954 *Transsexualism and Transvestism as Psychosomatic and Somatopsychic Syndromes,* as it would be another few years until the appearance of his well-known 1966 book *The Transsexual Phenomenon,* where he endeavors to cis-splain transsexuality to the lay population). Masters explains that, in his life, he has "been fortunate enough to know several persons who sincerely believed themselves to be females in male bodies" and follows this with the anecdote that he has "also known two persons—and in a sense there is an analogy—who firmly believed they were 'not human.'"[5] He then offers a brief analysis of this trans/nonhuman nexus, writing, "One's first impulse there, of course, is to diagnose schizophrenia, since schizophrenics report such feelings, but these two cases were different, the people very charming and well able to get along in the world."[6] In later correspondence, it becomes clear that Masters is interested in research on transsexual subjects not only as a sexologist but as someone increasingly interested in alterations of consciousness and psychosomatic schema. In 1967, he writes to Benjamin and encloses a questionnaire that he would "like to have filled out by the transsexuals and, since the comparison may be instructive, by the transvestites as well."[7] He asks Benjamin to have Virginia Prince—a former patient of

Benjamin's and a prolific trans activist who also performed secretarial work for Benjamin—submit these questionnaires to Benjamin's prospective patients when they visited the office, as an additive to their intake paperwork.

The questionnaire (which, to my knowledge, Benjamin never actually submitted to his prospective trans patients) was exclusively about the interface between transsexuality, transvestism, and LSD research. The first question was: "Do you believe that LSD might have special value for the transsexual or for the transvestite? What might that value be?" It then proceeds with a line of questioning about LSD as conversion therapy for trans folks, asking if they "think an LSD experience might 'cure' transsexuals or transvestites" and, moreover, if they would be interested in such a potential cure. If not, he inquires as to whether or not they might be interested in it for "therapeutic reasons," "just for the experience itself," or "as a means of personal growth and development" in order to "achieve better self-understanding."[8]

Masters sent this request and questionnaire to Benjamin in a moment of shifting trajectories in LSD research. By the mid-1960s, a major transition had occurred: researchers had ceased to utilize LSD as a means of inducing supposed psychotic or schizophrenic states, recognizing that the state induced by LSD was not a proxy for madness. Katherine Bonson, a controlled substances researcher with the Food and Drug Administration who has written a definitive short history of LSD clinical research in the United States, points out that "by 1956, Canadian psychiatrist and LSD researcher Humphrey Osmond concluded that LSD needed to be reframed away from its association with the induction of madness. He then created the new term 'psychedelic' (meaning 'mind-manifesting'), to replace 'hallucinogen,' which he felt conveyed that LSD produced a hallucinatory state of psychosis."[9] In other words, LSD was increasingly being used as an "adjunct to psychotherapy" that researchers believed could be of use in treating depression and other modes of psychological irregularity or purported maladjustment.[10] Use of the drug was consistent with trends in humanistic psychological practice that emphasized the role of the "unconscious" in processes of self-realization and self-actualization—in the parlance of the time, this was referred to as attaining and enhancing "human potential." Masters was interested in utilizing trans subjects in LSD research in order to explore or unlock their human potential and, importantly, to discover whether or not this process would "cure" their transness.

Though it seems strange from a contemporary vantage to posit that LSD could convince someone that they weren't trans, the notion that LSD could cure homosexuality—understood by mid-twentieth-century psychologists as a psychological disorder rooted in traumatic childhood experience—was an idea already circulating within the academic research circles utilizing acid. This investment in curative logic reaches a certain apotheosis in Timothy Leary's infamous 1966 interview with *Playboy* magazine. By the time of this interview, Leary, who had begun his LSD research at Harvard in 1960, had been fired from Harvard and gone on to become a guru figure in the counterculture of the 1960s, famously proselytizing the gospel of turning on, tuning in, and dropping out. Part of tuning in, it seems, had to do with recognizing a kind of cosmic truth of sex rooted in the tantric philosophy that had, by 1966, very thoroughly imbued the metaphysics of psychedelic research: that the path to enlightenment was routed through the supposedly profound unification of opposites experienced within cishetero penetrative sex. Religious studies scholar Jeffrey J. Kripal refers to this as a kind of "heteroerotic mysticism" and traces how this tantric imaginary is threaded throughout the human potential movement that emerged from psychedelic research circles in the 1960s.[11] A core belief of this movement, recounted by Kripal, is that "mystical life . . . was fundamentally about the restoration of a primordial unity that is temporarily lost in the biology of sex differentiation and the social injustices of gender construction and inequity."[12] You could fuck your way back to this primordial unity, but only if you did it the right way. Timothy Leary outlines the way, in no uncertain terms, in his 1966 interview:

Playboy: According to some reports, LSD can trigger the acting out of latent homosexual impulses in ostensibly heterosexual men and women. Is there any truth to that, in your opinion?

Leary: On the contrary, the fact is that LSD is a specific *cure* for homosexuality. It's well known that most sexual perversions are the result not of biological binds but of freaky, dislocating childhood experiences of one kind or another. Consequently, it's not surprising that we've had many cases of long-term homosexuals who, under LSD, discover that they are not only genitally but genetically male, that they are basically attracted to females. The most famous and public case of such cases is that of Allen Ginsberg, who has openly stated that the first time he turned on to women was during an LSD session several years ago. But this is only one of many such cases.

Playboy: Has this happened with Lesbians?

Leary: I was just going to cite such a case. An extremely attractive girl came down to our training center in Mexico.[13] She was a Lesbian and she was very active sexually, but all her energy was devoted to making it with girls. She was at an LSD session at one of our cottages and went down to the beach and saw this young man in a bathing suit and—flash!—for the first time in her life the cellular energy was flowing in her body and it bridged the gap. Her subsequent sexual choices were almost exclusively members of the opposite sex.[14]

While the historical record bears out that Ginsberg was, indeed, definitively not cured of his homosexuality by LSD, and this interview itself has come under intense scrutiny for misrepresenting the erotic dimensions of psychedelic experience, largely because Leary claims that "in a carefully prepared, loving LSD session, a woman will inevitably have several hundred orgasms," it more than adequately represents the cishetero bias that informed this first wave of academic psychedelic research.[15] It's not a far leap at all from believing LSD could cure homosexuality to believing it could cure transsexuality, as it, like homosexuality, was believed to be a psychological disorder similarly rooted in childhood trauma. Leary's commentary on how LSD unmasks the ostensible truth of both genital and genetic sex in the way it prompts a kind of reorientation toward heterosexuality is telling. In this imaginary, LSD unveils fundamental truths of selfhood, and the sexed and sexual metaphysics of such truth are rooted in the genetic microcosmos, which is a kind of prelapsarian idyll of cishetero desire where heterosexual attraction confirms genetic sex. You dose and drop directly into the heterosexual matrix.[16]

With this historical context in mind, it's not surprising that, in the year following Leary's interview, Masters would write to the preeminent expert on transsexuality and request that he ask his subjects about LSD. Though he was curious about its capacity to cure, he also seems to be more broadly interested in the relationship between trans experience and human potential, interested in whether or not trans psychosomatic experiences held a key to some form of human enlightenment, freedom, or awakening. Masters, like other participants in the human potential movement, was deeply affected by the work of humanistic psychologists like Abraham Maslow, Carl Rogers, and Frank Barron, which was adamantly nonpathologizing and, unlike behaviorist psychology, did not seek to reform or normalize subjects to bring them more firmly in line with hegemonic social and political orders. Keywords for humanistic psychologists are *empathy, choice, freedom,* and *transcendence.* For Masters, LSD could be utilized as part of the path toward self-actualization. This was the work he was increasingly invested in, through both his Foundation for Mind Research and the publication he coedited, entitled *Dromenon: A Journal of New Ways of Being.* Speaking further to Masters's decidedly nonpathologizing approach to understanding transsexuality is the fact that he ran a scathing review of Janice Raymond's infamous and deeply transphobic *The Transsexual Empire* in *Dromenon* shortly after the book's 1979 release. After a detailed and lengthy review that charts Raymond's belief that trans women are a patriarchal plot to infiltrate and take over feminist movement, his review concludes with a Shakespearean flourish wherein he refers to *The Transsexual Empire* as "a tale told by an idiot, full of sound and fury, signifying nothing."[17]

One way to interpret this years-long correspondence between Benjamin and Masters would be as a discourse between two avant-garde researchers pioneering a destigmatizing approach to trans subjects, both of whom were interested in facilitating transition and in what trans experience might tell us about forms of self-realization, the enhancement of human potential, and the role gender identity might play in the attainment of human self-actualization—or, perhaps, self-actualization beyond the conventional bounds of the human (cosmic consciousness, universal oneness, sacred spiritual union with the One-All, whatever). I think of this interface between LSD-enhanced psychotherapy, humanistic psychology, and mid-twentieth-century trans sexological practice as a kind of trans psychedelia that manifests across multiple terrains of gender and sex research. The focus is on pushing the limits of human embodiment and consciousness through interface with pharmaceutical and surgical innovations that ostensibly enhance one's quality of life. It's important to remember, with reference to this, that Benjamin's early research (before he shifted his focus to transsexuality) was in the field of endocrine gerontotherapy, which sought to enhance quality of life by delaying the effects of aging through the use of hormone therapy. While we're very familiar with this phenomenon now, as hormone replacement therapy is increasingly prescribed to aging cis men and peri- and postmenopausal cis women with great frequency, Benjamin was an early pioneer in this field and notably practiced endocrine gerontotherapy on himself, routinely injecting testosterone well into old age.

Masters and Benjamin, while both invested in testing the limits of human consciousness and embodiment in the name of enhanced livability, were also deeply racist. For me, this raises questions about the entwinement of ideologies of transformation and self-actualization with race. This entwinement matters deeply when considering the history of trans sexology because, as Jules Gill-Peterson makes clear, the field of endocrinology, so integral to emergent technologies of gender transition, is also steeped in eugenic logic. She details how the Austrian physiologists who pioneered the field, Eugen Steinach (who was a mentor, colleague, and friend to Harry Benjamin) and Paul Kammerer, undertook research on the morphological development of rats that sought to demonstrate how the endocrine system "mediated between the living organism and its environment," effectively modifying corporeal development based on the input of environmental conditions.[18] They discovered that "rats reared in warmer temperatures developed quicker than those in temperate environments . . . [and] apparently grew more prominent secondary sexual characteristics," which "also appeared to be heritable."[19] They then made the leap to arguing that "warm climate resulted in the hypersexualization attributed to non-European peoples by encouraging the overdevelopment, first, of the puberty glands and, consequently, of the secondary sex characteristics."[20] The hypersexualization of folks who live in or hail from what European colonists understood as "torrid zones"—that is, tropical climes—has a long and infamous history within Eurocentric scientific literature, from the natural histories of the eighteenth century to Darwinian accounts of racial difference, and is deployed over and over again as evidence of developmental backwardness with respect to a Eurocentric hierarchy of civilizational development. Hypersexualization has been linked to savagery, primitivity, languor, laziness, lack of rationality, and lack of self-control and has been consistently deployed as a justification for colonial domination, expropriation, and violence. It is not surprising that we see such logic appear in the correspondence of Masters and Benjamin, but it does indeed raise questions about the racial politics of who they understood as fit for transition and why it was that such fit candidates were overwhelmingly white.

In the midst of their correspondence, in an August 21, 1965, letter, Masters mentions the Watts Rebellion of 1965, a Black uprising against racist police harassment and violence enacted by the Los Angeles Police Department, which was one of the first militarized police departments in the nation. He writes, both callously and casually:

> How did they react to the Los Angeles uprising of the savages in San Francisco? Personally, I think freedom is a burden that weighs too heavily on the Negro, and the more he gets of it the more frightened he comes, so that the very thin veneer of Westernization falls away and we get this Mau Mau sort of thing. The debacle is only beginning and we "ain't seen nothin' yet."[21]

In his August 26, 1965, response to this missive, Benjamin writes:

> I cannot bring myself to have any sentimental attitude, pro-Negro or otherwise, about the Los Angeles mess. The fault lies undoubtedly on both sides but I missed in the various comments reference to the immature and somewhat child-like attitude that I have found so many Negroes to have, and that may explain their reaction to grievances that probably have a certain justification.[22]

Both Masters and Benjamin deploy tropes steeped in racial colonial violence to interpret the Watts Rebellion, shaped by anti-Black ideologies of atavism, anachronism, tribalism, and primitivity. Masters specifically links the Watts Rebellion to the explicitly anticolonial Mau Mau uprising in Kenya, which he frames not as a freedom struggle but as a proof of the inability of colonization and Westernization to ultimately "civilize" Black folks. Benjamin draws upon long-standing racial discourses of developmental delay in his commentary on the "somewhat child-like attitude" of "so many Negroes." It is clear that in this moment in the mid-1960s, in the midst of the civil rights movement and on the cusp of the formation of the Black Panther party, both men are invested in a centuries-long logic that undergirds white supremacy by framing bourgeois, white, Western culture as the apotheosis of civilization for reasons of environment, evolution, and heredity.

This interchange raises several weighty and difficult questions for contemporary scholars working at the juncture of trans studies, Black studies, and decolonial feminist thought. What does it mean that Benjamin, chief architect and proponent of mid-twentieth-century protocols of gender transition, was invested in such modern/colonial epistemes of race? To what extent does this allow us to read the (undeniably heterosexist) logics that determined supposedly viable candidates for gender transition as also thoroughgoingly shaped by companionate gendered logics of whiteness? If the archive of Western sexology is also a modern/colonial archive of racialized gender, how does this archive attest to the historical structuration of access to technologies of transition? How do these racist beliefs inform the human potential movement and related psychological and spiritual discourses on self-actualization that both Masters and Benjamin were deeply invested in? And finally, what does this legacy mean for those of us invested in decolonial and transfeminist strategies of survival, resistance, and flourishing?

For it wasn't just cishet sexological researchers that were delving into psychedelics, consciousness expansion, purportedly life-extending corporeal practices, and the cultivation of greater degrees of existential and cosmic awareness; it was a countercultural zeitgeist that swept up a great number of trans folks and, in many ways, laid the groundwork for contemporary practices of self-care taken up by trans folks attempting to heal from compounded forms of trauma, marginalization, and violence.

"INSTEAD OF THINKING ABOUT YOURSELF—BE": TRANS ENGAGEMENTS WITH NEW AGE SPIRITUALITY

In the same historical moment wherein Masters and Benjamin are corresponding about race riots and the potential of a psychedelic cure for transsexuality, the radical queer and trans youth of Vanguard, the San Francisco–based activist group that "organized young people of the Tenderloin's [San Francisco's long-standing vice district] streets—in particular those identified as hustlers and hair fairies, who exchanged sex for money and/or adopted unconventional gender roles—and emphasized the problems of police violence, exploitation, and discrimination" were self-publishing *Vanguard Magazine: The Magazine of the Tenderloin,* organizing mutual aid projects, and planning demonstrations.[23] As Susan Stryker recounts in *Transgender History,* their first major action, in July 1966, was to "confront the management of Compton's Cafeteria [a common Tenderloin hangout] over its poor treatment of trans women and street queens."[24] Vanguard first organized a picket line, and when that proved ineffective, "frustration boiled over into militant resistance," resulting in a trans and queer riot that predated the more famous Stonewall rebellion by three years.[25] The multi-issue activist work that Vanguard developed in the late 1960s remains strikingly prescient and necessary: they were protesting urban land-use policies and policing practices that targeted, surveilled, and punished sex workers, drug users, trans women, and low-income and unhoused people in the name of gentrifying an infamous port-city vice district on whose streets the members of Vanguard made home and built community.

They were also dropping acid.

In their seventh issue, Vanguard published a "dope sheet" that is a meditative and practical guide on how to take LSD for the first time. It ventriloquizes the wisdom of the original academic LSD researchers, emphasizing the importance of "set" and "setting"—that is, mindset and physical place—in order to avoid bad trips, stressing the necessity of being led through the experience by a guru figure who has extensive familiarity with the intricacies of psychedelic effects. They muse:

> Acid is a consciousness-raising drug & should be used as such. A standard error is to devote the trip to introspection, which is logically foolish & guaranteed to generate bad trips, at least in the early stages of the acid curriculum.

Self-knowledge is even more important than you think it is, but introspection is the last step in the process of knowing yourself. . . . Be with a beautiful person in a beautiful place doing beautiful things and being beautiful, & you will have a beautiful trip. Instead of thinking about yourself—be.[26]

This focus on presentness, on being in the moment, detached from introspection and instead fully inhabiting one's sensorium, is commonplace in psychedelic literature. Indeed, a large part of the appeal of LSD (and similar psychotropic drugs) lies in its unique ability to throttle one's self-awareness and, instead, steep the self in the sensorial, the hallucinatory.

This is a far cry—in some ways, the flip side—from the distantiating affective modes that I've written about thus far, which is why I'm so interested in trans experimentation with both psychedelics and the broader ensemble of practices that aim for embodied presentness, that support the cultivation of the ability to "be here now," as gay psychonaut and spiritual teacher Ram Dass put it in the title of his 1971 counterculture classic.[27] Even Michel Foucault, in the book-length account of his 1975 acid trip in Death Valley, attests to the evaporation of the capacity for critical reflexivity on acid. He is asked by a friend, toward the end of the experience, if he has had any philosophical insights; he reportedly replied, "Not really. I have not spent these hours reflecting on concepts. It has not been a philosophical experience for me, but something else entirely."[28] Similarly, author Michael Pollan, in his best-selling book on the contemporary resurgence of psychedelic research *How to Change Your Mind*, frames psychedelic use as an expressly mystical experience because it is both ineffable and comes coupled with "the conviction that some profound objective truth has been disclosed to you. . . . People feel they have been let in on a deep secret of the universe, and they cannot be shaken from that conviction."[29] Pollan points out that mystical experience is characterized by a dissolution of the subjective and objective, which is part of what makes verifying psychedelic experience so infamously difficult—it is phenomenological rather than empirically verifiable, but the phenomenological "I" is obliterated in the experience. He writes that "when our sense of a subjective 'I' disintegrates, as it often does in a high-dose psychedelic experience, it becomes impossible to distinguish between what is subjectively and objectively true. What's left to do the doubting if not your I?"[30] Indeed, the goal is to blast open the doors of consciousness in order to move past the defenses, critiques, paranoias, and fears of the self toward an epiphanic state. The human potential movement, and the New Age movement more broadly, have tended to consider this an important step in the process of self-actualization and both personal and collective evolution, a crucial practice undertaken in the attainment of a higher plane of consciousness.

A vacation from the "I" is deeply appealing, particularly for those of us whose I's are routinely gaslit, maligned, and maltreated (and to be clear, I cherish each one I've ever taken). But I also think of these vacations as a kind of psychic travel that is disproportionately accessible and perhaps disproportionately appealing to white folks because of the kinds of cultural circuits it runs through. The milieus in which psychedelic use has been taken up as part of the toolkit of self-actualization and metaphysical awakening, from the counterculture of the 1960s to our present-day culture of wellness retreats and transformational festivals, are overwhelmingly white. The hodgepodge of spiritual practices stemming from and associated with these spaces— yoga, breathwork, tarot, astrology—also tend to be white dominant. As trans folks have turned to these practices as a means of self-care and healing, they have also tended to entrench and intensify the operations of what anthropologist Arun Saldanha calls "white viscosity," which refers to how an aggregate of cultural practices work in concert in order to "make white bodies stick together and exclude others."[31] Saldanha specifically focuses on the psychedelic trance culture established in Goa, India, from the mid-1990s through the early 2000s but meditates throughout his text on the whiteness of psychedelic cultures more broadly, writing that "psychedelics—travel, music, drugs—is whiteness

accelerating, whiteness stuttering: either a deeper entrenchment into economic and cultural exploitation, or a shedding
of privilege, at least here and now."[32] What he means by this is
that psychedelic culture is envisioned as a spacetime in excess of
race, a site of unfaithfulness to the rules and norms of bourgeois
whiteness; involvement in such scenes is often imagined, by the
white folks involved, as either colorblind or, more egregiously, a
place of traitorousness to whiteness. Exoticizing engagements
with shamanism, the non-Western guru as devotional figure and
spiritual leader, extensive cultural appropriation of heteroclite
non-Western symbols and ritual practices, the romanticization
of ostensibly premodern spirituality and lifeways: this all works
in concert to convince white folks involved in such scenes that
they are simultaneously both aware of racism and somehow beyond its reach. Amanda Lucia, in her introduction to *White Utopias: The Religious Exoticism of Transformational Festivals*, provides
a vivid illustration of the appropriationist and exoticist through
lines that connect the counterculture of the 1960s to our present:

> In the New Age bookstores of my youth, I found transla-
> tions of the *Tibetan Book of the Dead* alongside Ram Dass's
> *Be Here Now* and translations of the *Dao de Ching*, shelved
> next to Motherpeace tarot cards, statues of Egyptian de-
> ities, Native American smudge sticks, and Pagan ritual
> manuals. This amalgamation was congealed in the religious
> explorations of the Transcendentalists in the 1840s, re-
> newed at the turn of the twentieth century, revived by the
> counterculture of the 1960s, and sold in the New Age book-
> stores of the 1990s—and today, nearly the exact same set
> of texts and ephemera of religious exoticism continue to
> inform the spirituality of transformational festivals.[33]

A motley amalgamation, indeed, and one that's also familiar to
me. It seems, these days, that the bookshelves of my and Lucia's
youth have become the social media feeds of our present, and
there's a resonance between her account of the woo bricolage of
the past with my current Instagram feed, which is full of trans and

queer discourse on self-care, healing practices, and boutique products for destressing from the compounding impacts of structural oppressions of varying kinds, life in the midst of an ongoing pandemic (I'm writing a draft of this in February 2021, nearly a year into the withdrawal of quarantine and social distancing), a collapsing (alright, collapsed) web of social safety nets, infinite debt, intimate and intergenerational trauma . . . I could go on. Just a quick snapshot from a scroll break taken while writing: trans artist Jonah Welch is announcing the start of their daily rosary ritual, the feminist stockists at Otherwild are selling Black-femme-made healing tinctures in honor of Black History Month, Lizzo is posting videos about the practice of blowing kisses to her fat belly and showering it with praises, a friend of mine is inviting everyone to their online sliding-scale queer and trans yoga classes, queer artist and maker Sweeney Brown is selling positive self-talk pillowcases that read "Your future self is proud of you" and "Your past is not your future," nonbinary tarot reader Edgar Fabián Frías is advertising classes on how to cultivate a gender-expansive tarot practice, and queer astrologer Chani Nicholas is urging me to pay attention to how Mercury's retrograde is highlighting my need to establish better boundaries and say no to what doesn't serve my higher self. My feed is filled with this kind of content every day, and of course it's in part a highly curated, potentially idiosyncratic example (I am putting my own woo on display here, I know), but I have a hunch that other folks' feeds are similarly replete with examples of the nexus of trans and queer culture with New Age ephemera, ritual, and practice.

I highlight this resonance because it raises questions about how the troubling racial politics of the New Age movement inform current dalliances with and deeper commitments to contemporary trans and queer iterations of spiritual practices. Every time a white, trans person charges their crystals during a full moon, moves through an asana, does a tarot reading for themselves or a friend, appeals to the stars for relationship advice, or considers traveling to the desert for a peyote retreat, we become further embedded in this long history of romanticization, piecemeal appropriation, and exoticizing commodification that has consistently resulted in the production of white viscosity.

To parse further how these practices entwine in order to produce white viscosity, I want to turn to a series of self-published newsletters from the turn of the twenty-first century that document an emergent community of trans Wiccans, ceremonialists, and self-proclaimed shamans who formed a loose collective through attending a series of retreats and small-scale transformational festivals in and around the southern Appalachian mountain city of Asheville, North Carolina. Asheville, with its long-standing reputation as a progressive, queer- and trans-friendly countercultural enclave in the mountain South, has long been a hub for such gatherings, though they are also held in smaller mountain communities in the Blue Ridge with similarly progressive reputations, like Hot Springs, North Carolina—a tiny resort town just off the Appalachian Trail, popular with thru-hikers and tourists who come to bathe in the springs—and Black Mountain, North Carolina, which was home to experimental Black Mountain College from 1933 to 1957, founded on the holistic and experiential educational principles of philosopher John Dewey and temporary intellectual home to a number of American avant-garde thinkers and artists, from architectural polymath Buckminster Fuller to the composer John Cage to the choreographer Merce Cunningham. Though the college shut its doors to students in the mid-twentieth century, Black Mountain has remained deeply associated with countercultural values and continues to play host to yoga retreats, jam bands, and world music festivals. As one participant in these New Age trans gatherings put it in 1999: "There is something magical here, something that keeps drawing me back to this place. . . . From all over North America, people are beginning to make pilgrimages here. No one can explain it. No one can lend proof to what is happening. Only the mountains and the Goddess know for sure."[34] In other words, the vibes in these worn and ancient mountains are, at least ostensibly, very, very good. Indeed, these vibes have fueled multiple waves of development and tourism since the 1980s, resulting in a current crisis of affordable housing prompted by one of the most rapid gentrification processes in recent U.S. history.

The newsletter that emerged out of this loose agglomeration of trans and gender-variant folks with an abiding interest in New Age ritual and practice who would gather periodically in the mountains of western North Carolina was entitled *Gender Quest: The Quarterly Journal of Kindred Spirits,* and it, as well as the community that it both documented and circulated among, was largely brought into being through the efforts of trans activist Holly Boswell, who had made Asheville her home in the late 1970s. She and white trans activist Jessica Britton cofounded the Phoenix Transgender Support Group in Asheville in 1986, establishing Asheville's trans-affirming reputation, and began organizing gatherings for trans and questioning folks in 1993 with another white trans woman, Yvonne Cook-Riley, who is better known for working with the International Foundation for Gender Education and its affiliated publication, *Transgender Tapestry* (initially called *TV/TS Tapestry*), one of the longest-running trans periodicals in the United States, beginning publication in 1979 and ending in 2008.[35] They named these gatherings "Kindred Spirits" and conceptualized them as a space "dedicated to the spiritual, emotional, intellectual, and physical well-being of all transgender people."[36]

It's imperative to mention, before analyzing the publications and ephemera associated with these gatherings, that both Boswell and Cook-Riley were instrumental in the popularization of the use of the term *transgender* in the late 1980s and early 1990s. The turn away from what they understood to be the overly pathologizing language of transsexuality and its concomitant emphasis on a binary understanding of gender and, by extension, transness was an important crux of both their activist work and, as we're about to see, their spiritual practice. Oral historian and literary scholar Amanda Wray, who is based in Asheville and overseeing the LGBTQIA+ Archive of Western North Carolina, provides a synopsis of Boswell's theorization of the term, culled from her publications and media interviews as well as oral histories provided by her friends and accomplices, in a detailed posthumous account of Boswell's life work:

> In 1991, Holly published "The Transgender Alternative" in *Chrysalis* and in IFGE's *Tapestry*, which is credited as one of the earliest, feminist texts deconstructing transgender identity. Keep in mind, at this time, academic scholarship continued to present transgender experience as a disordered way of feeling gender, given the DSM's language, with most medical research focused on sex change operations as a means for helping individuals fit into a gender binary. Holly's article explains: "I shall attempt to define transgender as a viable option between crossdresser and transsexual person, which also happens to *have a firm foundation in the ancient tradition of androgyny.*" After criticizing the ways gender and sex are conflated in modern medicine, everyday speech, and in academic scholarship, Holly describes gender androgyny as a "solace" for many, and she defines transgenderism as "identifying oneself across gender lines." Stryker and other LGBTQ+ historians cite Holly's short article as trailblazing work, which Holly says was intent on enabling individuals across the nation to "speak about themselves in *a more transcendent way.*" Moving past the stigmatizations associated with transexualism or transvestism during this time period, Holly talks of an *"anciently rooted"* blossoming "that defies and transcends the fallacious linkage between biological sex and gender expression."[37]

Boswell's articulation of transgender hinges on tropes of transcendence and transhistoricism that were widespread within trans activism in the United States at this particular cultural moment, rooted in a claim that refuted phobic iterations of trans embodiment as a late-modern medical-technical construct and form of subjectivity by a countervailing insistence on trans cultural presence since time immemorial, with a periodically suppressed or submerged historical lineage that connects, as the subtitle of Leslie Feinberg's 1996 *Transgender Warriors* has it,

"Joan of Arc to Dennis Rodman."[38] To be transgender, on this account, is to be part of an ancient and sacred lineage of individuals who transcended both binary instantiations of gender as well as the naturalized linkage between biological sex and gender expression. This is the birth of the "big tent" model of transgender identity, large enough to hold Jeanne d'Arc and Dennis Rodman, and it is conceived directly through an appeal to an ostensibly sacral, transhistoric, transcultural lineage of gender transgressors.

In an early issue of *Gender Quest*, in an essay entitled "The Spirit of Transgender," Boswell clearly articulates these linkages, situating the twentieth-century resurgence of trans visibility and organizing as a corrective to the patriarchal, war-oriented cultures that ostensibly displaced "the peaceful agrarian 30,000 year old Goddess cultures throughout Europe and the Mediterranean" during the Bronze Age (roughly 3000–1200 BC), driving Goddess culture underground and precipitating "the repression and persecution of transgendered people" over the course of the last 5,000 years.[39] She writes:

> The Transgender Spirit transcends the simplistic cultural dictum that anatomical sex is synonymous with gender expression. Gender should never be polarized. It is a rainbow that is far too splendorous in its diversity. The expression of one's whole gender must be intuitive, fluid, and in a perpetual state of becoming. There can be no rules to govern how Spirit must manifest. Widespread occurrences of hermaphroditism in plants, animals, and humans provide graphic evidence of Spirit expressing its diversity beyond the cultural constructs of bipolar gender. Transgendered people embody this Goddess-spirit of diversity integrated as one whole being. The inner <u>healing</u>, which means "to make whole," that we achieve can be outwardly applied to the imbalance and distress that surrounds us. We can serve as a bridge between polarities to help restore balance, integration, and wholeness.

Some Native American elders believe that there is an abundance of transgendered people being born at this time who can help heal our world. Gender is at the very heart of who we are as human beings. Our gender transitions— the very process of gender-shift—can be viewed as a kind of Vision Quest, addressing that age-old question: <u>who are we?</u> To transcend gender stereotyping is to dare to be fully oneself, fully human, as Spirit intended. . . . We *are* deities. We *are* Spirit manifesting in human forms. Let us live that truth, and help everyone see the beauty and strength that lies *beyond* the constraints of gender. And let us give thanks for the unique opportunity to do so.[40]

There's a lot to unpack here. Let's start with the just-so story of world-historical transformation that undergirds this tale of trans repression. On this account, the possibility of undisturbed trans existence is always allied to the ascendancy of a pacific, matriarchal hegemony, and trans life will thrive only with the resurgence of Goddess culture, conceived as an antidote to the last five millennia of global, militarized patriarchal hegemony. Moreover, the increasing visibility of and organizing undertaken by trans communities is a manifestation of the rise of a world-healing shift in consciousness, so much so that "Native American elders" (presented here as an amorphous, inspecific mass, rendering Indigeneity homogeneous, painted with the broadest of comprehensible strokes) are taking notice. This positions trans folks at the forefront of spiritual evolution: transition becomes a vision quest. Trans people become deities, emissaries, and handmaidens of the New Age sent to help the world awaken to a postbinary rainbow of gender, "splendorous in its diversity." Only in this New Age of matriarchal peace will gender diversity, in all its forms, be able to truly blossom, unharried and resplendent. Until then, all trans folks are shaman figures, leading the world toward the full manifestation of the Aquarian age, in this time but not of it, belonging both to the future and to a primordial premodernity. In this account of the metaphysics of trans being, there's no room for complicity with the violence of coloniality and racial capitalism, no way to interpret trans subjectivity outside of trans-as-spiritual-revelator, demonstrating to the world that the essence of being is irreducible to gender. It's no wonder that some trans folk find this New Age narrative appealing: it spins prophecy and chosenness out of conditions of discrimination and disenfranchisement. It's also no wonder that, in the images of Kindred Spirit gatherings reproduced in *Gender Quest*, there's not a single person of color in sight.

I cite this essay of Boswell's at length because it is a paradigmatic representation of trans New Age discourse: Indigenous spiritual practices are taken out of context and rendered roughly commensurable with Western esoteric spiritualities in order to position white trans folks as shamans and healers, in a revision of the "tantric heterosexuality" outlined by Kripal.[41] In this case, rather than union with the cosmic antinomies of masculinity and femininity being sought and found in heterosexual sexual union, they are instead reconciled in the psychic and physical embodiment of trans and gender-variant subjects. Troublingly, the figure of the "hermaphrodite," a term widely understood to be misleading, anachronistic, and pejorative when used with reference to intersex subjects, is repeatedly invoked as evidence of "Spirit expressing its diversity," and trans subjects are, by extension, theorized as roughly equivalent to intersex subjects. This conflation elides the specificity of, and important differences between, trans and intersex experiences and further contributes to the exoticization and fetishization of intersex embodiments. Finally, in its consistent figuration of trans folks as deities with a special mission to heal societal and political rifts, to "serve as a bridge between polarities to help restore balance, integration, and wholeness," it partakes of the structuring logic of white viscosity, which hinges on a discourse of unity undergirded by racial transcendence and colorblindness, whereby transformative experience in white counterculture is "considered a means to *overcome* one's kind or racial formation in order to embrace all of humanity or all of the planet."[42]

Throughout the issues of *Gender Quest,* participants in these trans gatherings refer to the mountains of western North Carolina as a kind of home, a space of safety and belonging wherein they can drop their defenses and relax, a space where they are able to fully and authentically just be. One contributor writes of turning to Holly Boswell at the end of a gathering and saying, "Thanks for my second home in North Carolina."[43] Another pens a long account, entitled "A Postcard from Home," of traveling to Hot Springs for a gathering—the author rhapsodizes about "coming home to Hot Springs and nearby Asheville" where "the energy is different," where the song of the mountains "reaches across time" to remind them of the finitude of their body and the lastingness of "timeless stone and living wood."[44] It's important to ask, in the face of such assertions, to what extent these reported senses of belonging and safety are predicated on racial (and other) forms of homogeneity, and thus to what extent these positive feelings are attained through—and thus further entrench—white viscosity. Who might not feel at home in these mountains, in counties that are nearly or over 90 percent white, in a region (southern Appalachia) so often represented as monolithically white and deeply racist? To what extent does the circulation of positive and ostensibly healing affect rely on racial homogeneity and white hegemony in the guise of unity and transcendence?

I'm suspicious—and I think we should all be—of practices of transformative healing that reproduce white viscosity and rely on the elision of crucial axes of difference between trans subjects that produce very, very different life chances and outcomes. In drafting *Side Affects,* other trans folks have told me over and over how relatable a book about, as I describe it in shorthand, "being trans and feeling bad" is. But I have also had many folks ask me why I choose to dwell on negative affect rather than, say, the experience of so-called gender euphoria experienced by subjects when their correct pronouns are used or when they engage in some kind of gender-affirming activity. My answer is this: when it comes to actually ameliorating the structural conditions that produce trans precarity and exacerbate transphobia, transmisogyny, and transmisogynoir, it doesn't matter all that much how great I—a white, educationally and economically privileged trans masc—feel about how often I am correctly gendered, about the gender-affirming outfits I put on, about looking in the mirror and not recoiling or dealing with a bout of dysphoric anxiety. Though my own positive affect about such things does indeed make it a bit easier to get up in the morning, and may even serve as a kind of possibility model to other (younger or emergent) trans folks, it doesn't make the ensemble of negative affects discussed throughout *Side Affects* disappear—at either the level of the individual or the collective—and it doesn't actually offer a model of or prod to coalition. I can't just exhort others to come feel good, like I feel good; I can't pretend happiness is contagious, and I definitely can't pretend that the cultivation of happiness makes any sense at all as a political aim. If and when I feel something akin to gender euphoria, it's surprising, dependent on factors well beyond my own agency, and also somewhat predictably predicated on axes of privilege that structure my quotidian experience. Moreover, it doesn't last. Often, what we call gender euphoria is just merely a pleasant experience. Euphoria is an outsize way of describing the pleasure of recognition and affirmation, which sits right alongside all sorts of negativity, rather than supplants it; the use of *euphoria* in such instances is thus unfaithful to the actual meaning of the word, which is bliss and the concomitant absolute (though temporary) obliteration of all bad feelings. .

The literature on the production of white viscosity in psychedelic and New Age spiritual movements points out, over and over again, that when folks deliberately seek out euphoria—which travels under many names in such movements, be it ecstatic union, self-actualization, feelings of wholeness, unity, and oneness, the sense of being able to forget the self and, to quote Vanguard once more, to "be with a beautiful person in a beautiful place doing beautiful things and being beautiful"—it's all too often predicated on the reproduction of sameness, the elision and tacit elimination of difference. Conflict and tension become avoided in the name of personal healing and transformation.

This involves the out-regulation of the presence of otherness in the form of what Sara Ahmed so convincingly terms the "affect alien": the figure who disrupts the ability of others to enjoy a scene or situation by "converting good feelings into bad" by virtue of their inability, or refusal, to be made happy by that which brings other happiness.[45] If the whole point of a gathering, a series of gatherings, or a movement is to produce and sustain euphoria and self-dissolution, it's no wonder that affect aliens aren't welcome. And while I wager that most trans folks understand intimately what it means to be an affect alien in cisnormative spaces, that doesn't mean we're immune from reproducing the very same dynamics in our attempts to pursue safety, belonging, and happiness. If there's a lesson to glean from the just-so story that emerges from *Gender Quest,* it's this: any account of trans existence that positions trans subjects as single-note prophets and healers is also invested in avoiding the actual complexities of trans lives, lives that inevitably include complicity with regimes of racial and settler colonial violence, lives that are flawed, imperfect, impure, and ethically intricate. Such a narrative is underwritten by a too-quick rush to heal that produces a misleadingly simple story of what it might take to get us, collectively, to a place of flourishing. Instead, as this book suggests, we might tarry with the negative and see what resonates across complex subjective and communal terrain, see what forms of solidarity emerge from that resonance.

When the topic of intergenerational trauma comes up, as it does unsurprisingly often in our home, my long-time partner (a lover of Russian literature—the more bleak, the better) paraphrases the opening line of Tolstoy's *Anna Karenina*: all happy families are the same, they say, but every unhappy family is unhappy in its own way. What they mean by this is that happiness is not actually all that interesting: there's nothing there to process, nothing there to illuminate, nothing that's particularly mysterious, enigmatic, confusing, or complex. Happiness is *nice,* that most lukewarm of adjectives, and in its niceness, it is also banal. They're saying, in these moments, that it's alright that we'll be processing trauma for the rest of our lives; it's to be expected, and it's from and through that collective processing that we'll be most able to approximate anything close to radical transformation, anything that remotely resembles healing. The only way around it is straight through.

ACKNOWLEDGMENTS

I write this at what I'm hoping is the tail end of a devastating pandemic that has relentlessly highlighted our collective precarity and fragile interdependency, as well as made plain precisely who is insulated enough to convince themselves that they exist otherwise than through such interdependency. I write in the midst of a predictable onslaught of transantagonistic legislation that seeks to have the cumulative impact of shaming trans kids into a conviction of the impracticability of living into themselves, which is to say that is seeks to shame them into not living, or at the very least to force them to live through and with the bitter recognition that much of the world believes they are impossible. I write it in the midst of the everyday depredations of racial capitalism and the relentless, quotidian onslaught of anti-Black violence, with the knowledge that resistance to such violence need be even more intensively relentless and quotidian. I write from the expropriated lands of the Susquehannock, Muncy, Iroquois, and Shawnee peoples, lands that now host monoculture farms, football fans, and a massive university whose land grant, the second largest in U.S. history, comprised tracts belonging to over 112 tribes across the territories of 16 states. I know, intimately, that my livelihood is irrevocably rooted in this expropriation, and many others.

The withdrawal and relative isolation that accompanies writing and research was intensified by Covid-19 over the months that I completed this book, yet my awareness and overwhelming

199

gratitude for those people without whom the thinking and writing, as well as the living, would have been impossible only deepened. I'll never again take for granted the imperative and the privilege that is thinking, talking, and sharing space and air and energy with these folks. What a gift it is. And what a miracle that dialogue remained possible, and provocative, while we sheltered in place. Enormous gratitude to all those brilliant colleagues, friends, and accomplices with whom I thought over the course of drafting this thing—in rooms, on screens, or just alone with their words: Jules Gill-Peterson, Cass Adair, Aren Aizura, Cam Awkward-Rich, Talia Bettcher, P. J. DiPietro, Shireen Roshanravan, Tushabe wa Tushabe, April Petillo, Abe Weil, Emmett Harsin Drager, Grace Lavery, Andrea Pitts, David Rubin, Amanda Swarr, Ann Cvetkovich, Zena Sharman, Greg Seigworth, Nathan Snaza, Hannah Bacon, Chris Barcelos, Tuck Woodstock, Wesley Flash, Matt Mager, Elizabeth Sharp, Emily Skidmore, Michael Faris, Jack Gieseking, Eliza Steinbock, Jian Neo Chen, Mia Fischer, Susan Stryker, Jo Hsu, Josh Price, Amy Marvin, A. J. Lewis, Wendy Truran, Matthew Arthur, Jina Kim, Emma Velez, Noah Zazanis, Shelley Park, Martin Manalansan, Cecilio Cooper, Eden Kinkaid, Cáel Keegan, J. Logan Smilges, Perry Zurn, Kyla Schuller, Avery Rose Everhart, Steven Thrasher, Aimi Hamraie, Moya Bailey, McKenzie Wark, Alexis Lothian, Cindy Cruz, Wanda Alarcón, Tim Johnston, Marquis Bey, Josh Franco, Gabriela Veronelli, Desiree Valentine, Phyllis Thompson, Stacy Keltner, Jennifer Purvis, Kelly Finley, Frances Henderson, Shenée Simon, Nick Clarkson, Sharon Holland, Tiz Giordano, Stephanie Evans, and so many others.

My colleagues at Penn State have been a joy to think and plot alongside. Much love to Sam Tenorio, Erin Heidt-Forsythe, Jill Wood, Daniel Susser, Kris Grey, J. Marlena Edwards, Timothy Griffiths, Amanda Scott, Ted Toadvine, Ben Jones, Nancy Tuana, Dara Walker, Alicia Decker, Ariane Cruz, Bénédicte Monicat, Pamela VanHaitsma, Karen Keifer-Boyd, Mariana Ortega, Amira Rose Davis, Eduardo Mendieta, Jonathan Eburne, Tracy Rutler, Hester Blum, Matt Tierney, Janet Lyon, Michael Bérubé, Heather

Froehlich, Sarah Clark Miller, Melissa Wright, Lori Ginzberg, Jennifer Wagner-Lawlor, Cynthia Young, and Terri Vescio. Deep thanks to the graduate students I've had the opportunity to think closely with: Brooklyn Leo, Kris McClain, Eric John Disbro, Ryan Pilcher, Liz Schoppelrei, Lars Stoltzfus-Brown, Corinne Lajoie, Austin Gaffin, Yi-Ting Chang, Miriam Gonzales, and Mercer Gary.

So much respect and gratitude for the artists, activists, and creators I've written about here: CeCe McDonald, Cassils, Torrey Peters, Casey Plett, Kai Cheng Thom, Rupert Raj, Dallas Denny, the members of Vanguard, Lou Sullivan, Cole Ray Davis, and Robert Eads. My endless appreciation to Shawn Wilson at the Kinsey Institute and to K. J. Rawson, who has gifted us the Digital Transgender Archive. My editor at the University of Minnesota Press, Jason Weidemann, provided crucial encouragement, support, and regularly posted photos of his dog, which all aided in the drafting of this thing in their own crucial ways.

This book is for the sprawling multispecies fam: Jocelyne, Suzie, Dawson, Stephen, Khren, Jackson, Tobias, Gabriel, Ryan, James, Jim, Leo, Oshi, Simmy, Pinot, Capote, Howie, Bear, Sweet Pea, and so many other lovely critters I'm lucky enough to share life space with. For Lib, for always. For María Lugones, who left us too soon, and left an immeasurable wealth of knowledge, love, and fuel for resistance in her wake. For trans folks, in all our complexity, with all the rough edges.

NOTES

INTRODUCTION

1. Andrea Long Chu, "My New Vagina Won't Make Me Happy," *New York Times*, November 24, 2018.
2. Chu, "My New Vagina."
3. Daniel Stern, *The Interpersonal World of the Infant: A View from Psychoanalysis and Developmental Psychology* (New York: Basic Books, 2000), 138.
4. Kathleen Stewart, *Ordinary Affects* (Durham, N.C.: Duke University Press, 2007), 2.
5. Stewart, *Ordinary Affects*, 3.
6. Ann Cvetkovich, "Public Feelings," *South Atlantic Quarterly* 106, no. 3 (2007): 464.
7. Cvetkovich, "Public Feelings," 464.
8. Cvetkovich, 464.
9. Raymond Williams, *Marxism and Literature* (New York: Oxford University Press, 1977), 128.
10. Hil Malatino, *Queer Embodiment: Monstrosity, Medical Violence, and Intersex Experience* (Lincoln: University of Nebraska Press, 2019), 111.
11. Adam Frank and Elizabeth Wilson, *A Silvan Tomkins Handbook: Foundations for Affect Theory* (Minneapolis: University of Minnesota Press, 2020), 63.
12. Eric Stanley, "The Affective Commons: Gay Shame, Queer Hate, and Other Collective Feelings," *GLQ: A Journal of Lesbian and Gay Studies* 24, no. 4 (2018): 490.
13. Lauren Berlant and Jordan Greenwald, "Affect in the End Times: A Conversation with Lauren Berlant," *Qui Parle* 20, no. 2 (2012): 77.
14. Stanley, "Affective Commons," 491.

15. Stanley, 489.
16. Stanley, 490.
17. Stanley, 503.
18. Brian Massumi, *Parables for the Virtual: Movement, Affect, Sensation* (Durham, N.C.: Duke University Press, 2002), 28.
19. John Protevi, *Political Affect: Connecting the Social and the Somatic* (Minneapolis: University of Minnesota Press, 2009), 49, 51.
20. Gilles Deleuze, *Expressionism in Philosophy: Spinoza* (New York: Zone Books, 1990), 242.
21. Lauren Berlant, *Cruel Optimism* (Durham, N.C.: Duke University Press, 2011).
22. Lauren Berlant, "Structures of Unfeeling: *Mysterious Skin*," *International Journal of Politics, Culture, and Society* 28, no. 3 (2015): 191–213.
23. Gayle Salamon, *Assuming a Body: Transgender and Rhetorics of Materiality* (New York: Columbia University Press, 2010).
24. Sianne Ngai, *Ugly Feelings* (Cambridge, Mass.: Harvard University Press, 2005), 126.
25. Lou Sullivan, *We Both Laughed in Pleasure: The Selected Diaries of Lou Sullivan, 1961–1991,* ed. Ellis Martin and Zach Ozma (New York: Nightboat Press, 2019); and Paul Preciado, *Testo-Junkie: Sex, Drugs, and Biopolitics in the Pharmacopornographic Era* (New York: Feminist Press, 2013).
26. Sara Ahmed, *Living a Feminist Life* (Durham, N.C.: Duke University Press, 2017); Sara Ahmed, *The Promise of Happiness* (Durham, N.C.: Duke University Press, 2010); María Lugones, *Pilgramages/peregrinajes* (Lanham, Md.: Rowman and Littlefield, 2003); Judith Butler, *Senses of the Subject* (New York: Fordham University Press, 2015); and Susan Stryker, "My Words to Victor Frankenstein above the Village of Chamounix," *GLQ* 1, no. 1 (1994): 237–54.
27. Hil Malatino, *Trans Care* (Minneapolis: University of Minnesota Press, 2020).
28. Arun Saldanha, *Psychedelic White: Goa Trance and the Viscosity of Race* (Minneapolis: University of Minnesota Press, 2007), 50; and Amanda J. Lucia, *White Utopias: The Religious Exoticism of Transformational Festivals* (Oakland: University of California Press, 2020), 12.

1. FUTURE FATIGUE

1. Lauren Berlant, *Cruel Optimism* (Durham, N.C.: Duke University Press, 2011).

2. Tobias Raun, "Archiving the Wonders of Testosterone via YouTube," *TSQ* 2, no. 4 (2015): 701–9; and Laura Horak, "Trans on YouTube: Intimacy, Visibility, Temporality," *TSQ* 1, no. 4 (2014): 572–85.

3. Jasbir Puar, "In the Wake of It Gets Better," *Guardian,* November 16, 2010, https://www.theguardian.com/commentisfree/cifamerica/2010/nov/16/wake-it-gets-better-campaign.

4. Raun, "Archiving the Wonders of Testosterone," 702–3.

5. Raun, 704.

6. Raun, 705–6.

7. Raun, 707.

8. J. F. Miller, "YouTube as a Site of Counternarratives to Transnormativity," *Journal of Homosexuality* 66, no. 6 (2019): 7–8.

9. Miller, "YouTube as a Site of Counternarratives," 8.

10. Miller, 5.

11. Sandy Stone, "The *Empire* Strikes Back: A Posttranssexual Manifesto," in *Body Guards: The Cultural Politics of Gender Ambiguity,* ed. Julia Epstein and Kristina Straub, 280–304 (New York: Routledge, 1991); Dean Spade, "Resisting Medicine, Remodeling Gender," *Berkeley Women's Law Journal* 15 (2003): 15–37; Julian Carter, "Embracing Transition, or Dancing in the Folds of Time," in *The Transgender Studies Reader 2,* ed. Aren Aizura and Susan Stryker, 130–44 (New York: Routledge, 2013); Jules Gill-Peterson, "Implanting Plasticity into Sex and Trans/Gender," *Angelaki* 22, no. 4 (2017): 47–60; and C. Riley Snorton, *Black on Both Sides* (Minneapolis: University of Minnesota Press, 2017).

12. Eric Stanley, "Near Life, Queer Death: Overkill and Ontological Capture," *Social Text* 29, no. 2 (2011): 15.

13. Horak, "Trans on YouTube," 580.

14. Horak, 581.

15. Lee Edelman, *No Future* (Durham, N.C.: Duke University Press, 2004).

16. Horak, "Trans on YouTube," 580.

17. Berlant, *Cruel Optimism,* 26.

18. Gayle Salamon, *Assuming a Body* (New York: Columbia University Press, 2010), 62.

19. Salamon, *Assuming a Body,* 62.

20. Gilles Deleuze and Félix Guattari, *A Thousand Plateaus* (Minneapolis: University of Minnesota Press, 1987). For its use in trans studies, see, for instance, Lucas Cassidy Crawford, "Transgender without Organs? Mobilizing a Geo-affective Theory of Gender Modification," *Women's Studies Quarterly* 36, nos. 3–4 (2008): 133; and Nikki Sullivan, "Transmogrification: (Un)Becoming Other(s),"

in *The Transgender Studies Reader,* ed. Susan Stryker and Stephen Whittle (New York: Routledge, 2006): 560–61.

21. Todd May, "When Is a Deleuzian Becoming?," *Continental Philosophy Review* 36, no. 2 (2003): 150.

22. Susan Stryker, Paisley Currah, and Lisa Jean Moore, "Introduction: Trans, Trans-, or Transgender?," *Women's Studies Quarterly* 36, nos. 3–4 (2008): 12.

23. Stryker, Currah, and Moore, "Introduction," 13.

24. Heather Love, *Feeling Backward* (Cambridge, Mass.: Harvard University Press, 2009), 9.

25. Carter, "Embracing Transition," 142.

26. Carter, 142.

27. Gwen Benaway, "A Body Like a Home," *Hazlitt,* May 30, 2018, https://hazlitt.net/longreads/body-home.

28. Benaway, "Body Like a Home."

29. Atalia Israeli-Nevo, "Taking (My) Time: Temporality in Transition, Queer Delays, and Being (in the) Present," *Somatechnics* 7, no. 1 (2017): 38.

30. Kai Cheng Thom, *Fierce Femmes and Notorious Liars: A Dangerous Trans Girl's Confabulous Memoir* (Montreal: Metonymy Press, 2018); and Torrey Peters, *Infect Your Friends and Loved Ones* (self-pub., 2017).

31. Thom, *Fierce Femmes and Notorious Liars,* 20.

32. Thom, 21.

33. Thom, 40.

34. Thom, 40.

35. Alexis Lothian, "A Speculative History of No Future: Feminist Negativity and the Queer Dystopian Impulses of Katharine Burdekin's *Swastika Night,*" *Poetics Today* 37, no. 3 (2016): 448.

36. Walidah Imarisha, Adrienne M. Brown, and Sheree R. Thomas, *Octavia's Brood: Science Fiction Stories from Social Justice Movements* (Oakland, Calif.: AK Press, 2015), 10.

37. Britni de la Cretaz, "Author Kai Cheng Thom on Writing a New Kind of Transgender Memoir," *Teen Vogue,* April 5, 2017, https://www.teenvogue.com/story/author-kai-cheng-thom-on-writing-a-new-kind-of-transgender-memoir.

38. Thom, *Fierce Femmes and Notorious Liars,* 2–3.

39. Michel Foucault, *Society Must Be Defended: Lectures at the Collège de France, 1975–1976* (New York: Picador, 2003), 239.

40. Thom, *Fierce Femmes and Notorious Liars,* 178.

41. Thom, 178–79.

42. Thom, 179–80.

43. Berlant, *Cruel Optimism*, 262.
44. Susan Stryker, "Transgender History, Homonormativity, and Disciplinarity," *Radical History Review* 100 (2008): 148.
45. John Money and Margaret Lamacz, "Gynemimesis and Gynemimetophilia: Individual and Cross-Cultural Manifestations of a Gender-Coping Strategy Hitherto Unnamed," *Comparative Psychiatry* 25, no. 4 (1984); and J. Michael Bailey, *The Man Who Would Be Queen* (Washington, D.C.: Joseph Henry Press, 2003).
46. Stryker, "Transgender History," 148.
47. Talia Mae Bettcher, "Evil Deceivers and Make-Believers: On Transphobic Violence and the Politics of Illusion," *Hypatia* 22, no. 3 (2007): 43–65.
48. Chela Sandoval, *Methodology of the Oppressed* (Minneapolis: University of Minnesota Press, 2000), 57.
49. *Tongues Untied,* directed by Marlon Riggs (San Francisco: 1989); and Radicalesbians, "The Woman-Identified Woman" (Know, Inc.: 1970).
50. Peters, *Infect Your Friends,* 25.
51. Peters, 28.
52. Peters, 28.
53. Paul Preciado, *Testo-Junkie* (New York: Feminist Press, 2013); and Jack Halberstam, "F2M: The Making of Female Masculinity," in *The Lesbian Postmodern,* ed. Laura Doan (New York: Columbia University Press, 1994), 226.
54. Peters, *Infect Your Friends,* 52.
55. Peters, 54.
56. Peters, 54.
57. Peters, 54.
58. Eve Kosofsky Sedgwick, *Epistemology of the Closet* (Berkeley: University of California Press, 1990).

2. FUCK FEELINGS

1. Sara Ahmed, *Queer Phenomenology* (Durham, N.C.: Duke University Press, 2006), 156.
2. Ahmed, *Queer Phenomenology,* 156.
3. Ahmed, 157.
4. Ahmed, 157.
5. Ahmed, 158.
6. Ahmed, 158.
7. Alice Dreger, "What to Expect When You Have the Child You Weren't Expecting," in *Surgically Shaping Children: Technology,*

Ethics, and the Pursuit of Normality, ed. Erik Parens, 253–66 (Baltimore: Johns Hopkins University Press, 2006).

8. María Lugones, *Pilgrimages/Peregrinajes* (Lanham, Md.: Rowman and Littlefield, 2003), 77.

9. Ahmed, *Queer Phenomenology,* 159.

10. Lauren Berlant, "Structures of Unfeeling: *Mysterious Skin,*" *International Journal of Politics, Culture, and Society* 28, no. 3 (2015): 194.

11. Berlant, "Structures of Unfeeling," 194.

12. Berlant, 193.

13. Berlant, 193.

14. Berlant, 195.

15. *Southern Comfort,* directed by Kate Davis (Q-Ball Productions, 2001), DVD.

16. *Deep Run,* directed by Hillevi Loven (New York: Women Make Movies, 2015), DVD.

17. Berlant, "Structures of Unfeeling," 210.

18. Casey Plett, *Little Fish* (Vancouver, B.C.: Arsenal Pulp Press, 2018).

19. Plett, *Little Fish,* 11.

20. Plett, 12.

21. Plett, 103, 204, 141.

22. Plett, 186.

23. Plett, 89.

24. Tom Roberts, "Feeling Nothing: Numbness and Emotional Absence," *European Journal of Philosophy* 27, no. 1 (2019): 189.

25. Roberts, "Feeling Nothing," 187.

26. Roberts, 190.

27. Plett, *Little Fish,* 70, 58, 119, 192, 199.

28. Plett, 49.

29. William Horn, "Making Your Own Choices: An Interview with Casey Plett," *Columbia Journal,* July 25, 2018, http://columbiajournal.org/casey-plett-making-your-choices-an-interview/.

30. Plett, *Little Fish,* 212.

31. Plett, 213.

32. Plett, 213.

33. Plett, 216.

34. Maurice Merleau-Ponty, *Phenomenology of Perception* (New York: Routledge, 1962).

35. Gail Weiss, *Body Images* (New York: Routledge, 1999), 17.

36. Gayle Salamon, *Assuming a Body* (New York: Columbia University Press, 2010), 62.

37. Plett, *Little Fish,* 218.

38. Plett, 218, 219.

39. Weiss, *Body Images,* 13.
40. Plett, *Little Fish,* 227.
41. Plett, 229.
42. Leonore F. Carpenter and R. Barrett Marshall, "Walking While Trans: Profiling of Transgender Women by Law Enforcement, and the Problem of Proof," *William & Mary Journal of Women and the Law* 24, no. 1 (2017): 6.
43. Salamon, *Assuming a Body,* 32.
44. Salamon, 32.

3. FOUND WANTING

1. Lou Sullivan, *We Both Laughed in Pleasure: The Selected Diaries of Lou Sullivan, 1961–1991,* ed. Ellis Martin and Zach Ozma (New York: Nightboat Press, 2019), 25.
2. Sullivan, *We Both Laughed in Pleasure,* 45.
3. Sullivan, 93.
4. Carter Sickels, "Finding a More Tender, Queer Masculinity in 'The Outsiders,'" *Catapult,* June 24, 2020, https://catapult.co/stories/finding-a-more-tender-queer-masculinity-in-the-outsiders-journey-transgender-masculinity-ralph-macchio-carter-sickels.
5. Amos Mac and Rocco Kayiatos, *Original Plumbing: The Best of Ten Years of Trans Male Culture* (New York: Feminist Press, 2019), xv.
6. *Oxford English Dictionary Online,* 3rd ed. (2007), s.v. "envy," http://www.oed.com/.
7. *Oxford English Dictionary Online,* s.v. "envy."
8. Sianna Ngai, *Ugly Feelings* (Cambridge, Mass.: Harvard University Press, 2004), 126.
9. Ngai, *Ugly Feelings,* 128, 127, 129.
10. Ngai, 129.
11. Mari Ruti, *Penis Envy and Other Bad Feelings* (New York: Columbia University Press), ix.
12. Noah Zazanis, "On Hating Men (and Becoming One Anyway)," *New Inquiry,* December 24, 2019, https://thenewinquiry.com/on-hating-men-and-becoming-one-anyway/.
13. Zazanis, "On Hating Men."
14. Cam Awkward-Rich, "Trans, Feminism: Or, Reading Like a Depressed Transsexual," *Signs* 42, no. 4 (2017).
15. Salamon, *Assuming a Body,* 122; and Janet Halley, *Split Decisions: How and Why to Take a Break from Feminism* (Princeton, N.J.: Princeton University Press, 2006), 262, 273.

16. Bobby Noble, *Sons of the Movement: FtMs Risking Incoherence on a Post-Queer Cultural Landscape* (Toronto: Women's Press, 2006).

17. Thomas Page McBee, *Man Alive* (San Francisco: City Lights, 2014); and *Amateur: A Reckoning with Gender, Identity, and Masculinity* (New York: Scribner, 2018).

18. Zazanis, "On Hating Men."

19. Awkward-Rich, "Trans, Feminism," 831, 834–35.

20. Jack Halberstam, *In a Queer Time and Place: Transgender Bodies, Subcultural Lives* (New York: New York University Press, 2004), 179.

21. Sassafras Lowrey, *Lost Boi* (Vancouver, B.C.: Arsenal Pulp Press, 2015), 1.

22. Awkward-Rich, "Trans, Feminism," 835.

23. Virginie Despentes, *Baise-Moi* (New York: Grove Press, 2007).

24. Paul Preciado, *Testo Junkie: Sex, Drugs, and Biopolitics in the Pharmacopornographic Era* (New York: Feminist Press, 2013), 90.

25. Preciado, *Testo Junkie*, 90.

26. Preciado, 98.

27. Preciado, 34–35.

28. Preciado, 94.

29. Preciado, 91.

30. Jordy Rosenberg, "The Daddy Dialectic," *LA Review of Books*, March 11, 2018, https://lareviewofbooks.org/article/the-daddy-dialectic/.

31. Rosenberg, "Daddy Dialectic."

32. Jamison Green, *Becoming a Visible Man* (Nashville, Tenn.: Vanderbilt University Press, 2004); Jennifer Finney Boylan, "The Trans Memoir Comes of Age," *New York Times*, June 13, 2017, https://www.nytimes.com/2017/06/13/books/review/critics-take-queer-writing.html; and *Becoming Chaz*, directed by Fenton Bailey and Randy Barbato (World of Wonder Productions, 2011), DVD.

33. T. Garner, "Becoming," *TSQ* 1, no. 1–2 (2014): 30–32.

34. Gilles Deleuze and Félix Guattari, *A Thousand Plateaus* (Minneapolis: University of Minnesota Press, 1987), 238.

35. Ngai, *Ugly Feelings*, 162.

36. Melanie Klein, *Envy and Gratitude and Other Works, 1946–1963* (London: Virago Press, 1988), 193.

37. Klein, *Envy and Gratitude*, 193.

38. María Lugones, *Pilgrimages/Peregrinajes* (Lanham, Md.: Rowman and Littlefield, 2003), 151.

39. Lugones, *Pilgrimages/Peregrinajes*, 152, 151.

40. Lugones, 160, 154.

41. Lugones, 160.

42. Lugones, 152–53.

43. Kalvin Garrah, "Why Buck Angel Threatened Me (But Now We're Good)," December 20, 2018, YouTube video, 8:43, https://youtu.be/aAo8zRNmwgU.

44. A. Finn Enke, "The Education of Little Cis," in *The Transgender Studies Reader 2,* ed. Aren Aizura and Susan Stryker (New York: Routledge, 2013), 242.

45. Enke, "Education of Little Cis," 244.

4. TOUGH BREAKS

1. Antonio Pascual-Leone, Phoenix Gilles, Terence Singh, and Cristina Andreescu, "Problem Anger in Psychotherapy: An Emotion-Focused Perspective on Hate, Rage, and Rejecting Anger," *Journal of Contemporary Psychotherapy* 43 (2013): 83–92; and George Eifert and John Forsyth, "The Application of Acceptance and Commitment Therapy to Problem Anger," *Cognitive and Behavioral Therapy* 18, no. 2 (2011): 241–50.

2. For a paradigmatic example, see Bonnie Berry, *Social Rage* (New York: Routledge, 1999).

3. Sara Ahmed unpacks the concept of "orienting affects" in both *Queer Phenomenology* (Durham, N.C.: Duke University Press, 2006) and *The Promise of Happiness* (Durham, N.C.: Duke University Press, 2010).

4. María Lugones, *Pilgramages/peregrinajes* (Lanham, Md.: Rowman and Littlefield, 2003), 103.

5. Ahmed, *Promise of Happiness,* 45.

6. Ahmed, 45.

7. Ahmed, 49.

8. Judith Butler, *Undoing Gender* (New York: Routledge, 2004).

9. Ahmed, *Promise of Happiness,* 97.

10. Judith Butler, *Sense of the Subject* (New York: Fordham University Press, 2015), 97.

11. Butler, *Sense of the Subject,* 67.

12. Butler, 67.

13. Jay McNeil, Sonya J. Ellis, and Fiona J. R. Eccles, "Suicide in Trans Populations: A Systemic Review of Prevalence and Correlates," *Psychology of Sexual Orientation and Gender Diversity* 4, no. 3 (2017): 341–42.

14. Chérie Moody and Nathan Grant Smith, "Suicide Protective Factors among Trans Adults," *Archives of Sexual Behavior* 42, no. 5 (2013): 740.

15. Moody and Smith, "Suicide Protective Factors," 741.
16. Butler, *Sense of the Subject*, 67.
17. Gilles Deleuze, *Expressionism in Philosophy: Spinoza* (New York: Zone Books, 1990), 242.
18. Butler, *Sense of the Subject*, 9–10.
19. Teresa Brennan, *The Transmission of Affect* (Ithaca, N.Y.: Cornell University Press, 2004), 3; and Claudia Card, *Lesbian Choices* (New York: Columbia University Press, 1995).
20. Eve Kosofsky Sedgwick, *Epistemology of the Closet* (Berkeley: University of California Press, 1990), 23.
21. Lugones, *Pilgramages/peregrinajes*, 103.
22. Susan Stryker, "My Words to Victor Frankenstein above the Village of Chamounix," *GLQ* 1, no. 3 (1994): 237–54.
23. Gloria Anzaldúa, *Borderlands/la frontera* (San Francisco: Aunt Lute Books, 2012); and Lugones, *Pilgramages/peregrinajes*.
24. Lugones, *Pilgramages/peregrinajes*.
25. Brennan, *Transmission of Affect*, 3.
26. John Protevi, *Political Affect* (Minneapolis: University of Minnesota Press, 2009), 33.
27. Protevi, *Political Affect*, 35.
28. Lugones, *Pilgramages/peregrinajes*, 117.
29. Human Rights Campaign and the Trans People of Color Coalition, *A Time to Act: Fatal Violence against Transgender People in America in 2017* (Human Rights Campaign Foundation, 2017), 4.
30. Cece McDonald, "Go beyond Our Natural Selves: Letters from the Minnesota Correctional Facility—St. Cloud," *TSQ: Transgender Studies Quarterly* 4, no. 2 (2017): 243.
31. McDonald, "Go beyond Our Natural Selves," 258.
32. McDonald, 258 (emphasis added).
33. James C. Scott, *Domination and the Arts of Resistance* (New Haven, Conn.: Yale University Press, 1990), 183.
34. Scott, *Domination and the Arts of Resistance*, 184.
35. Nel Noddings, *Starting at Home* (Berkeley: University of California Press, 2002); and Fiona Robinson, *Globalizing Care* (Boulder, Colo.: Westview Press, 1999).
36. Beth Richie, *Arrested Justice* (New York: New York University Press, 2012), 12.
37. *Check It,* directed by Dana Flor and Toby Oppenheimer (Macro Pictures, 2017).
38. Sarah Schulman, *Conflict Is Not Abuse: Overstating Harm, Community Responsibility, and the Duty of Repair* (Vancouver, B.C.: Arsenal Pulp Press, 2016), 280.

39. Schulman, *Conflict Is Not Abuse,* 31.
40. Butler, *Sense of the Subject,* 63.
41. Butler, 89.
42. Audre Lorde, *Sister Outsider* (Trumansburg, N.Y.: Crossing Press, 1984), 128.
43. Lorde, *Sister Outsider,* 127.
44. Lorde, 131.
45. Lorde, 130, 131.
46. Kenta Asakura, "Paving Pathways through the Pain: A Grounded Theory of Resilience among Lesbian, Gay, Bisexual, Trans, and Queer Youth," *Journal of Research on Adolescence* 27, no. 3 (2016): 521.
47. Stryker, "My Words to Victor Frankenstein," 249.
48. Harlan Weaver, "Monster Trans: Diffracting Affect, Reading Rage," *Somatechnics* 3, no. 2 (2013): 302.
49. Kelly Oliver, "Witnessing and Testimony," *Parallax* 10, no. 1 (2010): 82.
50. McDonald, "Go beyond Our Natural Selves," 255.
51. Sara Ahmed, *Living a Feminist Life* (Durham, N.C.: Duke University Press, 2017), 234.
52. Ahmed, *Living a Feminist Life,* 234.
53. Ahmed, *Living a Feminist Life,* 234.
54. Cassils, "Becoming an Image," February 13, 2013, YouTube video, 2:03, https://www.youtube.com/watch?v=TzM8GTL2WGo.
55. Kevin Coffey, "'Omaha Is Lucky to Have [Her]'—After Homelessness and Prison, R & B Singer Became an Advocate for Others," *Omaha World-Herald,* November 7, 2016, http://www.omaha.com/living/omaha-is-lucky-to-have-him-after-homelessness-and-prison/article_d34851bf-e416-57c5-babf-0e438d50698b.html.
56. Karen Emenhiser-Harris, "A 1,900-Pound Sculpture Pushed through the Streets of Omaha, in Tribute to Its LGBTQ History," *Hyperallergic,* May 5, 2017, https://hyperallergic.com/377494/.
57. Susan Stryker, "Opening Remarks," Trans*Studies: An International Transdisciplinary Conference on Gender, Embodiment, and Sexuality, Tucson, Ariz., September 2016.

5. BEYOND BURNOUT

1. Anne Helen Petersen, *Can't Even: How Millenials Became the Burnout Generation* (Boston: Houghton Mifflin Harcourt, 2020), xvi.
2. Petersen, *Can't Even,* xvi.
3. David E. Smith, "The Free Clinic Movement in the United States:

A Ten-Year Perspective (1966–1976)," *Journal of Drug Issues* 6, no. 4 (1976): 344.

4. Matthew Hoffarth, "The Making of Burnout: From Social Change to Self-Awareness in the Postwar United States, 1970–82," *History of the Human Sciences* 30, no. 5 (2017): 32.

5. Hoffarth, "Making of Burnout," 35.

6. Christina Maslach, *Burnout: The Cost of Caring* (Englewood Cliffs, N.J.: Prentice-Hall, 1982), 4.

7. Joanne Meyerowitz, *How Sex Changed: A History of Transsexuality in the United States* (Cambridge, Mass.: Harvard University Press, 2002), 222.

8. Meyerowitz, *How Sex Changed,* 256.

9. Adele E. Clark, Laura Mamo, Jennifer Ruth Fosket, Jennifer R. Fishman, and Janet K. Shim, "Biomedicalization: A Theoretical and Substantive Introduction," in *Biomedicalization: Technoscience, Health, and Illness in the U.S.,* ed. Adele E. Clarke, Laura Mamo, Jennifer Ruth Fosket, Jennifer R. Fishman, and Janet K. Shim, 1–46 (Durham, N.C.: Duke University Press, 2010), 2.

10. Adele E. Clark, Laura Mamo, Jennifer Ruth Fosket, Jennifer R. Fishman, and Janet K. Shim, "Biomedicalization: Technoscientific Transformations of Health, Ilness, and U.S. Biomedicine," in Clarke et al., *Biomedicalization,* 58.

11. Correspondence from Alice Webb to prospective patient, 21 June 1989, box II, series IV, folder 1, Harry Benjamin International Gender Dysphoria Association Archives, Kinsey Institute for Research in Sex, Gender, and Reproduction, Inc., Indiana University, Bloomington, Indiana.

12. Correspondence from Alice Webb to prospective patient, 3 May 1986, box II, series IV, folder 1, Harry Benjamin International Gender Dysphoria Association Archives, Kinsey Institute for Research in Sex, Gender, and Reproduction, Inc., Indiana University, Bloomington, Indiana.

13. David Valentine, *Imagining Transgender: An Ethnography of a Category* (Durham, N.C.: Duke University Press, 2007), 21 (emphasis added).

14. Valentine, *Imagining Transgender,* 107.

15. Miranda Joseph, *Against the Romance of Community* (Minneapolis: University of Minnesota Press, 2002), 5.

16. Moya Bailey, "New Terms of Resistance: A Response to Zenzele Isoke," *Souls,* 15, no. 4 (2014): 341.

17. Dean Spade, "Resisting Medicine, Re/modeling Gender," *Berkeley Women's Law Journal* 15 (2003): 23.

18. Rupert Raj, Moving Trans History Forward Conference, Victoria, British Columbia, 2016.

19. Rupert Raj, *Metamorphosis Magazine* 6, no. 3 (1987): 3, Digital Transgender Archive, https://www.digitaltransgenderarchive.net/files/m326m182n.

20. Raj, *Metamorphosis Magazine*.

21. Dallas Denny, *Chrysalis Quarterly* 1, no. 1 (Spring 1991): 2, Digital Transgender Archive, https://www.digitaltransgenderarchive.net/files/6682x392q.

22. Photocopy of page from *FTM International Newsletter*, Fall 1995, sent to Alice Webb, box 1, series III, folder 1, Harry Benjamin International Gender Dysphoria Association Archives, Kinsey Institute for Research in Sex, Gender, and Reproduction, Inc., Indiana University, Bloomington, Indiana.

23. Photocopy of page 18 from *TV/TS Tapestry* 69 (Fall 1994), sent to Alice Webb, box 1, series III, folder 1, Harry Benjamin International Gender Dysphoria Association Archives, Kinsey Institute for Research in Sex, Gender, and Reproduction, Inc., Indiana University, Bloomington, Indiana.

24. Sharon Satterfield to Alice Webb, 15 December 1994, box 1, series III, folder 1, Harry Benjamin International Gender Dysphoria Association Archives, Kinsey Institute for Research in Sex, Gender, and Reproduction, Inc., Indiana University, Bloomington, Indiana.

25. Dallas Denny to Rupert Raj, 9 August 1994, box 1, series III, folder 1, Harry Benjamin International Gender Dysphoria Association Archives, Kinsey Institute for Research in Sex, Gender, and Reproduction, Inc., Indiana University, Bloomington, Indiana.

26. Walter Bockting to Alice Webb, 30 January 1995, box 1, series III, folder 1, Harry Benjamin International Gender Dysphoria Association Archives, Kinsey Institute for Research in Sex, Gender, and Reproduction, Inc., Indiana University, Bloomington, Indiana (emphasis added).

27. Adele Clarke, "From the Rise of Medicine to Biomedicalization: U.S. Healthscapes and Iconography, circa 1890–Present," in Clarke et al., *Biomedicalization*, 105.

28. Dallas Denny, *Chrysalis Quarterly* 1, no. 1 (Spring 1991): 2, Digital Transgender Archive, https://www.digitaltransgenderarchive.net/files/wh246s128.

29. Denny, *Chrysalis Quarterly*, 5.

30. Denny, 5.

31. Dallas Denny, *Chrysalis Quarterly* 1, no. 2 (Summer 1991): 13, Digital

Transgender Archive, https://www.digitaltransgenderarchive.net/files/wh246s128.

32. Denny, *Chrysalis Quarterly*, 3.
33. Denny, 13.
34. Denny, 13.
35. Lauren Berlant, *Cruel Optimism* (Durham, N.C.: Duke University Press, 2011), 199.
36. Berlant, 199.
37. Berlant, 199.
38. Berlant, 199.

6. AFTER NEGATIVITY?

1. Ann Cvetkovich, *Depression: A Public Feeling* (Durham, N.C.: Duke University Press, 2012), 15.
2. Cvetkovich, *Depression*, 15.
3. Joanne Meyerowitz, *How Sex Changed: A History of Transsexuality in the United States* (Cambridge, Mass.: Harvard University Press, 2002).
4. Review of *The Homosexual Revolution,* by R. E. L. Masters, *Kirkus Reviews,* May 1, 1962.
5. Robert Masters to Harry Benjamin, 7 February 1962, box 9, series IIe, folder 9, Harry Benjamin Archives, Kinsey Institute for Research in Sex, Gender, and Reproduction, Inc., Indiana University, Bloomington, Indiana.
6. Masters to Benjamin, 7 February 1962.
7. Robert Masters to Harry Benjamin, 28 May 1967, box 9, series IIe, folder 9, Harry Benjamin Archives, Kinsey Institute for Research in Sex, Gender, and Reproduction, Inc., Indiana University, Bloomington, Indiana.
8. Masters to Benjamin, 28 May 1967.
9. Katherine Bonson, "Regulation of Human Research with LSD in the United States (1949–1987)," *Psychopharmacology* 235, no. 2 (2018): 593.
10. Bonson, "Regulation of Human Research with LSD," 593.
11. Jeffrey J. Kripal, *Esalen: America and the Religion of No Religion* (Chicago: University of Chicago Press, 2007), 227.
12. Kripal, *Esalen*, 221.
13. Leary organized a series of summer retreats to Zihuatanejo, Mexico, in the early 1960s for the purposes of psychedelic research.
14. "Timothy Leary," in *Playboy Interviews* (Chicago: Playboy Press, 1967), 138–39.

15. "Timothy Leary," 134.
16. Judith Butler, *Gender Trouble: Feminism and the Subversion of Identity* (New York: Routledge, 1990), 45.
17. Robert Masters, "Bookmarks," *Dromenon: A Journal of New Ways of Being* 2, no. 2 (1979): 34.
18. Jules Gill-Peterson, *Histories of the Transgender Child* (Minneapolis: University of Minnesota Press, 2018), 51.
19. Gill-Peterson, *Histories of the Transgender Child,* 51.
20. Gill-Peterson, 51.
21. Robert Masters to Harry Benjamin, 21 August 1965, box 9, series IIe, folder 9, Harry Benjamin Archives, Kinsey Institute for Research in Sex, Gender, and Reproduction, Inc., Indiana University, Bloomington, Indiana.
22. Harry Benjamin to Robert Masters, 26 August 1965, box 9, series IIe, folder 9, Harry Benjamin Archives, Kinsey Institute for Research in Sex, Gender, and Reproduction, Inc., Indiana University, Bloomington, Indiana.
23. Christina Hanhardt, *Safe Space: Gay Neighborhood History and the Politics of Violence* (Durham, N.C.: Duke University Press, 2013), 73.
24. Susan Stryker, *Transgender History: The Roots of Today's Revolution* (New York: Seal Press, 2017), 95.
25. Stryker, *Transgender History,* 96.
26. *Vanguard Magazine* 1, no. 7 (May 1967), Digital Transgender Archive, https://www.digitaltransgenderarchive.net/files/3r074t94h.
27. Ram Dass, *Be Here Now* (San Cristobal, N.M.: Lama Publishing, 1971).
28. Simeon Wade, *Foucault in California* (Berkeley, Calif.: Heyday Press, 2019), 62.
29. Michael Pollan, *How to Change Your Mind* (New York: Penguin, 2018), 41.
30. Pollan, *How to Change Your Mind,* 42.
31. Arun Saldanha, *Psychedelic White: Goa Trance and the Viscosity of Race* (Minneapolis: University of Minnesota Press, 2007), 50.
32. Saldanha, *Psychedelic White,* 198.
33. Amanda J. Lucia, *White Utopias: The Religious Exoticism of Transformational Festivals* (Oakland: University of California Press, 2020), 12.
34. *Gender Quest* (Summer 1999), Digital Transgender Archive, https://www.digitaltransgenderarchive.net/files/ft848q60n.
35. Amanda Wray, "Holly Boswell: Asheville's Social Justice Warrior, Voices from the LGBTQIA+ Archive of Western North Carolina," *Journal of Appalachian Studies* 26, no. 2 (2020): 180.

36. *Gender Quest* (Autumn 1998), Digital Transgender Archive, https://www.digitaltransgenderarchive.net/files/0c483j37r.

37. Amanda Wray, "Holly Boswell: Asheville's Social Justice Warrior, Voices from the LGBTQIA+ Archive of Western North Carolina," *Journal of Appalachian Studies* 26, no. 2 (2020): 182 (emphasis added).

38. Leslie Feinberg, *Transgender Warriors: Making History from Joan of Arc to Dennis Rodman* (Boston: Beacon Press, 1997).

39. *Gender Quest* (Summer 1998), Digital Transgender Archive, https://www.digitaltransgenderarchive.net/files/0c483j37r.

40. *Gender Quest* (Summer 1998).

41. Kripal, *Esalen*, 110–11.

42. Saldanha, *Psychedelic White*, 72.

43. *Gender Quest* (Summer 2000), Digital Transgender Archive, https://www.digitaltransgenderarchive.net/files/1r66j1131.

44. *Gender Quest* (Summer 1999), Digital Transgender Archive, https://www.digitaltransgenderarchive.net/files/ft848q60n.

45. Sara Ahmed, *The Promise of Happiness* (Durham, N.C.: Duke University Press, 2010), 49.

INDEX

absence, emotional, 66–67

access to health care, 21; activism for, 154; patient-consumer model of, 141; to trans biomedicine, 141

access to transition, 152, 164; difficulties of, 24; dissociation in, 35; easy, 98; envy of, 97, 98; limits on, 14; politics of, 27, 134; stratification in, 8; structural impossibilities in, 143; technological, 27, 38, 47, 96, 101, 102, 139, 147, 151, 183. *See also* gatekeeping; surgery, transsexual; transition; transition, medical

activism, trans: for accessibility, 154; ethics of care in, 120; medical gatekeeping and, 140, 157; mutual care in, 159; transcendence tropes of, 191. *See also* gender workers, voluntary; militancy, trans

affect: "aliens," 197; cognition and, 11; conversion into language, 94; distantiating, 185; eliding of nuance in, 171; imposition of structure on, 13; intensive, 12; liberal regulation

of, 6–7; passing between subjects, 116; prepersonal intensities of, 11; shaping of trans lives, 169–70; shifts in, 1–2; side, 7–12; transmission of, 115–16

affect, flat, 14; in affective commons, 58; of depression, 56; retreat in, 62; risk in, 63; survival through, 58; underperformance in, 57–58; withdrawal in, 58

affect, negative: amplification between trans subjects, 9; awareness of, 11; bad feelings in, 11; of caring interrelationality, 4; cisheteropatriarchy and, 5; in conatus, 111; development of resilience through, 130; driving worldmaking projects, 123; factors modulating, 5; forms of, 4; framing of trans lives, 5; in gender mismatch, 2; healing for, 171; in *Infect Your Friends and Loved Ones,* 43; marginalization in, 33; medical establishment's intensification of, 163; narrativizing of, 171; ongoing manifestations of, 8;

Deleuze, Gilles, and Félix Guattari: *A Thousand Plateaus*, 13, 30, 95

demonology, in trans living, 1

Denny, Dallas, 147–53; American Educational Gender Information Service of, 153; as community liaison, 153–54, 164–65; on "good" trans persons, 162–64; HBIGDA and, 157; letter to Raj, 157; in reconfiguration of HBIGDA Standards, 154; trans care labor of, 154; on transition fraud, 161

desire, 77; to be alone, 114; frustration of, 20; juncture with envy, 80–81; for life, 109, 111, 121; for masculinity, 85; shaped by deprivation, 98; to transition, 79

Despentes, Virginie: *Baise-moi,* 90

détournement, t4t, 44, 45–46

Dewey, John, 189

Diagnostic and Statistical Manual: "transsexualism" in, 140

disequilibrium: in misrecognition, 76; phenomenological experience of, 76–77

disorientation, 51–56, 75; affective modulation of, 76; of body-in-the-world, 55–56; crisis of motility in, 55; effects of, 53; emotional underperformance in, 56; intercorporeality of, 56; misrecognition in, 53–55; presence/absence in, 54–55; receding from surroundings during, 52; reorientation and, 52, 53; responses to, 56; self-understanding and, 54; shaping of embodiment, 76; social withdrawal in, 56;

tolerance for, 55; vital experience of, 51–53

dissociation: trans experience of, 35–36; in transphobia, 34–35

documentaries, on white Southern trans men, 58–63

dominance, sex/class-based understandings of, 85

doulas, for transition, 147, 165

drag, temporal, 33

Dromenon: A Journal of New Ways of Being, 179

drop-out culture, health care for, 136–37

Dustan, Guillaume: advocacy of barebacking, 91

dysphoria, gender, 1, 2; as constitutive criteria of transness, 102; individuating, 103; range of effects, 102; role in trans legitimacy, 101; similes for, 3; subjects not experiencing, 101; "uninvited dilemma" of, 151. *See also* feelings, bad; negativity, trans

dystopias: speculative, 37; in trans fiction, 36–37

Eads, Robert: documentary on, 58–59; estrangement of, 62–63; unemployment of, 59. *See also Southern Comfort*

eggs (pre-recognition trans people), 70

ego, vacation from, 186

embodiment, 7, 11; affective experience of, 30; disorientation in, 76; informed by memory, 77; as intercorporeal, 72; medical-technical construct of, 191; negative affects of, 56; non-cis, 117; overlapping experiences of, 34; racial privilege

Gender NetWorker (newsletter), 148, 152

Gender Quest (newsletter), 17, 171, 190; Kindred Spirit gatherings in, 194, 195

gender services, "good consumers" of, 160–67

gender transivity, envy and, 84

Gender Worker (consultancy group), 148

gender workers, voluntary, 147–53; affective interchanges among, 153; affective labor of, 151; burnout among, 166; carer/recipient boundaries of, 152; compassion fatigue among, 150, 152; lack of recognition for, 151, 166; lack of support for, 148–49; remuneration for, 150; social death of, 152; transfer of negative affects, 153. *See also* care labor

Gill-Peterson, Jules, 25, 181

Goddess culture, patriarchal displacement of, 192, 193

Green, Jamison: *Becoming a Visible Man,* 94–95

gurus: as devotional figures, 187; for psychedelic use, 184

Haight Ashbury Free Clinic (San Francisco), 135–36

Halberstam, Jack: boy figures of, 89; Peter Pan stories of, 96; *In a Queer Time and Place,* 33; on transsexuality, 46–47

Halley, Janet, 87

happiness, banality of, 197–98

Harris, Karen Emenhiser, 130

Harry Benjamin International Gender Dysphoria Association (HBIGDA), 153, 156; administrative violence of, 157; advocacy of medical transition, 173; archives of, 133–34, 142, 173; authority of, 174; communication malfunctions of, 156; as community/medical establishment arbiter, 156–57; control over trans people, 155; crises of 1990s, 154–55; Department of Human Services, 156; dissatisfaction with, 155–56; origin of, 140; patient crises of, 156; patient/therapist correspondence of, 142–44; recruitment of trans community leaders, 133; rejection of psychotherapy, 173; sexual harassment charges in, 156; SRS coordination, 156; suicidality associated with, 156; trans loss of faith in, 158

Harry Benjamin International Gender Dysphoria Association, Standards of Care, 142–43; AEGIS and, 154, 157; categories in, 143; debates over, 154; protection of consumers, 155; reconfiguration of, 154–55; trans dialogue on, 158; unrealistic, 157. *See also* World Professional Association for Transgender Health

healing, 171; collective, 172; discourses of, 171; elimination of difference in, 196; racial homogeneity and, 195; rituals of, 171; simplistic narratives of, 197; in social media streams, 188; trans-inclusive, 18; trans/queer discourse on, 188; wholeness in, 192

health care: for drop-out culture,

in, 102; privatization of, 139;
streamlined access to, 151
Teen Beat (magazine), 81
teen heartthrobs, desire for, 81
temporality: of becoming, 94; in
Little Fish, 63–64; of progress,
26; of rage, 170; of transition
process, 19–36. *See also* lag,
temporal; time, trans
Tenderloin district (San Francisco), LSD use in, 184
TERF (trans exclusionary radical
feminist) wars, 86–87
t4t (trans4trans): as Craigslist
category, 43, 44, 45; desire
for, 146; as détournement, 44,
45–46; intimacy of, 43, 46;
praxis of love, 14, 20, 47, 48–49;
proto-trans-separatist space of,
45; transphobic logic of, 44
Thom, Kai Cheng: dystopic
imaginary of, 20, 36; on trans
memoir genre, 39. See *Fierce
Femmes and Notorious Liars*
Thomas, Sheree René, 37
time: enfolded, 36; hormone,
25–28, 64; straight-cis, 64;
unfolding of difference in, 30
time, trans, 33; activities of, 65;
enfolded, 36; in *Little Fish,*
63–64. *See also* temporality
Time to Act, A (report, 2017), 117
Tinsley, Omise'eke Natasha, 117
Tolstoy, Leo: *Anna Karenina,* 197
Tomkins, Silvan, 9
trances, psychedelic (Goa, India),
186
"Trans-" (*Women's Studies Quarterly,* 2008), 31–32
transantagonism: affective orientation to, 11; dealing with, 14;
existential impacts of, 7

transcendence: in transgender,
191; white hegemony as, 195
transcendentalism, nineteenth
century, 187
trans communities: capitalist
modes of production and, 144;
effect of medical gatekeeping
on, 159; horizontal hostility in,
97; peer support in, 144–47;
publications of, 21; sharing of
rage, 131; substance abuse in,
67; support groups, 141–42;
transformation of medical
practice, 158, 159; work with
HBIGDA, 133
Trans Day of Remembrance, 125
trans experience: constitutive
criteria for, 103; criteria for belonging, 101; grounding commonality for, 101; hegemonic
narratives of, 10; *longue durée*
of, 1; medico-juridical determinations of, 101–2; negative
affect in, 3; suffering in, 102;
tropes of representation, 2
transformation, embodied, 15
transformation festivals, spirituality of, 187
trans frustration, mobilizing of,
153–59
transgender: popularization of
term, 190–91
Trans Happiness™, 2
"trans-ing," practice of, 31–32
transition: affective politics of,
30; affective temporalities of,
19–36; agential relation to, 47;
antediluvian, 37, 47; anticipatory emotions of, 24; becoming in, 31, 33–34; colonial
racist epistemes of, 183; coming home in, 34; "completed,"

Trans People of Color Coalition, 117

transphobia: antifeminist, 126; cumulative effects of, 131; dissociation in, 34–35; in employment, 143; everyday, 171; exacerbating factors for, 195–96; institutional neglect in, 61; internalized, 163; during temporal lag, 28; in t4t, 44

"transsexualism," in *Diagnostic and Statistical Manual*, 140

transsexuality: LSD as cure for, 176, 179; in LSD research, 176; pathologizing language of, 190; psychedelic cure for, 183; as schizophrenia, 175; transgender and, 98–99. *See also* surgery, transsexual

trans validity, hierarchies of, 98

trans visibility: hypervisible, 1; social costs of, 74–75

trauma: collective, 125–26; collective processing of, 198; communal criticism of, 120; deindividuated, 125; different registers of, 6; emergence into present, 36; everyday/ catastrophic, 6; intergenerational, 197; military, 126–27; mundane, 6; protection by anger, 106; psychedelic use for, 172; rage as response to, 121; resilience in face of, 37, 127; secondary, 152; shared, 48; transformed into militancy, 126; transmutation to strength, 125; vicarious, 150, 152

triggers: avoidance of, 15; by misrecognition, 76

TSQ—Transgender Studies Quarterly, 95

TV/TS Tapestry (journal), 190, 191; role in trans communal formation, 155

uncertainty, emotive response to, 57

University of Minnesota Program in Human Sexuality, 155

Valentine, David, 147; *Imagining Transgender*, 144–46

Vanguard (activist group, San Francisco), 183, 196; LSD use guide, 184–85

Vanguard Magazine, 184

Velvet Whip (band), 80

violence: capitalist, 9–10; of dominant culture, 122; gendered, 110; multivalent impacts of, 129; necropolitical, 75; police, 118; queer/transphobic agents of, 129; against trans women, 118; against women, 117

virtue signaling, white leftist, 1

vision quests, transitions as, 193

vlogs, trans, 13, 20–24; affective surround of, 24; care labor of, 21; critiques of trans experience, 24; damaging expectations in, 24; educational tropes of, 23; function of, 21; medical information in, 21, 22; promissory narratives of, 22–23; proximity to medical industry, 22; structuring principle of, 23; transnormative tropologies of, 24; visual coaching in, 23; worldbuilding work of, 24–25; on YouTube, 23. *See also* transition narratives

Watts Rebellion (Los Angeles, 1965), 181–82
Weaver, Harlan, 124
Webb, Alice, 155; patients' correspondence with, 142–44
Weiss, Gail, 71
Welch, Jonah, 188
whiteness: in countercultures, 194; gendered logics of, 183; in psychedelic culture, 186–87; of trans gatherings, 195
white supremacy, discourse of civilization in, 182
white viscosity, 17, 186; in New Age spirituality, 189, 194, 195, 196; in psychedelics, 196; structuring logic of, 194; of transformative healing, 195
wholeness, trans discourses of, 171
Williams, Raymond, 8
Wilson, Elizabeth, 9
Wilson, Shawn, 173
women, male power over, 85
women, Black: racist typologies of, 117
women, trans: in the academy, 96; archetypes of, 39–40; correspondence with therapists, 142; dysfunctional, 68; exploitation of, 161; as masculinist aggressors, 87; memoirs of, 39; non-hormonally transitioned, 160; oppression of, 85; performance of deference, 40–41; in service economies, 163; silicone injections for, 161–62; social punishment of, 163; stealth, 162; as threat to feminism, 180; violence affecting, 118
women of color: anger among, 113, 121–22; violence against, 117
women of color, trans: HIV-positive, 144; suffering of, 1
"woo" (believer in New Age philosophy and practice), 172, 188
World Professional Association for Transgender Health (WPATH), 16, 173. *See also* Harry Benjamin International Gender Dysphoria Association
Wray, Amanda, 190–91
writing, withdrawal from world in, 52

YouTube: privileged subjects of, 24; trans vlogs on, 23

Zazanis, Noah: "On Hating Men," 88